# Sexidemic

# Sexidemic

## A Cultural History of Sex in America

LAWRENCE R. SAMUEL

ROWMAN & LITTLEFIELD PUBLISHERS, INC.
*Lanham • Boulder • New York • Toronto • Plymouth, UK*

Published by Rowman & Littlefield Publishers, Inc.
A wholly owned subsidary of The Rowman & Littlefield Publishing Group, Inc.
4501 Forbes Boulevard, Suite 200, Lanham, Maryland 20706
www.rowman.com

10 Thornbury Road, Plymouth PL6 7PP, United Kingdom

British Library Cataloguing in Publication Information Available

**Library of Congress Cataloging-in-Publication Data**
Samuel, Lawrence R.
  Sexidemic : a cultural history of sex in America / Lawrence R. Samuel.
    p. cm.
  Includes bibliographical references and index.
  ISBN 978-1-4422-2040-9 (cloth : alk. paper) — ISBN 978-1-4422-2041-6 (electronic) 1.
Sex—United States—History. I. Title.
  HQ18.U5S26 2013
  306.70973—dc23
                                                                                    2012036125

∞™ The paper used in this publication meets the minimum requirements of
American National Standard for Information Sciences—Permanence of Paper for
Printed Library Materials, ANSI/NISO Z39.48-1992.

Printed in the United States of America

# Contents

# Introduction

For a people who supposedly love sex, Americans have had no shortage of problems with it. Since the end of World War II, in fact, we've had a contentious relationship with sexuality, and the subject has been a source of considerable tension and controversy on both an individual and societal level. Rather than being a simple pleasure of life, something to be enjoyed, sex has served as a challenging and disruptive force in many Americans' everyday lives for the last two-thirds of a century. Our love affair with sex has thus been a rocky one, filled with bumps in the road that have caused major instability across our cultural landscape. A very wide range of social, economic, and political factors—the domestic conformity of the postwar years, the excesses of the counterculture, the overexposure and fragmentation of sexuality, the self-help movement, the AIDS crisis, the rise of celebrity culture, an obsession with money and materialism, the emergence of "political correctness" and an increasingly litigious society, the "midlifing" of the baby boomers, an explosion of entertainment options and alternative sensory pleasures, and the flourishing of Internet-related sex, to name just some—were instrumental in creating what can be considered a crisis in sexuality of epidemic proportions. Our individualistic, competitive, consumerist, and anxious national character is both reflected in and reinforced by this "sexidemic," something few have recognized or perhaps want to admit.

That is the bold thesis of *Sexidemic: A Cultural History of Sex in America*. *Sexidemic* is the first real cultural history of sexuality in the United States since the end of World War II, filling a large gap in our literary landscape. That a dedicated cultural history of sexuality in America over the past two-thirds of a century has yet to be published is very surprising; this alone is justification for such a book (especially here in our allegedly "oversexed" society). Like our other great taboo, death, sex has no doubt suffered (in a historical sense) from the strong emotions we have assigned to it. "Excavating the past is never easy, but this is especially true when it comes to sex, a subject often surrounded by silence, shame, distortion, and bravado," explains Kathy Peiss in her *Major Problems in the History of American Sexuality*, a good assessment of the unfortunate situation.[1] Complicating matters has been the unreliability of sex research, a problem even before the publication of the infamous "Kinsey Report" in 1948. "Sexual behavior is a volatile and sensitive topic, and surveys designed to reveal it have both great power and great limits," writes Julia A. Ericksen in her *Kiss and Tell: Surveying Sex in the Twentieth Century*. In Ericksen's study, both researchers' preconceptions about what questions to ask and respondents' ability and willingness to answer truthfully would have been difficult at best.[2] Sex research has also always been considered a suspect, dubious enterprise, even within the scientific community, and this hinders its status as a legitimate field of inquiry. Finally, as editors Laura M. Carpenter and John DeLamater show in their *Sex for Life*, the fact that human sexuality changes throughout a lifetime has also made the subject difficult to study and understand. Sexualities among those on either side of the age spectrum—children and the elderly—is a particularly thorny topic, further hampering the field.[3]

Sexuality is unarguably central to the American experience, however, making a book fully dedicated to its cultural history worth writing and, I hope, worth reading. "Sexuality has an *American* history," exclaims Elizabeth Reis in her *American Sexual Histories*, and is "a story of great importance and complexity."[4] While other books in the field have tended to focus on specific dimensions of sexuality, for example, birth control or gay culture, this one addresses its broader cultural dynamics since World War II, an admittedly ambitious undertaking. Such an undertaking is well worth the effort, I believe. Tracing the narrative of America through the lens of sexuality offers us a new and different way of understanding who we are as a people, and this is the ultimate purpose of *Sexidemic*. "Intimate relations have shown continuity but also dramatic change over time in America," Reis observes, "and it is our challenge . . . to analyze these significant but elusive matters with care and imagination."[5]

To say that sex plays a major role in everyday life in America would be an understatement (particularly because it is the source of life itself). Sexuality is a mainstay of American popular and consumer culture; the adage "sex sells" is taken to heart by marketers of all kinds of products and services. Advertising and entertainment are filled with sexuality, with books, television, movies, and the Internet delivering a constant barrage of sex-related content. Recreation too is heavily steeped in sex, with millions of us spending inordinate amounts of time and money on middlebrow erotica, online porn, lap dances, and the world's oldest profession. Self-help has long been enamored with sexuality, many of us thinking our sex lives could and should be improved by learning some kind of secret, magical "how-to." A plethora of therapies have been put forth over the years, each of them catering to our perceived deficiencies surrounding this most intimate of experiences and promising to heal whatever we think is wrong (or just different) with us.

The breadth and depth of sexuality is truly remarkable, which we learn by combing through its cultural history. For better and worse, sexual desire leads to many of the decisions we make, and I firmly believe our primal urge is directly responsible for much of what we do. (Some social scientists and historians contest this view, but brain research in many fields is proving that how we behave and even what we believe is overwhelmingly biologically and genetically determined.) All of us are hardwired for sex; after all, our instinct to reproduce and perpetuate the species is perhaps the most basic. Sexual desire does not follow the rules of reason, as history has shown over and over, with many a marriage and career (and occasional empire) ruined in the pursuit of lust. Today, sex makes its presence known in education ("sex ed"), politics (scandals), and the legal sphere (harassment suits), a fair reflection of its tendency (or insistence) to drive much of human behavior. The medical arena regularly crosses paths with sex, whether through methods of birth control (e.g., the pill), treatments for sexually transmitted diseases (STDs), the battle against AIDS, or drugs for low desire or impotence (e.g., Viagra). Gender roles are heavily shaped by sex, of course, with many gays and lesbians using their sexuality as a primary source of identity and community.

"Attitudes toward sex play a significant role in setting and maintaining the frontiers of gender, ethnicity, race, class, and religion," notes Reis, and "even the threshold that separates childhood from adulthood."[6] Sex has also been seen as a litmus test of our values at any given time, with its status as either a cultural taboo or an expression of free speech providing a good indicator of the country's relative moral temperament.

The Zelig-like nature of sexuality in America becomes apparent from a sweeping survey like this one. As media proliferated and the communications universe expanded, the subject of sexuality consistently grew in volume, playing an ever more central role in American society. A bird's-eye view reveals that there has been no single narrative of sexuality in the United States, that is, that its role has been highly dependent on the values of a particular time (and, often, place). Sexuality in the United States has thus hardly been a straight line; its story is filled with sharp twists and turns. "Sexuality has been continually reshaped by the changing nature of the economy, the family, and politics," observe John D'Emilio and Estelle B. Freedman in their *Intimate Matters: A History of Sexuality in America*, the paradigm of how sex has shape-shifted considerably over the past four centuries in North America. In broad strokes, sexuality was family- and reproduction-centered in the colonial era, marriage-based and romanticized in the nineteenth century, and individualized and commercialized in the twentieth, illustrating its profound ability to both shape and reflect different cultural climates.[7] With digitalization, sex is taking on new forms in the early years of the twenty-first century, something that will no doubt continue as technology plays an even more integral role in our lives. Online pornography is turning out to be the proverbial "game-changer," radically altering the sexual behavior of many men (and, as a result, women). Authors of a growing number of books including Gail Dines's *Pornland*, William M. Struthers's *Wired for Intimacy*, Robert Jensen's *Getting Off*, and Pamela Paul's *Pornified* all argue that the proliferation of pornography is transforming relationships and, as a rule, not for the better.[8]

Given how central sexuality is in America, it makes perfect sense that a comprehensive exploration of the subject over the past two-thirds of a century offers fresh insights leading to a reexamination of our national identity. By charting its cultural trajectory since the end of World War II, we learn how the country's continual woes with sexuality helped make us an anxious, insecure people. The sex lives of many, perhaps most, Americans have been in a perpetual state of crisis, a constant source of concern. We've fretted over every dimension of it, with problems in both quality and quantity. We were either having too little of it or too much of it—never just right. Others were doing it more frequently or better. Our body parts were seen as somehow deficient, and our technique was wrong. Homosexuality and bisexuality have been routinely viewed as immoral or even pathological despite study after study showing that many of us (particularly young women) are naturally "bi-curious."[9] With this unhealthy view of sexuality, it was not surprising that we felt we needed a variety of potions and gadgets to make it happen or be pleasurable. It was also not surprising that our bipolar approach to sexuality oozed out in a steady stream of "dysfunctional" behavior. Low libido and sex addiction emerged as common disorders, and sex scandal after sex scandal have made headlines, especially over the last couple of years. (American history is, of course, marked by sex scandals involving prominent men, e.g., Henry Ward Beecher, Fatty Arbuckle, and Charlie Chaplin.) Only money has surpassed sex as a source of stress for Americans, something few of us likely realize.

America's "sexidemic" is hardly a new phenomenon or a radical idea. (There have been concerns about our "oversexed" society since the early twentieth century; in 1913, for example, a popular magazine declared it was "Sex O' Clock" in America.) More than half a century ago, the notable American psychologist Albert Ellis wrote a book about what he viewed as an "anti-sexual culture" in the United States, claiming that most Americans were living in a state of "sex-love-marriage poverty." It was our upbringing that was at fault for leaving Americans "emotionally maimed" when it came to sex, he maintained, with psychotherapy the only possible cure for our sexual repressions and "antagonisms." Importantly, the "American sexual tragedy," as he titled his book, was culturally rather than personally constructed. "The sabotaging of human sex-love relations is a problem which is socially rather than individually created, and which therefore cannot be solved on a broad scale without widespread societal changes in sex attitudes," Ellis wrote, meaning sexual impairment was endemic to Americans. Ellis was not optimistic about America's sexual future. "The American sexual tragedy can be expected to continue its three century long run, and in some respects even to become more tragic, until a pronounced social effort (along with sporadic individual rebellions) is made to end it," he concluded, a prophecy that I believe has so far been realized.[10]

Negative attitudes toward sexuality have been a permanent fixture in this country, of course, especially those articulated by authoritarian, morally based institutions and organizations, notably organized religion. The reach of the Vatican's "Congregation for the Doctrine of Faith" extends to American Catholics, many of whom struggle with the church's official stance that sexual pleasure outside of procreation is sinful.[11] Public libraries have consistently banned books deemed too erotic for patrons to borrow, the most recent example being the racy best seller *Fifty Shades of Grey*.[12] Through laws prohibiting certain kinds of sexual acts, federal, state, and local governments also have contributed to making certain expressions of sexuality seem wanton and "dirty." Given this country's guiding principles, it is surprising and disheartening that the government has played an active role in shaping the way we have viewed and practiced sexuality. "Nowhere in our founding documents is there any mention of regulating anything considered immoral, disgusting, or sinful," notes Marty Klein in his *America's War on Sex: The Attack on Law, Lust, and Liberty*, and governmental intrusion in sexuality is contrary to the United States being "founded on the idea that people could choose what to do and with whom."[13] In his next book, Klein, a leading sex therapist, proposes that each of us has a kind of "sexual intelligence" (whose "quotient" can be raised), a wonderful concept that should be advanced rather than repressed by those in positions of power.[14]

One does not have to be an expert to recognize that American public schools have also largely been antisex. Sex ed in this country has been a battle between those who think kids will inevitably have sex and thus should be protected from its dangerous consequences and those who think it is too hazardous to allow them to do, with almost no promoting of its pleasures. It is thus not surprising that for many teens a conversation about sexuality with their parents, doctor, or even partner remains the "most awkward talk ever!" as *Human Sexuality Newsletter* recently put it.[15] The media too have over the past few decades played a key role in fueling a crisis in sexuality through what Roger N. Lancaster calls "sex panics." The teen male prostitution scares of the 1970s, apocalyptic AIDS scenarios and day care abuse cases of the 1980s, and pedophile threats and priest abuse scandals of the 1990s were just some examples of how the media sensationalized sexuality to boost readership and ratings, Lancaster argues in his *Sex Panic and the Punitive State*.[16]

The medical community has also served as an agent of sexual confusion and insecurity. Psychiatrists and physicians have long invested themselves in the sexual arena, each profession influencing patients' sex lives in the name of good mental and physical health. This was particularly true in the 1950s and early 1960s, when sexuality went well beyond being seen as a contributing factor to personal well-being and, rather incredibly, became a matter of national security. "Medical practitioners in the United States . . . situated themselves as the guardians of the sexual well-being of Americans in the early decades of the Cold War," writes Carolyn Herbst Lewis in her *Prescription for Heterosexuality: Sexual Citizenship in the Cold War Era.* Both psychiatrists and physicians subscribed to consensus thinking that "sexually satisfied partners were more likely to stay married, to produce well-adjusted families, and to form the building blocks of a moral and stable national community." When comfortably housed in a private home in the suburbs, a heterosexual couple with children was seen as a "fortress against the anxieties provoked by the Cold War," Lewis explains, with sexuality thus linked to the American Way of Life. Physicians and people with PhDs considered sexualities that did not conform to this rather narrow standard to be not only symptomatic of some kind of mental flaw but also, quite possibly, subversive and dangerous. Things have thankfully changed considerably over the past half century, but some suspicion toward sexuality falling outside the boundaries of married heterosexuals remains, a legacy of our Puritan past.[17]

All this naturally raises the question of why sex has been so problematic in America. Psychiatrists, especially those with psychoanalytic training, would no doubt have a lot of theories, but I approach it through a wider lens. Our Puritan roots have obviously played a role in our love/hate relationship with sex, this cultural heritage still shaping our ambivalence toward the subject. (Puritans certainly had restrictions on sex, but they also believed it was an important part of marriage, and individuals who transgressed were quickly absorbed back into the community with no lasting negative effects after confessing and accepting their punishment.) More than that, however, much of Western, and especially American, culture is antithetical to healthy attitudes toward sexuality. We are a competitive people and society, something that is simply not conducive to good sex lives. We tend to take our ethos of achievement and drive for success into the bedroom, leading to pressure to be beautiful and "perform" or to prove our virility. Our obsession with the individual or self has also caused considerable chaos within the arena of sexuality, which is also contrary to an experience that is by definition collaborative. Regardless of the reasons, the result has been an overemphasis on sexuality in everyday life in America, our external expressions of sex obscuring our internal discomfort and insecurities surrounding it. "Almost everyone agrees that American society is a hypersexual society, a society in which sexual discourse, erotica, and pornography are pervasive," observes Kenneth C. W. Kammeyer in his *Hypersexual Society: Sexual Discourse, Erotica, Pornography in America Today*, noting that this common belief crossed all social, economic, and political divisions.[18]

Finally, I argue that America's widespread sexual crisis is a product of sex being perceived as something to consume, a commodity, a view that is also inconsistent with a healthy concept of sexuality. "Our national conversation about sex now suffers from a tremendous impoverishment," wrote Dagmar Herzog in her *Sex in Crisis: The New Sexual Revolution and the Future of American Politics*. Herzog finds plenty of advice on sexual techniques and considerable alarm over teens' behavior but not much substantive discussion. "There is much titillating talk about sex in America, yet there is very little talk about sex that is morally engaged and affirmative," she continues; the superficiality of our treatment of the subject is entirely consistent with our disposable society.[19] "Sex in our society today has, indeed, been naturalized and demystified," agrees Edwin M. Schur in his *Americanization of Sex*, suggesting that "our culture and social system may be pushing sexuality very far in the direction of an emotional emptiness."[20] Again, sex is not unlike money, the problem being that someone else always has (or is believed to have) more. Like one's bank account, viewing sex as relative rather than absolute is bound to lead to dissatisfaction. Popular culture has not helped, fueling our inferiority complex and making us mistake fantasy for reality. "The public image of sex in America bears virtually no relationship to the truth," state the authors of *Sex in America: A Definitive Survey*, and the myths and unrealistic misconceptions at play are capable of doing real damage to individuals' self-esteem, relationships, and health.[21] Sex is almost always better on screen (and now on our computers) than in daily life, making it no wonder that many of us find the real thing not especially exciting. In short, sex in America is now just one more thing by which to be entertained, a (hopefully) pleasurable experience largely devoid of any deep meaning or significance except perhaps when trying to conceive.

A very brief survey of sexuality in America helps us understand how and why the sexual woes of the latter half of the twentieth century and first decades of the twenty-first came to be. Sexual morality became "a conspicuous and controversial issue" in all of the American colonies in the early 1600s, notes Richard Godbeer in his *Sexual Revolution in Early America*, with casual promiscuity banned as the church prescribed abstinence for couples until they officially wed. Even then, however, sex was viewed as a complex and complicated affair. Early Americans "consider[ed] sex to be important as a social, economic, political legal, moral, and religious issue," he adds, hardly limited to a simple act of procreation. Before this country was a country, in other words, sex was viewed less as a marker of personal identity (that would come later) and more as a strong thread in the total cultural fabric. Sexuality in the seventeenth century thus was not tied to the individual but rather "a component of spirituality, cultural identity, and social status," according to Godbeer, and a powerful force of community that is difficult for us to even understand in these overtly self-centric times.[22] Because of its predominant communal and public orientation, sexuality often intersected with issues of race, gender, and class, with sex considered an agent of control by white, wealthier men over women, people of color, and the working class.[23]

As D'Emilio and Freedman explain in their tour de force *Intimate Matters*, sexuality in America became increasingly privatized in the eighteenth and nineteenth centuries, moving away from its communal orientation in the colonial or preindustrial era. Sex also moved beyond its reproductive role over the course of these two hundred years, with intimacy and eroticism (and homosexuality) added to the equation. Regulation of sexuality by the church and state eroded, and the individual was now assigned primary control over his or her sexual desires. Within the rapidly developing consumer-based economy, sex-related products and services emerged, with marital advice, contraceptives, abortions, prostitution, sexual entertainment, and sexual material all for sale. Sex in America thus appeared to be following the same path as in Europe in the seventeenth and eighteenth centuries, when, as Faramerz Dabhoiwala argues in his 2012 *Origins of Sex*, the "first sexual revolution" took place.[24] However, deep concerns about what D'Emilio and Freedman call "the free market of sex" also developed over this span of time, as some members of society feared the rise of rampant, immoral sexuality. In order to maintain social order, or at least the appearance of it (prostitution, for example, was considered "a necessary evil"), women assumed the duty of keeping sexuality and its public expression in check. Matters of class were in play, of course: the upper and middle classes exerted a kind of power over the working class and its perceived more licentious ways. Out of these "antivice" sexual politics sprang a countercultural "free-love" movement, foreshadowing another utopian interpretation of sexuality by a century or so.[25]

Sexuality took another major shift in the early decades of the twentieth century as modernity enhanced values of youth, leisure, and individualism. The term "sex" now meant not just gender but also sexuality, signaling a new kind of reception toward expressions of love and eroticism, particularly by women. In her informative and entertaining *Straight: The Surprisingly Short History of Heterosexuality*, Hanne Blank (author of the equally engaging *Virgin: The Untouched History*) convincingly argues that "heterosexuality" as a form of identity emerged around the turn of the twentieth century due to the research, theories, and writings of Sigmund Freud, Richard von Krafft-Ebing, and other leading figures of psychology.[26] By the "Jazz Age" of the 1920s, the clear separation between public and private sexuality had largely dissolved, with sexuality now a staple of American popular and consumer culture. Much of the social stigma attached to premarital sex had also faded, with sexual attraction considered a primary factor in selecting a mate and new methods of birth control practiced. Sex was, rather suddenly, seemingly everywhere, with Freudian psychoanalysis, short skirts, suggestive "confession" magazines, and (pre–Hays code) movies all bringing sexuality into the open. And with one of those new, affordable Model Ts, one could escape the stuffy parlor room (and supervising parents) and more fully enjoy the company of a date while "motoring." The movie house was, of course, also an opportune development for necking (especially because it was air-conditioned!).

The idea and practice of sexual freedom fit nicely into a cultural climate praising the notions of happiness, self-gratification, and fulfillment; the (superficial) primness of Victorian days was gone for good. In an era heavily defined by dirty politics, big business, and frenzied urbanism, physical pleasures, especially sex, were seen as one of the few remaining refuges for the individual. Many Americans took full advantage of their newfound liberties as the nation enjoyed another "sexual revolution."[27] (In her *Sexuality in Europe*, Herzog cites the advent of contraception and pornography as the catalyst for Europe's twentieth-century sexual revolution.[28]) As Christina Simmons shows in her *Making Marriage Modern*, however, a good number of problems were associated with sex in America in the 1920s. Experts, for example, reminded married couples not to engage in the "female on top" position because it represented an inappropriate and possibly destructive reversal of ideal gender roles, suggesting perhaps that sex was as problematic as ever and that the changes associated with this period were not all that revolutionary. Likewise, while women may have regained their desire in this period, they were also more vulnerable to sexual assault (or at least more on their own to handle these problems).[29]

During the hard times of the Great Depression, it became clearer that there was trouble in paradise. In a much more sober social and economic climate, more traditional gender roles returned, bringing with them a backlash against the sexually liberated ways of the single woman. Nice girls now did not have sex or at least did not enjoy it, a reversal of the sexual progress made by women in the 1920s. ("Bad girls," like the roles played by Mae West, Greta Garbo, and Marlene Dietrich, reinforced this idea.) Among the married, sexual difficulties were on the rise, as concerns about money (and having another baby) influenced goings-on in the bedroom.[30] The seeds of the American crisis in sexuality were thus firmly planted in the 1930s as the country's collective libido suffered from a loss of confidence. Wartime pressures, including the separation of husbands and wives for years and physical and mental trauma, only added to sexual insecurities and tensions when couples were reunited. GIs and sailors, both single and married, may have had some fun with prostitutes during the war, but these experiences did little to advance their knowledge of female sexuality. In fact, as Marilyn E. Hegarty observes in her *Victory Girls, Khaki-Wackies, and Patriotutes*, female sexuality was deemed "disturbing, even dangerous" to federal officials during the war, with prostitution regulated and repressed as a means to control venereal disease. The government promoted a "militarized type of masculine sexuality," Hegarty writes, not an especially good approach to developing a happy sex life between couples.[31]

As men and women settled into domestic life after the war, they were indeed typically ill prepared for what was sometimes referred to as the "marital

union." A socially prescribed, family-oriented form of sexuality was an essential part of the "domestic containment" of the postwar era, explains Elaine
Tyler May in her *Homeward Bound: American Families in the Cold War
Era*.[32] The rigidity of postwar society and drive to "keep up with the Joneses"
would also intensify sexual anxieties. The tensions surrounding sexuality in
the United States during the postwar years could most easily be detected in
the publication of the two Kinsey reports. "In 1948 and 1953, the United
States was rocked by events that observers compared to the explosion of the
atomic bomb," writes Miriam G. Reumann in her *American Sexual Character: Sex, Gender, and National Identity in the Kinsey Reports* about the two
publications. The surveys produced by the Indiana University zoologist and
his team revealed that American sexuality was significantly less "contained"
than people liked to think. That the books themselves were considered, in
Reumann's words, "immoral, perverse, and damaging to the reputation of the
United States" vividly illustrated postwar Americans' public discomfort with
any form of sexuality residing outside the narrow boundaries of traditional
gender roles and family life.[33] What Americans were actually doing behind
closed doors was a whole different matter, a prime example of the nation's
complex and conflicting attitudes toward sexuality.

The lid on the nation's sexual bottle could and would not stay closed for
long. "Well before the 'Summer of Love' or the gay liberation movement or
even the bestselling sex manual *The Joy of Sex*, Americans were already talking about sexual revolution," notes Beth Bailey in her *Sex in the Heartland*.
By the early 1960s (if not earlier), major changes in Americans' attitudes and
behaviors toward sex could be detected, even in the country's "heartland."
Citizens of towns like Lawrence, Kansas, were very much a part of the budding sexual revolution, Bailey shows, and were active players in the social
and cultural upheaval that was in play.[34] The sexual revolution of the sixties
(which some believe continues to this day) would not prove to be the panacea
for Americans' problems in the bedroom, however. "In the 1960s and '70s
many tried, but most failed . . . to sustain a consistent political point of view
regarding sex," David Allyn writes in his definitive study of the sexual revolution *Make Love, Not War*. "The problem of sexuality remains critical for the
nation," Allyn declared in 2000, with all kinds of factors—the definition of
marriage, gender differences, STDs, sex education, and many others—being
"unresolved issues in American society."[35] Bailey concurred: "Decades later

we are still fighting about sex and its legitimate expression, those battles complicated by the scourge of AIDS, by the problems of teenage pregnancy and motherhood, by emerging medical technologies that offer new possibilities and new questions about ethics and morality."[36]

*Sexidemic* tells its story chronologically, beginning at the end of World War II and going right up to today, when the subject of sex is arguably more problematic than ever. While I frequently cross paths with gay and lesbian culture, the topic is obviously too expansive to fully accommodate in this book, and readers would be better served by consulting one of the many books in the burgeoning field of what is sometimes called "queer studies." As well, I spend little or no time on criminal aspects of sex, which also deserves its own dedicated study. This book is about the history of American sexuality, so I devote little attention to those of other countries as, again, they warrant their own examination. Regarding sources, the spine of *Sexidemic* relies primarily on contemporary, popular magazines and newspapers. Hundreds of different sources, many of them forgotten, are used, drawing from journalists' writing of "the first draft of history." Journalistic sources were prioritized not only because this is a work of cultural history but also because they were typically filtered, vetted, and fact-checked, and offer a relatively objective and balanced perspective. Books and journal articles are used to frame the story and provide valuable context. Sex has of course played a recurring role in books, movies, and television, this too serving as prime fodder in the book.

The first chapter, "Pillow Talk," looks at sexuality in America in the late 1940s and 1950s, when the repressive cultural climate of the postwar era led to the formation of a crisis in sexuality: i.e., a "sexidemic." Chapter 2, "Easy Rider," examines sexuality in the 1960s, when this crisis became a matter of national concern against the backdrop of the counterculture and sexual revolution. Chapter 3, "Carnal Knowledge," explores sexuality in America during the 1970s, when the crisis intensified through overexposure and what can be considered overindulgence. Chapter 4, "Fatal Attraction," investigates sexuality in the 1980s, when a new disease turned sex into one of Americans' biggest concerns. Chapter 5, "Indecent Proposal," considers sexuality in America in the 1990s, a decade in which sex became an area of society fraught with moral and possibly legal hazards. The final chapter, "Ice Age," reflects on sexuality since 2000, when the signs of our sexual pathology can be found everywhere.

Sex in this country may become even chillier in the future, I propose in the conclusion of the book, as advancing technology continues to allow sexual experiences not requiring the presence of other people. Still, Americans have an opportunity to heal from their "sexidemic," I believe, and recover some of the magic and mystery of this special part of life.

# 1

# Pillow Talk

I'm yours tonight. My darling, possess me.

—*Jan Morrow (Doris Day) to Brad Allen (Rock Hudson) in the 1959 film* Pillow Talk

In June 1957, a book hit the shelves that quickly became the stuff of cocktail party chatter. As its title suggested, Robert Elliot Fitch argued in his *Decline and Fall of Sex* that much of the romance of sexuality had been lost in the modern age. Contemporary novels and plays by the likes of Norman Mailer and Tennessee Williams made this all too clear, their works and others of the postwar years a long way from the kind of eroticism depicted in *Tristan and Iseult* or *Romeo and Juliet*. The anatomical details provided in the two Kinsey reports did a lot of damage to sex, of course, as did all-the-rage Freudian psychoanalysis. "When sex is separated from love and honor it sinks into the slime," Fitch, a Congregational minister, wrote, and American sexuality is now cold, sterile, and passionless.[1]

Fitch's thesis mirrored the views of many other more worldly social critics. Sex was not what it used to be, more people were saying and thinking in the 1950s, and the consensus was that the shift had begun immediately after the war. Contrary to what one might think, the graphic information to be found in the Kinsey reports and the torrent of sexuality in popular and consumer culture that followed had not provided most Americans with a solid foundation in the basics of sex. In fact, there was abundant evidence that Americans remained largely ignorant in the subject. Both children and adults had to be educated about sex, postwar experts agreed, since this particular arena of life was considered too important to be left to chance. Although the accuracy of Kinsey's findings would be challenged, both then and now, it could not be disputed that the books were instrumental in stimulating the nation to openly and frankly confront sexuality for the first time. Sexuality during the postwar years could be said to be polarized or "schizophrenic," with this divide accounting for many of Americans' growing problems in the bedroom. "Official" sex was that within marriage, a good part of it revolving around procreation. Blessed by both church and state, marital sex was considered "normal," part of the era's conformist ways that were centered on domestic life. Underneath the veneer of socially sanctioned postwar sex was "unofficial" sexuality, however, a backlash to the cultural containment of the times. Whether official or unofficial, references to sexuality could be found virtually everywhere in the 1950s, from Bettie Page erotica and Elvis's gyrating hips to strip clubs and the giant fins on a Cadillac. The first publication of *Playboy* in 1953 canonized America's fascination with sex, with no better choice than the world's top sexpot, Marilyn Monroe, as the first centerfold. The unbridled "pillow talk" of the postwar years would serve to pave the way for the sexual revolution that was to come and mark the true beginnings of the American "sexidemic."

## FALLACIES, FACTS, AND PROBLEMS

The nation's budding sexual epidemic could be detected in various ways as soon as the war was over. Young people were especially misinformed and underinformed about sex, and looked for any and all opportunities to become more familiar with the subject. At the University of California at Berkeley, for example, students flocked in droves to the "Youth and Marriage" course being offered there, attracted by its reputed frankness. The university had bowed to student pressure to offer the course, which turned out to be one of the most popular on campus. (A group of medical students had begun delivering unauthorized lectures on "Freudian sex theories," effectively forcing university officials to take action when local churchgoers protested.) Most exciting, students were invited to ask any question they liked in class (written down for anonymity), although particularly sensitive subject matter was relegated to private discussion in the professor's office.[2]

A good number of college students in the late 1940s were of course veterans taking advantage of the GI Bill. Common belief was (and remains) that America soldiers became quite sexually experienced during the war, especially those who served in Europe with its purportedly sophisticated women. (The same was said to be true after World War I.) The results of an investigation led by Dr. Fred Brown of Mount Sinai Hospital in 1946 suggested this was not at all true, however. Brown and some colleagues traveled throughout the German occupation zone to speak to GI audiences about sex, finding that the soldiers were hardly fluent in the subject. After the team gave a lecture called "Sex: Fallacies, Facts and Problems" to more than twenty thousand American troops, the soldiers were encouraged to ask the experts questions, something of which they took full advantage. The GIs most frequently asked questions revolved around birth control, specifically about the effectiveness of the "rhythm method." (Difficulty finding contraceptives likely made this top of mind for soldiers stationed in Germany after the war.) Soldiers were also very interested in whether exposure to radar or flying at high altitudes would make them sterile, as well as whether they or their wives would suffer psychological damage from remaining abstinent during their long separation. By the end of the six-month lecture tour, the team of experts had fielded no fewer than 1,127 different questions from the troops, more evidence that American men were not very well educated in the subject. Brown published the findings in an article in the *Journal of Social Psychology* titled "What American Men Want to Know About Sex," which, it turned out, was quite a bit. There was a need "for reliable sex information in America," Brown wrote, since the "marriage and family" and "sex hygiene" courses offered by some public schools and colleges were clearly not sufficient.[3]

In fact, most American men at midcentury gained their knowledge of sex from other men or as boys from other boys, research showed, with schools, ministers, and parents playing a minor role in their sexual education. Some fathers had the "facts of life" talk with their sons, but such lectures were often too vague to be of much value. (These conversations only reinforced kids' belief that their parents themselves did not know much about the subject.) Chats among friends in playgrounds did not provide a sound education in sexuality, however, something men would later readily admit. Even married men felt they did not know much about sex; the fact that one was having it did not necessarily mean that one knew what one was doing. Ideally, men would learn about sex before they got married, of course, and such thinking leads to the conclusion that there was considerable need for more formal education in the subject.[4] Studies also showed that girls and women also got most of their information about sex from friends. Mothers might have the "menstruation conversation" with their daughters, but fathers were even more reluctant to talk frankly about sex with them than with their sons. "I don't think anyone ever gave me the wrong ideas, but I was pretty vague on what they didn't tell me," said one University of Oklahoma coed; thus, misconceptions about sexuality were just as common among young women as men.[5]

Young adults' lack of knowledge about human sexuality became most apparent in marriage, which quite often was the first time both men and women had sex on a regular basis. Marriages could perhaps withstand one partner being sexually illiterate, but when both were, serious trouble frequently followed. Classic sexual problems—men experiencing premature ejaculation or erectile issues and women suffering from low desire or response—had the potential of ruining the relationship and people's lives. "There is no greater personal tragedy than that of a normally ardent man married to a woman who is cold and unresponsive," wrote Amram Scheinfeld in 1948, and this is a major reason for everything from divorce and broken homes to alcoholism and "psychological crackups." So little was known about female sexuality that it was difficult to say when a woman should be considered "frigid," but the condition was believed to be on the rise. Never having had sexual intercourse, much less having had it with their future spouse, many men and women were no doubt surprised by their spouse's behavior in the bedroom early in their marriages. It was more difficult to tell when a woman was sexually satisfied than a man, making the matter that much more confusing. With no information suggesting otherwise, a good number of men measured their wife's satisfaction by the male standard, that is, orgasm in about five minutes. If and when this did not occur, a husband could conclude he was unattractive or insufficiently virile, while the wife might think there was something wrong with her physically or psychologically. Recognizing that females' menstrual cycle and hormonal changes influenced their sexual response was helpful but hardly solved the problem. A wedding could not resolve the years of being told sex was not something nice girls did, a comment marriage counselors heard over and over from women, and the risk of an unwanted pregnancy in these pre–birth control pill days was another big turnoff. (While the pill was not yet around, in the United State a considerable number of middle-class couples were in fact using some form of contraception as early as the mid-nineteenth century.)[6]

The rapidly increasing number of resources dedicated to resolving such problems often failed to offer couples much comfort. Men were routinely advised by marriage counselors to display plenty of affection toward their wives to get them in the proper emotional state for sex and to spend lots of time on foreplay to make sure the act did not end prematurely for her. Many men viewed regular, socially approved sex as one of the primary benefits of getting hitched, however, and were thus especially excited to participate in the conjugal bliss they were guaranteed. Such a state unfortunately tended to make lovemaking during the first few years of marriage a quite abbreviated affair. Women received much of the blame for this "two ships passing in the night," however, since the overwhelming dominance of men in the medical and psychiatric professions lent a decidedly male-centric perspective to marriage counseling.[7]

In addition to offering possible ways to improve things in the bedroom, marriage counselors (and other authority figures) assumed the responsibility of reining in unchecked sexuality among the unmarried. Not just the well-being of individuals was at stake, they believed, but also the welfare of American society as a whole was being jeopardized. Both polls and anecdotal evidence revealed that moral standards, including those relating to sex, were relaxing after the war just as they had after World War I. Fearing another "Jazz Age" and the licentious behavior that came with it, professionals in various fields issued warnings about the hazards of sexual intercourse before marriage. Premarital sex, particularly for women, was presented as a threat to the cornerstone of American society—marriage and family—and thus was strongly discouraged by all kinds of experts. "Even if conception and infection are successfully avoided, mental conflicts which destroy all serenity and peace of mind often result from illicit love affairs," stated Mario A. Castallo, a physician and author of *Woman's Inside Story*, adding that "serious psychological consequences are among the penalties of premarital sex relations."[8]

## WHEN CHILDREN ASK ABOUT SEX
The generally sorry state of sexuality in America at midcentury could be traced back to the lack of education in the subject at an early age. No sex ed in

public schools was required at the district or state level, but there were some trailblazers in the nascent field that had emerged in one form or another decades earlier. Oregon, of all places, was leading the way in K–12 sex ed in the late 1940s, with thousands of twelve- and thirteen-year-olds (sixth to ninth graders) in that state shown a film called *Human Growth*. Although the film had a scientific name and was only twenty minutes long, it was considered quite a breakthrough at the time. (*Life* called it "epoch-making," while *Time* described it as an effort "to take sex education out from behind the barn and into the class room.") Ten years in the making and produced by actor Eddie Albert (best known then for starring in the 1938 movie *Brother Rat*, with his lead role in the popular *Green Acres* television show two decades in the future), *Human Growth* represented a "new approach to [the] delicate problem" of teaching kids about sex, noted *Life*. Extra care was taken to avoid the embarrassment and self-consciousness that typically came with the subject, explaining why the film focused on the growth of the human body, the development of the glands, and the biology of the reproductive process. And by using an animated cartoon (done by two ex-Disney artists) and diagrams rather than actual human bodies, *Human Growth* certainly achieved its objective to avoid embarrassing both students and teachers. The film had about as much to do with actual sexuality as *Bambi*, however, serving as a good example of how the American education system was failing young people when it came to the subject of sex.[9]

Fledgling programs like that in Oregon were a reaction to the consensus that parents were failing to teach their children adequately about sex. A litter of puppies or kittens served as an ideal lesson in sexuality; it was even better if children lived on a farm and could observe cows or pigs reproduce. When human sexuality was concerned, however, it was a much different matter. Parents' answers to their children's almost inevitable question, "Where do babies come from?" were indeed vague in the years following the war. A 1949 pamphlet published by the Public Affairs Committee, "How to Tell Your Child About Sex," for example, recommended that parents answer the question by simply saying, "Babies grow inside their mothers." More important was to instill through behavior the idea among children that sexuality was "natural" rather than by having those awkward, embarrassing conversations. Have siblings dress in the same room and bathe and go to the toilet together, the pamphlet suggested, with seeing neighbors' and relatives' babies bathe also being a good idea. Letting children see their parents undressed was presented as an effective way to teach sexuality as well, much better than the oft-told stories that babies arrived via a stork or in a doctor's bag.[10]

Some parents, however, believed that any method of teaching children about sex at home was better than what was taking place in some public schools. Sex education was "an integral part of the parent-child relationship," argued Ruth Hawthorne Fay in the *Reader's Digest* in 1950, not happy to see the American school system gradually take over the job. It may have been true that parents did not do a very good job of teaching kids about sex, but that did not mean schools had the right to assume the responsibility. If you must, teach us how to teach our children about sex, Fay and likeminded parents suggested, which would be a much better alternative than holding classes on anatomy and reproduction in between math and geography lessons. Sex taught in the classroom left out the key ingredient of love, opponents justifiably felt, taking issue with social scientists' claim that the subject should be approached academically like any other subject. In short, sex education was a family responsibility, Fay insisted, telling school officials to "leave my child alone!"[11]

The intense debate over sex ed in the early 1950s resembled the most recent kerfuffle over children watching television. A sure way to ensure good attendance at a PTA meeting was to put a discussion on sex ed on the agenda, something that educators increasingly did as the debate heated up. Parents, educators, doctors, and religious leaders had discussed the subject since the early part of the century, but now, with the "baby boom" in full swing, the consensus was that some action had to be taken.[12] As with the television issue, pros and cons were passionately put forth, the central issue being whether kids would benefit or suffer from exposure to a new kind of information. Most experts agreed children would ideally indeed learn about sex in the home from their parents, but this simply did not typically take place. Explaining human sexuality was a lot more difficult and uncomfortable than explaining, say, why it rained or snowed, with most parents having little idea what they should and should not tell their wee ones when asked about anatomy or reproduction.[13]

The "birds and the bees" conversation between parent and child had already become something of a cliché mocked in popular culture by midcentury. The ways in which it took place varied, but it typically was an utter failure, with little useful information delivered because of parents' discomfort discussing sex. If pregnant dogs and cats were nowhere to be found, an aunt or neighbor having a baby was considered an excellent opportunity to bring the subject up in order to be done with the unpleasant but necessary business. A scene with a pregnant woman in a movie or television show could also prompt a mother or father to bring up the facts of life with a child. Parents were especially reluctant to describe the act of sexual intercourse and did not know which words to use or avoid. Some parents took down a medical dictionary from their bookshelf and proceeded to give a lecture on obstetrics to their glassy-eyed child, the latter more often than not more confused than ever.[14] Other parents were frustrated that, years after having what they thought was a perfectly fine sex chat with a child, the same questions would pop up a few years later. Nine- or ten-year-olds had heard a different, much stranger story from their friends than the one their parents had told them a few years earlier, it often turned out, making them keen on clearing up the matter once and for all. At this point, pamphlets or books from the library were provided for the child to read, or the family doctor was asked to intervene, the issue now beyond the parents' abilities.[15]

Recognizing that many parents were in such a pickle, a variety of institutions and organizations stepped into the sex education fray to offer assistance. School boards developed lecture series for parents seeking advice, for example, with four thousand people attending such a program offered by the Bridgeport, Connecticut, Board of Education in the spring of 1951. Seeing both a spiritual void and business opportunity, the Christophers, a Christian organization, decided to sell a four-part, age-specific series of long-playing records called "Sex Instruction" for teachers and parents. (Individual titles were "How Babies are Born," "Menstruation," "Problems of Growing Boys, and "The Marriage Union.")[16] Home-study courses in the subject were also available for parents, and state governments developed material for them as well. New York's Department of Education published a pamphlet called "The Gift of Life," for example, which was distributed to churches and synagogues throughout the state.[17] Literature was also available from organizations like the Child Study Association. That organization published a pamphlet called "When Children Ask About Sex," which many parents hurriedly produced from a drawer when the subject came up.[18]

By teaching parents how to effectively teach their children about sexuality, sex ed could remain in the home where it belonged, this line of thinking of went, skirting the controversy over whether the subject should be incorporated into public school curricula. Some parents, not satisfied with the usually dry-as-a-bone materials made available by the government, religious organizations, and associations, took matters into own hands. In the new suburb of Levittown, Long Island, for example, one housewife decided to develop her own sex-ed course for parents in her neighborhood. Groups of parents (twelve or fewer) met in Mrs. Dolores Keller's home one night a week for ten two-hour sessions, with the host (a part-time college biology teacher) helping her neighbors overcome their own misinformation and lack of knowledge about sex. The course was so good that the adult education division of her school district eventually adopted it.[19]

The row over sex ed and the efforts to find a good way to teach human sexuality to children were, in retrospect, a painful but productive experience. By the mid-1950s, it was clear that there had been a complete shift in thinking about sex education in America over the past quarter century. Before the war, it was commonly believed that children had no need to be concerned with anatomical differences between boys and girls or the process of reproduction, meaning little or no education was needed. A decade after the war, however, experts agreed not only that most children naturally thought about human sexuality but also that any and all questions they had about it should be answered as honestly and directly as possible.[20] Instruction focused on conveying the naturalness of anatomical differences between men and women and biological processes, explaining why family nudity and leaving bathroom doors open were considered acceptable. Through this kind of approach, children would have less need to engage in "sex play," it was believed, since their questions about the human body would already be answered. Because younger children lived in a state of innocence and wonder, no harm could come to them from seeing Mommy, Daddy, or siblings naked, it was believed. Any embarrassment or discomfort would be limited to parents, this being true as well when discussing the facts of life objectively and nonemotionally. Hurriedly covering up in the shower should a child walk in would instill the idea that nudity was shameful, something that could cause long-term damage to the boy's or girl's sexual development. Experts were beginning to back off somewhat on this "modern" position, however, thinking some children could be confused or made uncomfortable by parents taking an approach to sex education grounded in complete freedom and openness.[21]

The midcentury movement for sex education either at home or in public schools could be also seen as part of the era's devout faith in logic and planning. If the biological facts of life were taught to young people, problems related to sexuality would disappear, experts believed; students' understanding of the details of human reproduction would clear up any confusion. These same experts were convinced that curiosity in this area of life was considered potentially "unwholesome." Youngsters' penchant to investigate and experiment with their own sexuality (or, worse, that of others) was especially disturbing. Through effective home instruction or ten or so lectures in either "Family Living" or science courses, the problematic subject of sex could be neatly tied up, allowing children to focus on more constructive extracurricular pursuits like sports and hobbies. By the late 1950s, however, it was clear that this simplistic approach to sex education was not working out as well as expected. Many young people at all ages continued to struggle with the idea and practice of sexuality despite receiving scientific information, a puzzle to those thinking their rational approach should and would work. As well, studies were showing that both elementary and high school sex-ed programs had almost no influence on students' sexual behavior in college.[22] Unlike what a popular television show of the time, *Dragnet*, suggested, "just the facts" were apparently not enough when it came to sexuality. Sex was a lot more complicated than reading, writing, and arithmetic, educators were now realizing, and a description of human anatomy and the technical details of reproduction was simply not enough to produce sexually well-adjusted young adults. Sex education "is not a subject that can be approached as a single problem since sex is related to the spiritual, emotional and physical development of the individual as well as to the social aspects of the community at-large," wrote Catherine T. Dennis of the North Carolina State Department of Education, a view that pointed to the direction the field would eventually take.[23]

## THAT BOOK BY THAT INDIANA PROFESSOR

The sea change in sex education and sexuality as a whole that took place in America soon after the war had much to do with the efforts of one man: Alfred C. Kinsey. Kinsey's interest in human sexuality had begun in 1938, when some students of his asked him some questions about it, particularly as pertaining to its role in marriage. Feeling he was unqualified to provide scientific answers, the professor of zoology (whose expertise was in gall wasps) read dozens of books on the subject, finding them all unsatisfactory. Kinsey began doing his own research of sexuality among students and faculty members at Indiana University (as well as among some personal friends), eventually getting grants from the National Research Council and Rockefeller Foundation to more formally pursue the work. Applying the same kind of "taxonomic approach" that he used to study bugs, Kinsey dove headfirst into the world of human sexuality, soon creating a dedicated sex research lab in Bloomington.[24] Kinsey's mission was to "accumulate an objectively determined body of fact about sex which strictly avoids social or moral interpretations," something that clearly did not exist in the sexually repressive 1930s.[25] Kinsey would receive much criticism for viewing sexuality through an allegedly pure scientific lens, with many believing it was impossible to adequately understand the subject without taking into account its ethical dimensions, not to mention love. (He actually had a clear social agenda in his work, as the foreword to his male volume illustrated.) Precisely the same would be said to be true a generation later of William Masters and Virginia Johnson's work, just one of many remarkable parallels between history's most celebrated (and scorned) sex researchers.

Over the course of nine years, Kinsey and his co-researchers at Indiana University, psychologist Wardell B. Pomeroy and statistician Clyde E. Martin, interviewed 5,300 American men about their sexuality and published the findings in *Sexual Behavior in the Human Male*. With its detailed look at the sex histories of men of various ages, occupations, educational levels, and economic classes, the 1948 book instantly became a sensation. "Not only as a marathon best-seller but more as a phenomenal source of talk and controversy, *Sexual Behavior in the Human Male* within a few months virtually has attained the status of a new American institution," *Life* magazine exclaimed, despite costing twice as much as the typical new book (and, at three pounds, weighing at least twice as much). The book quickly became known as the "Kinsey Report" (or just the "Report"), with some in publishing circles predicting that one million copies could eventually be sold in the United States alone (meaning one out of every forty-three American households would own a copy). The Kinsey Report was said to be the most popular scientific book since Charles Darwin's *On the Origin of Species* was published in 1859, the two technical publications having a major cultural impact and "crossover" appeal.[26] Booksellers had not seen such a rush to buy any book in a dozen years, when *Gone With the Wind* caused a similar literary frenzy.[27]

Although it was designed to simply start a conversation about one of our primary taboos rather than purport to have all the answers, *Sexual Behavior in the Human Male* sparked a firestorm of controversy surrounding the subject of sex in America. The nation's journalistic landscape became littered with every kind of literary form in response to the publication of the book, with forums, roundtables, and debates also held to discuss its merits and flaws. (Some were broadcast on the radio.) Newspaper cartoonists had a field day, with husbands routinely presented as wolves in sheep's clothing now that the truth was known about their sexual proclivities. Comedians also benefited from a windfall of fresh material, with a nightclub act in the late 1940s or early 1950s almost guaranteed to include a series of jokes about some Kinsey finding. Two related books, Albert Deutsch's *Sex Habits of American Men* and Morris Ernst and David Loth's *American Sexual Behavior and the Kinsey Report*, were quickly published to capitalize on the phenomenon. Others capitalized on the phenomenon for different aims. In New York, some men pretending to be Kinsey associates began interviewing women about their sex lives at Columbia University and at an office building that happened to house a top modeling agency. A liquor manufacturer called the Kinsey Distilling Corporation reported a significant increase in sales and made no effort to dispel a widespread belief that it was somehow affiliated with the researcher from Indiana. Most important, however, was the effect the book had in everyday discourse. "As a subject of conversation," *Life* observed, "the Report can be depended on to nose out [Progressive Party presidential candidate Henry A.] Wallace, Russia, the elections and the high cost of living for the better part of an evening."[28]

The Kinsey Report phenomenon was all the more amazing given that the publisher, which specialized in medical books, considered not releasing the volume publicly because of the outrage it expected would follow. (Wellesley women were not allowed to buy a copy at the campus bookstore without a note from a professor, a good indication of how shocking the book was considered to be.) The publisher's decision to go ahead with a first printing of five thousand and make it available to the general public turned out to be a wise one. Reprint after reprint was required to keep up with the demand, with more than 250,000 copies soon sold. Positive public sentiment toward the Report reflected its huge sales figures. Gallup polls showed that Americans approved of the book's publication by a ratio of about five to one, with much of lay readers' criticism limited to their belief that the Report would have been more pornographic than scientific. (Publishers considered it "the least-read bestseller.")[29] Men and women tended to ask for the book at bookstores in different ways. Women boldly requested a copy, mentioning the book by its official title, while men asked for it in hushed tones and referred to it as "that book by that Indiana professor" or "you know, that Report." (An exception was one man from Miami Beach, who bought fifty copies of the book and sent them to all his women friends.)[30] Europeans were puzzled by the uproar the book had caused in America, not understanding why so much fuss was being made about some research on sexuality. What new insights could there possibly be in a book written by some academics about a subject as old and familiar as sex? they reasonably asked, not quite appreciating how taboo the topic remained in the United States and how little many Americans actually knew about it.[31]

With many people at the time reluctant to talk about their sex lives, Kinsey went anywhere and everywhere to find subjects for his study, including prisons, reformatories, and college fraternities. He would justifiably be criticized for such selective sampling, as members of such institutions were hardly representative of the general population. Kinsey's statistical method, which relied generally on the mean rather than the median or mode, also tended to overstate men's sexual behavior. Subjects came almost exclusively from cities in the Northeast and Midwest, meaning there was a geographic bias as well. All findings in *Sexual Behavior in the Human Male* thus had to be taken with a large grain of salt (something true for all major sex studies of the next few decades, including those of Masters and Johnson). Interviews (with white males only, meaning there was a racial and economic bias as well) averaged ninety minutes and consisted of anywhere from three to five hundred questions. Kinsey's research was thus based exclusively on recollections, which alone was reason enough for skepticism, given individuals' habit of misremembering events, especially those from childhood.[32]

Still, the Kinsey Report offered considerable insight into a dimension of the human experience where no one had previously dared to venture. If there was any single, grand revelation in the book, it was that sexuality in men developed earlier and continued later in life and took more forms than commonly believed. Actual sexual behavior among men (and, it could be assumed, women, since that was with whom most of the activity was taking place) stood in stark contrast to the nation's Puritan values. The figures regarding the incidence of socially discouraged sexuality, that is, premarital sex, unfaithfulness to wives, and patronage of prostitutes, were especially startling (85 percent, 50 percent, and 70 percent, respectively). In fact, 95 percent of American men would be in prison if all the laws regarding sexuality were rigidly enforced, Kinsey suggested, and the gap between what we thought and said about sex and what we actually did is a large one.[33] (Oral-genital contact, an activity in which 59 percent of men had reportedly taken part, for example, was a felony in a number of states. Having intercourse with animals, as 17 percent of "farm boys" were reported to have done, may or may not have been a criminal offense, but most readers, especially city folk, found the act repugnant.)[34] These numbers were, again, highly suspect, given who was providing the answers to Kinsey's questions and how the data were gathered and analyzed, but the Report provided a fascinating window into male sexuality and how it appeared to differ significantly from moral standards.

The critical response to *Sexual Behavior in the Human Male* was, as might have been expected, highly polarized. Some reviewers consciously or unconsciously described the impact of the book in sexual language, apparently swept up in the excitement of the subject. "It has stimulated a frank discussion of sex that has had the character of an explosion and has provided a wholesome release," wrote Martin Gumpert in the *Nation*, the book thus functioning not unlike a national orgasm. Some critics, however, were not pleased about the climactic reaction Kinsey had produced. With the House Un-American Activities Committee's hearings going in full swing, some felt that Kinsey should be called before an equivalent congressional committee concerned about un-American sex activities. Support for Kinsey and his work was equally ardent. Kinsey was often compared with Darwin, while historian and journalist Albert Deutsch likened him to Socrates and Copernicus. His research, like that of the famed British biologist, was viewed as an act of bravery because it dared to challenge prevailing beliefs. "The most distorted and maltreated of sciences, the study of sex, has been largely freed from intolerance, superstition, frivolity, and morbidity,"

Gumpert observed, and this was the real contribution of the book. As significant, supporters of Kinsey like Gumpert argued, the book allowed ordinary
Americans to discuss a subject that had generally been the exclusive domain
of two very different but equally authoritarian institutions—religion and
psychoanalysis. It was members of these two fields who served as the most
vocal critics of *Sexual Behavior in the Human Male*, not coincidentally;
neither the clergy nor the shrinks were pleased to see their control of the
taboo topic diminished. Readers of the book reported a therapeutic effect
similar to that realized from a church service or session on the couch; in
fact, some of their guilt and shame associated with sexuality was alleviated
through the knowledge that many others shared the very same "abnormal"
or "perverted" interests.[35]

## A MORAL BEING

While some individuals were happy to learn their sexual inclinations were
hardly unique, others were not sanguine that the publication of Kinsey's research had changed the ways Americans thought and talked about sex. Like
it or not, the Kinsey Report brought sex into the national conversation as no
other single book, film, or event had ever done. As in the 1920s when, stirred
up by popular Freudian theory, Americans talked about sexual repression and
neuroses over Gin Rickeys and Singapore Slings, ordinary folks were discussing what people did behind bedroom doors (or did not do because they were
"maladjusted"). Bringing sex out into the open was a good thing, most agreed,
but did seemingly every conversation or magazine article have to bring up
the subject? Opinions on politics, business, and sports were regularly being
diverted to matters of sexuality over the dinner table and at parties, some
complained, all the more annoying because the chatter was approached from
a scientific versus romantic angle. Words or phrases never uttered by laypeo-
ple like "chromosomes," "emotional zones," and "mutual satisfaction" were
now commonly heard, and anatomical details bandied about with amazing
accuracy. Advertisers too appeared to have caught the sexual bug, with many
products now plainly pitched as vehicles for attracting a lover. "The white-hot
spotlight we've turned on sex has probably illuminated a lot of dark corners,
but do we have to leave it burning 24 hours a day?" asked Robert Thomas Allen in the *Reader's Digest* in 1950, hoping Americans could pay attention to
other, equally important matters.[36]

Not only had the Kinsey Report made Americans sex crazy, but some considered the zoology professor's "taxonomic approach" the wrong way to study the subject. Protestant theologian Reinhold Niebuhr found Kinsey's reduction of sex to biological impulses "distressing" and worried that his statistics would become accepted as the norm for sexual practices. Christians were hardly perfect, especially when it came to attitudes toward sex, but viewing humans as animals in their sexuality was a truly grievous development.[37] The Reverend William J. Gibbons, a leading Jesuit, agreed, believing that, because man was "a moral being," he could and should use reason to dictate his sexual behavior. "Man, not being governed by the . . . instincts of lesser animals, would find his tendencies running wild were he not to regulate them by reason," Gibbons said in 1950, especially concerned about Kinsey's figures regarding premarital sex.[38] Should there be any doubt, Pope Pius XII reinforced the Roman Catholic's position on sexuality. Not only was premarital sex a sin, he announced in 1951, but any sexual activity between married couples "to satisfy sensuality" was also prohibited for Catholics. Interfering with the normal processes of conception and birth, whether by contraceptives, abortion, or the "rhythm method," was forbidden; only sex with the purpose of "the fecundity of union" was allowed.[39]

Most academics, not surprisingly, thought otherwise about Kinsey's findings and viewed the gnashing of teeth among the faithful as factually unwarranted. George Peter Murdock, an anthropologist at Yale, for example, found the fact that most Americans were not virgins when they married was entirely consistent with most human societies, and thus premarital sex should be seen as natural. Seventy percent of the 250 cultures around the world Murdock studied permitted sexual experimentation before marriage, making its prevalence in the United States not socially dangerous, as many of the religious professed. In fact, Murdock argued that there were some clear advantages to adolescents having sex. Less guilt, a mastery of sexual technique, and the establishment of "normal heterosexual habits" were just a few of the reasons to approve of teen sexuality, he explained, adding that this would be an effective way to get more young people to go to church should it endorse such behavior. It was Protestants who had led sexual reform by removing the taboo of ecclesiastical celibacy, after all, and Murdock saw "no inherent reason why they could not lead a second reform of equal magnitude and importance."[40]

Based on some Protestants' response to Kinsey's research, it was highly unlikely that Murdock's proposal that the church should advocate teen sexuality would move forward. After reading Kinsey's first book and hearing a second on female sexuality was in the works, Missouri Synod Lutherans decided to do some research of their own to challenge the findings of the famous "sexologist." With a $25,000 budget and a twenty-five-person team, the evangelical group surveyed about five thousand members of their own flock and uncovered some very different findings. Only 16 percent of teenage boys belonging to the synod engaged in premarital sex, the researchers found, much fewer than Kinsey's closest figure. (Eighty percent of nonchurchgoing Protestant high school boys had had sexual intercourse, he found.) Infidelity among married teenage men was also much more rare among their own kind than what Kinsey reported of that segment of the general population (4 percent versus about 40 percent). Perhaps sharing Niebuhr's fear that Kinsey's figures would be seen as normal and thus shape actual sexual behavior, the Missouri Synod made it clear that not all Americans were as promiscuous as he claimed.[41]

Not just the religious but also marriage counselors pronounced that Kinsey's findings should not be assumed to be "normal." Kinsey's revelation that one in two married men and one in four married women under forty years old had committed adultery was particularly disturbing to those in the business of keeping couples happily together. Abraham Stone, coauthor with his late wife of the widely read *Marriage Manual: A Practical Guide-Book to Sex and Marriage*, was one such counselor quick to make a strong case against marital infidelity. Law, social custom, and religion in the United States mandated monogamy, Stone reminded those who perhaps thought the apparent popularity of extramarital relations made it acceptable. Getting caught by one's spouse typically had disastrous results, he explained in the *Reader's Digest* in 1954; the fact that humans (especially males) were by nature promiscuous was not justification to sleep with one's secretary or the next-door neighbor just because the opportunity presented itself. Some psychiatrists went further, seeing infidelity as an emotional disturbance or form of neurosis. "Infidelity, like alcoholism or drug addiction, is an expression of a deep basic disorder of character which has its roots in childhood experiences," wrote Frank Caprio, author of *Marital Infidelity*, implying that there were quite a few emotionally crippled Americans if Kinsey's findings were at all accurate.[42]

Even worse, perhaps, Kinsey and the sea of sexuality in popular and consumer culture he helped create was believed to be overshadowing other vital
dimensions of the human experience, namely, love. The tail was wagging
the dog, in other words; an expression of love (sex) was now seen as more
important than love itself. Sociologists like Paul H. Landis tried to set things
straight by emphasizing that physical contact was merely a symbol of love and
that Americans should not be distracted by this new glorification of sexuality. Sex was the result of a caring relationship, not the cause, Landis clarified,
something Americans were beginning to forget. And by focusing on the
technical aspects of sex, Kinsey was putting pressure on couples to achieve a
level of satisfaction that was, in most cases, not reachable. Both husbands and
wives were preoccupied with the latter having an orgasm each time they had
sex (ideally simultaneously with the former), an expectation that was ruining
many an otherwise good marriage.[43]

What some saw as the elevation of sex over love and marriage carried
major social implications. The Kinsey Report was not just the most egregious
example of America's preoccupation with sex, these critics believed, but also
the most visible signs of the nation's moral laxity. Pitirim Sorokin, a professor of sociology at Harvard, was one such critic; the immigrant from Russia
thought the country was becoming dangerously obsessed with sexuality. "A
consuming interest in sex has so penetrated our national culture that it has
been estimated we encounter some kind of sexual lure every nine minutes of
our waking day," Sorokin wrote in *This Week* magazine in 1954, convinced we
were fast approaching the depravity of ancient Greece or Rome. Kinsey's objective reporting of the incidence of a wide variety of sexual behaviors helped
to legitimize them, he argued, since the Indiana researcher's data equated
commonality with acceptability. In other words, just because a good percentage of the population did something did not make it right, indirectly referencing men's penchant for infidelity, prostitution, and homosexuality. According
to Sorokin, America's problem with sex went far beyond the Kinsey Report,
however. Pop culture (notably Mickey Spillane's detective stories) was strewn
with sexuality, something that jeopardized the mental health of individuals
and society as a whole. Pervasive sexuality was causing many Americans to
attribute their unhappiness to a bad sex life, he suggested, with all kinds of
negative consequences (e.g., crime, insanity, and suicide) as the result.[44]

Sex still on his mind, Sorokin decided to expand his thoughts on the matter. In his 1956 *American Sex Revolution*, the Harvard professor (now head

of the university's Research Center in Creative Altruism, which he created) continued his diatribe on the nation's fixation with sex. "Americans are becoming victims of a sex mania as malign as cancer," he wrote, claiming sexual bribery and blackmail were part of this disease sweeping the country. America's 120 million adults were guilty of not just decadence but also "sexual anarchy," he posited, with our collective debauchery causing major social mayhem. Sexual indulgence also shortened one's lifespan, Sorokin maintained, although his methodology for making such an assertion was less than scientific. (He compared the age of death of European monarchs, who were presumably promiscuous, with those of saints, who were likely not.) Everything from juvenile delinquency to divorce could be traced back to our insatiable appetite for sex, he reiterated, an opinion that many book reviewers challenged with vigor. Sorokin was clearly overstating the effects of his book's title, but he can be credited for anticipating the actual sexual revolution that would take place in a decade or so. (Few if any postwar social critics foresaw the looming counterculture, much less the sexual revolution.) As well, Sorokin used and probably coined the term "sex addiction" in his book, this too something that was considerably ahead of its time.[45]

Although Sorokin's viewpoint was extreme, he was not alone in thinking that the country had gone overboard in bringing sex out of the shadows and into the light. "We have only to look about us to realize that, as a nation, we are preoccupied—almost obsessed—with the superficial aspects of sex, with sex as a form of amusement," thought Goodrich C. Schauffler, a notable gynecologist, who blamed popular and consumer culture for the dramatic increase in pregnancies and venereal disease among unmarried teenagers as well. The writhing of Elvis Presley, the backbeat of rock 'n roll, racy illustrations on the covers of magazines, comic books, pulp fiction novels, and torrid love scenes in movies were making teens want to have sex, Schauffler concluded, with girls eventually yielding to boys' persistent demands. Adults had only themselves to blame for tolerating the use of sex as a selling device, with the chickens now coming home to roost.[46]

## HOMOSEXUALS AND OTHER MORAL PERVERTS

Kinsey justifiably received most of the credit and most of the blame for exposing the nation's sexuality, but more than a hundred other scientists had in fact done work in the field since the 1920s. Given the findings of some of these scientists, it was not surprising that Kinsey's research stood out like a sore thumb. One sex researcher had discovered a remedy for arthritis, for example, while another had developed a treatment for cancer of the prostate gland—worthy achievements but lacking the literal sex appeal of Kinsey's work.[47] Contemporaries of Kinsey did make important contributions to the field, however. Donald Webster Cory's *Homosexual in America*, Clellan S. Ford and Frank A. Beach's *Patterns of Sexual Behavior*, and Albert Ellis's *Folklore of Sex* (all published in 1951) each illustrated the wide range of sexual activity in the United States and like Kinsey's work were welcome information to some but disquieting to others. More conservative critics believed that the simple awareness of what many American adults were up to could cause anxiety to those whose sex lives were not as active or adventurous. The eminent anthropologist Margaret Mead, rather surprisingly, was one such person who viewed the public knowledge of such a personal and intimate area of life as potentially harmful to certain individuals and to society at large. Knowing that premarital virginity and marital fidelity were in decline, as Kinsey's and these other books showed, might encourage some to adopt those behaviors, this contingent argued; a Pandora's box of sexuality would be opened up through such in-depth sex research.[48]

Even Kinsey could not anticipate the reaction some politicians would have to his (and Cory's) research regarding male homosexuality. With Cold War fear and paranoia raging, not just Communists were viewed as enemies of the State but homosexuals as well. In 1950, a Senate subcommittee led by Clyde Hoey, a Democrat from North Carolina, somehow determined that no fewer than thirty-six of fifty-three branches of the federal government employed "homosexuals and other moral perverts." Hoey and his colleagues were concerned that these workers could become traitors if foreign agents threatened to expose them, their reasoning based on a 1913 case involving an Austrian spy named Alfred Redl. Almost five thousand of the 3.5 million federal workers had been identified as fitting this description, most of them in the armed forces. (None were found in the White House office, thankfully.) It was unclear how Hoey and his colleagues knew these employees were perverts, but some had quit their jobs under pressure to do so or had already been fired.[49]

Kinsey's findings regarding the incidence of homosexuality within the male population presented a problem for the Senate subcommittee charged with investigating the employment of "homosexuals and other moral perverts" by the federal government. If Kinsey's numbers were even close to accurate, the

government would have to get rid of tens of thousands of civil service employees for fear they would present a security risk (being subject to blackmail
by Communists). Four percent of white American adults were "exclusively
homosexual," according to Kinsey, meaning 56,787 of government workers
fit that description if they were representative of the general population (with
no reason to believe otherwise). That same figure meant that twenty one
senators and representatives were homosexual—even more troubling given
that they presented a far greater security risk than your average civil service
employee. Should Kinsey's figure regarding the number of American white
adults who had had any homosexual contact over the course of their lives (37
percent) be within the range of validity, the risks to national security would
be truly staggering. Over half a million federal employees would have to get
the ax, as would 192 members of Congress; such a scenario was perhaps more
damaging to the country's well-being than anything the Communists could
devise. A probe into not just homosexuality but other "perversions" would
further deplete the number of Americans eligible to work for Uncle Sam.
So-called sexual abnormalities and participation in socially taboo acts were
as common among successful men, including politicians, as any other group,
Kinsey had found, meaning the nation would barely have a working government should it achieve its goal.[50] By 1953, the State Department had fired
more than three hundred employees on moral charges; their loyalty to the
United States was questioned on the basis of their sexual preference.[51]

Kinsey's revelation that a sizable percentage of American men had some
homosexual contact in their lives went far beyond issues of national security.
While all agreed that most of this activity was simply related to childhood
curiosity—a brief stage that would quickly and thankfully pass—much concern was reserved for those boys (or, more rarely, girls) who did not "grow
out of it." Signs that a son or daughter was legitimately sexually attracted to
people of his or her own gender were considered deeply disturbing to parents in the 1950s. More attention was being paid to the causes and possible
cures of homosexuality in the early 1950s as concerns about "abnormalities"
of all kinds intensified, a byproduct of Cold War anxieties and the nation's
reverence for conformist values. Rather than a disease (or glandular defect,
as once thought), homosexuality was a symptom of an underlying emotional
disorder, most psychiatrists agreed, a conclusion that was certainly troubling
but better than if it was an inherited condition. The degree of the problem

could range from a common neurosis to something much worse. "The victim may be a psychopathic personality, with a defective conscience or inadequate sense of responsibility toward others," *Time* wrote of homosexuals in 1953, and if this was so, successful treatment was unlikely. Schizophrenic "victims," that is, those with a "split personality," however, responded to treatment for homosexuality, psychiatrists and doctors believed. All of this was part of mainstream psychological thought at midcentury.[52]

Just as he had stirred up America's sexual pot in the 1920s, Sigmund Freud's thoughts regarding homosexuality continued to reverberate in the 1950s. Freudian-based psychoanalytic theory, still dominant within the psychiatric community in the postwar years, located the onset of homosexuality among adolescents squarely within the parental relationship. Homosexuality developed when a child failed to "identify" with the parent of his or her own gender, it was generally believed based on Freudian theory, and this rejection caused him or her to "over-identify" with the other parent. Boys thus became homosexuals because they embraced feminine characteristics, girls because they embraced masculine ones. (A popular play that ran on Broadway between September 1953 and February 1955, Robert Anderson's *Tea and Sympathy*, addressed this very theme.) "What did we do wrong?" asked many parents in this position, as their child was quickly whisked off to a shrink to try to remedy the situation. "He will help the boy to see how his emotional growth has been stunted or twisted by factors that he did not understand," explained *Time*, the development of a whole personality causing any and all homosexual inclinations to disappear. Best of all, prolonged analysis was not required to repair this particular neurosis. "If the boy is in his early teens and not set in his ways, a few hours of give and take interviews may suffice," the magazine reported, although the "habit" would be much more difficult to break if the "deviate" was a few years older. If that was the case, therapy was prescribed to help the young man adjust to society, not for his own benefit but in the hope he would not harm others through his affliction. It was considered important not to bully a young homosexual or label him a "pervert," lest he strike out in violence. One New York City teenager had reportedly murdered his parents in December 1953 because his mother had called him a "fairy," a warning to others suspecting they could be in the presence of a homosexual.[53]

Although there were undoubtedly times and places in which it would have been worse to be homosexual, postwar America was definitely not a good cultural climate to have, as *Newsweek* put it in 1954, "the delicate problem." (*Time* described it as "the hidden problem.") Homosexual relations were a criminal offense (sodomy) in forty-six of the forty-eight states at the time, with northeastern liberal arts universities being one of the few public settings where "deviants" or "inverts" were generally tolerated. Half a million homosexual men and women were estimated to live in New York City alone, however, making the "delicate problem" something impossible to ignore. As well, homosexual culture could be found in books, magazines, and drama with increasing frequency, making it clear that the issue was not going to simply disappear through a few hours of psychotherapy. (Besides *Tea and Sympathy*, *The Children's Hour* and *The Immoralist* were homosexually themed plays running on Broadway, and a magazine called *One* was wholly dedicated to the subject.) A scandal involving a relationship between the actor Sir John Gielgud and Lord Montagu of Beaulieu had recently rocked British society, illustrating that the United States was hardly alone in its condemnation of homosexuality. Deemed antithetical to Christian doctrine (specifically the reference to Sodom in Genesis 19:4–7) and regarded as a disgusting, horrible vice by its most outspoken enemies, homosexuality remained one of the few major taboos in Western society.[54]

Much of the blame for individuals not fighting off what was sometimes referred to as an "irresistible urge" was placed squarely on the man who wrote extensively about it, Sigmund Freud. By defining homosexuality as a complex rather than a sin, Freud had given homosexuals free rein to pursue their perversion, critics believed. Contemporary psychologists and psychiatrists basically agreed with this assessment, viewing homosexuality not as evil but as an unfortunate condition stemming from childhood. A recent article in the *Journal of Social Hygiene* titled "The Problem of Homosexuality" confirmed as much. Knowing they would never get married or have children, homosexuals were unhappy and discontented people, according to Karl M. Bowman and Bernice Engle of the University of California Medical School, but they had no intention to harm others or bring down American society as some believed. A "fixation" and a "weak father" were the major ingredients that produced a homosexual, although some doctors thought that some methods of child raising and coeducation could trigger the "pattern." Some parents and teachers thus limited contact between girls and boys in order to prevent this from taking place, especially among shy children. Socially insecure children were particularly vulnerable to the formation of an interest in homosexuality, this theory went, accounting for some of the gender-specific classrooms and playgrounds in America in the 1950s.[55]

Going against the grain, two psychiatrists, Adelaide M. Johnson of the University of Minnesota and David B. Robinson of the Mayo Clinic, believed parents were indeed at fault for their child's sexual deviance. Not just homosexuality but also sadomasochism, exhibitionism, voyeurism, fetishism, transvestitism, and even bestiality were all a result of "parental seduction," they theorized in a 1957 article in the *AMA Journal*, causing quite a wave in psychiatric circles. Parental seduction could take many forms, the two argued. Their view was reflective of the backlash to the free and open form of sex education that had been popular in the years after the war. Discussing sex with children in frank terms, appearing naked before them, bathing or sleeping with them, and even a caress could lead to their sexual arousal, Johnson and Robinson proposed, the larger problem being that there was no proper outlet to relieve these drives. Repression and regression were the sad fate for children growing up in such an unhealthy climate, a cure for which was unlikely.[56]

## AN AREA OF VAST DARK IGNORANCE

With the impact of *Sexual Behavior in the Human Male* still very much felt five years after its appearance, Kinsey's second volume in his planned series of books about sex in America was published. Like the first volume, *Sexual Behavior in the Human Female* would shock Americans through its unflinching examination of an aspect of society typically relegated to the margins. Kinsey interviewed about six thousand (again, all white) women to write his much-anticipated follow-up to his 1948 study about men; this second volume was coauthored by Pomeroy, Martin, and anthropologist Paul H. Gebhard. Women talked about sex significantly less than men, nearly everyone agreed, making interest in the second Kinsey Report that much greater. Some writers referred to the publication date of the book as "K-Day," and some newspapers made its release their lead story on their front pages (beating out such others as the verification of a Soviet hydrogen bomb blast and the return of

Adlai Stevenson from a global peacekeeping mission). *Newsweek* declared it "the hottest news story of the year," a bold claim given that events like the announcement of Jonas Salk's polio vaccine, the coronation of Elizabeth II, and the execution of the Rosenbergs had already occurred. More than a hundred reporters accepted an invitation to read advance galleys of the book on-site at Indiana University, all of them required to sign a three-page contract that they would not spill the beans before the official publication date. (Three years earlier, *Redbook* had somehow been able to publish an unauthorized "first preview" of the book.)[57] The book's findings were expected to be "so explosive as to make the [nuclear bomb] tests on the Nevada flats look like the fireworks display of a county," wrote George Milburn in the *Nation*, quite a buildup for the release of a scientific book written by a zoologist teaching at a midwestern university. Women's magazines like *Women's Home Companion* and *Collier's*, bastions of traditional domestic life, offered complete reports on Kinsey's latest findings in their September 1953 issues, allowing housewives to know whether or not they were keeping up with the Joneses, sexually speaking.[58]

The findings of the new book (nicknamed "All About Eve") were, it turned out, both expected and surprising. "The range of variation [of sexual behavior] in the female far exceeds the range of variation in the male," Kinsey and his colleagues wrote; that women developed earlier sexually and had more erogenous zones than men was one of the more interesting bits of news.[59] The data (recorded on two hundred thousand IBM punch cards) revealed that married women in their late teens had sex with their husbands 2.8 times per week; thirty-year-olds, 2.2 times; and forty-year-olds, 1.5 times. Some women at all age levels reported having sex four or more times a day every day of the week, rather remarkably. About half of the married women in the study were not virgins when they wed; this was one of the bigger surprises in the book. Class, religion, and education level made little difference in whether women chose to have sex while single, although there was a generational difference. Younger women—those born during or after the Roaring Twenties—were more than twice as likely as those middle-aged (those born before) to have slept with a man before they got hitched. (Women born before 1900 referred to petting as "courting," "bundling," "spooning," "smooching," "larking," and "sparking.") Married women were about twice as faithful as married men, Kinsey reported in his new book, with about a quarter of wives admitting they had strayed (versus half of husbands).[60] In general, men were consider-ably more interested in sex than women, Kinsey concluded, so much so that he found it almost a miracle that "married couples are ever able to work out a satisfactory sexual relationship." Age alone was a cruel trick of nature when it came to gender differences in sexuality, he also observed, since the male peaked a decade or two earlier than the female.[61]

If the second Kinsey Report was as well received as the first for its intrigu-ing insights, it was similarly attacked for its suspect methodology. Sampling and statistical problems plagued *Sexual Behavior in the Human Female*, mak-ing the findings in the book less than fully reliable (some would say totally unreliable). As in Kinsey's first volume on men, younger, better educated, and urban subjects were overrecruited (some defended the book by saying, "Women were women"). Class differences, which were notable among men (lower-class men viewed higher-class men's devotion to foreplay as "per-verted," for example), were indeed significantly less apparent among women. But even with its flaws, *Sexual Behavior in the Human Female* was a rare peek into the sex lives of American women; this alone for many made the consider-able retail price of $8 worthwhile. "The statistics, if not perfect, are at least the only statistics in town," *Life* noted, "and the first good strong ray of light into an area of vast dark ignorance." Readers found the fact that ninety-nine out of every one hundred women had engaged in some sort of sexuality by age 35 intriguing, for example, and that a full third of married women had previ-ously "petted" with more than ten men (some more than one hundred). Still, a primary motivating factor for men to get married was for sexual purposes, something that did not generally hold true for women. Many women could take or leave sex, readers learned, while most men made it one of life's priori-ties and spent much of their day thinking about it. Marilyn Monroe's breathy passion was apparently a big act, men might have concluded from reading *Sexual Behavior in the Human Female*; real women were not nearly as sex obsessed as the movies made them out to be.[62] Kinsey himself was admittedly amazed by the variation in women's capacity for sexual pleasure, which he thought was actually far greater than men's.

As or more important than Kinsey's findings about women's sex lives, however, were his views on the role of sexuality in American society. No institution was doing a good job in teaching women about sex, he surmised, and only experience itself helped them learn about it in a positive way. "It is petting rather than the home, classroom or religious instruction, lectures or books, classes in biology, sociology or philosophy, or actual coitus," Kinsey wrote, "that provides most females with their first real understanding of a heterosexual experience." Not only were parents, educators, and ministers of little or no use in teaching young women about sex, but also they were hindering the process, he believed. "The church, the home and the school are the chief sources of the sexual inhibitions, the distaste for all aspects of sex, the fears of the physical difficulties that may be involved in a sexual relation-ship, and the feelings of guilt which many females carry with them into their marriage," he stated, implying that all institutions do more harm than good in this arena.[63] (Kinsey's observations were spot on, but it should be kept in mind that married women knew enough about sex to create the baby boom.) Like Freud and social critics such as Theodore Dreiser, Sherwood Anderson, and Bertrand Russell, Kinsey was a strong advocate for sexual liberty and sharply criticized moral conventions of the day; his second book was an ideal platform to voice his informed views.[64]

Another of Kinsey's aims in his second book was to dispel much of the information offered in what was the primary repository of sex advice at the time, the marriage manual. (In addition to the Stones' *Marriage Manual*, books such as Havelock Ellis's *Studies in the Psychology of Sex*, Oliver M. But-terfield's *Marriage and Sexual Harmony*, Fred Brown and Rudolph K. Kemp-ton's *Sex Questions and Answers*, Helene Deutsch's *Psychology of Women*, and Allan Fromme's *Psychologist Looks at Sex and Marriage* were commonly recommended to couples.) Such books typically assumed that women inher-ently had less capacity for sexual response, a fallacy according to Kinsey's research. That women also needed to be kissed, caressed, and romanced more than men was also wrong, he believed, the former physically able to climax just as quickly and easily (and a lot more frequently) than the latter. (Studies of women's "self-gratification" proved this, as did research into the sex lives of "lower educational groups," who reportedly spent less time on foreplay.) Long periods of petting before intercourse—one of the staple pieces of wisdom in most marriage manuals—was thus unnecessary, Kinsey argued, a mythology about female sexuality that harkened back to ancient times. (Some bawdy English folk songs praising the sexual readiness of women were a lot more accurate, he pointed out.) Any problems with female sexuality were not biological but social, he added, because girls were often taught that physical contact with boys (or with oneself) was a bad thing. This accounted for marriage manuals' standard recommendation for the need for husbands to "warm up" their "chilly" wives. From this perspective, Kinsey could be said to have been an early feminist, using scientifically based facts to identify socially based gender inequalities. Kinsey took particular issue with the commonly used word "frigidity," seeing it as a purely social construct rather than a biological one.[65]

Kinsey was equally determined to set the record straight when it came to teenage sexuality. American adults' generally negative stance toward sexual activity among adolescents was also a product of social mores rather than anything to do with the human body. Teenage boys were at the peak of their sexual powers, in fact, meaning their desire and urge to act on it was perfectly normal. "It is the increasing inability of older persons to understand the sexual capacities of youth which is responsible for the opinion that there is a rise in juvenile delinquency," he explained, adding that some of the great romances in literature involved the very young (Juliet was thirteen, Helen of Troy a year younger). As with women, society was responsible for making adolescents feel badly about their sexuality, and this shame or guilt was something that could carry into adulthood.[66]

## LA PETITE MORT

Because *Sexual Behavior in the Human Female* was the second installment in what was ambitiously envisioned as a multipart series about sex in America, Kinsey took advantage of the opportunity to make some comparisons between men's and women's sexual psychology. Men became more sexually excited and more often by external stimuli than women, for example. Of thirty-three different "prompts," in fact, only three were found to be more arousing for women: romantic movies, romantic literature, and being bitten by a lover. (Everything from the sight of a nude woman to a stocking got men's juices flowing.) Transvestitism was far more common among men than women, as was homosexuality. However, from a purely biological standpoint, men and women had more in common sexually than popularly believed, Kinsey made clear. (He also pointed out that both male and female humans shared many sexual traits with other mammals, much to some critics' dismay.) The physical effects of the orgasm, notably, were quite similar for men and women. The French nicknames for the orgasm—"la petite mort" ("the little death") and "la mort doux" ("the sweet death")—had a legitimate basis in biology. In addition to a faster pulse and breathing rate, senses became dulled at the point of climax. All vision could be briefly lost, and some even became unconscious for a few seconds. Loss of a sense of pain was also part of the orgasm experience, since the brain was in a very peculiar state when in the throes of ecstasy. A scientist from Buenos Aires, Abraham Mosovich, found that brain waves during orgasm were remarkably similar to those of a person having an epileptic fit, proof enough of the intense power of sex.[67]

Despite the popularity of the second Kinsey Report among the general public and positive reviews by most critics, the information contained in it was simply too much for the prudish. Mining the sexual histories of men was bad enough, but documenting those of women was reprehensible, some thought. One person clearly offended by *Sexual Behavior in the Human Female* was Representative Louis B. Heller, a Democrat from Brooklyn, New York, who proposed a congressional investigation of the book and its authors. Kinsey was "hurling the insult of the century" at American women and contributing "to the depravity of a whole generation, to the loss of faith in human dignity . . . to the spread of juvenile delinquency, and to the misunderstanding and confusion about sex," Heller stated a week before the book was officially published, obviously not happy to learn that about half of younger women were not virgins when they got married and that a quarter had cheated on their husbands. Heller was trying to get the U.S. Post Office to stop delivering the book until Congress had time to consider "the value of such studies, if any"—the beginning of a lengthy censorship battle with the federal government. (U.S. Customs did not take kindly to Kinsey's importing pornographic films a few years later.) Undeterred, Kinsey continued to promote his new book by holding press conferences and giving talks to various groups. Two-thirds of married Americans had some kind of sexual problem, he told audiences, much of this due to the fact that men knew little about women's sexuality and vice versa. This was why his research was so important, he reiterated, countering critics like Heller who believed exploration of human sexuality was immoral and harmful to society.[68]

A year after his book about female sexuality was published, Kinsey turned his attention to an even more controversial subject—the sexual behavior of children. Kinsey revealed the subject of his next book to a group of leaders in the fields of family counseling, child care, and sex education in New York in February 1954. "Many a child who knows nothing about reproduction, or about the differences between the male and female, has developed definite attitudes and responses toward sex at the age of 2 or 3," he told the audience of five hundred people, some of whom were no doubt a bit uncomfortable to hear this news. Kinsey had discussed child sexuality in each of his two reports, but dedicating a whole study of it was an especially bold thing to do given the taboo surrounding the subject. Kinsey had already collected data on several hundred children under the age of five, finding that some of their sexual "personality" had been well established as toddlers. Children at a young age were typically aware of the normalcy of heterosexuality and of the physical differences between boys and girls (and thus men and women), for example, and such knowledge paved the way for their future sex lives. Children's sexuality was proving to be a lot more difficult to test than that of adults, however, making Kinsey use play techniques to get answers to his questions. Even infants of two or three months responded to sexual stimuli, he was finding, confirming what other researchers (notably Sigmund Freud) had proposed. Clinging to and snuggling with the mother was a baby's initiation into sexuality, Kinsey argued, and discouraging this at a certain point was something that could lead to trouble in the bedroom decades later.[69]

In late 1955, Kinsey went to Europe to spread his gospel of American sexuality, lecturing before medical groups and meeting with psychiatrists and other interested parties. Kinsey was particularly struck by the openness toward sexuality in Scandinavia, and how laws governing it there were much closer to actual behavior than in the United States. When he returned in December of that year, Kinsey told the press that he now planned to publish twenty more books on the subject over the next decade, the best part being that he and his colleagues had already completed all of the research for them. With some eighteen thousand sexual histories of what he considered to be a diverse group of Americans (they ranged, in his words, from "the Junior League to the New York garment district"), his institute had all the raw data it needed to publish a veritable library of American sexual behavior. With some card punching, analysis, and editing, volumes on everything from abortion to transvestism would come forth, completing his life's work. And after working for the past seventeen years in the basement of a building on campus that dated back to 1884, Kinsey and his team were moving to the brand-new

Jordan Hall of Science, which included a "sex library" of more than seventeen thousand books, twenty thousand prints, a huge collection of photographs, and thousands of feet of film.[70]

In just eight months, however, Kinsey would be dead at age 62 from a heart ailment and pneumonia, his grand mission cut short. The trustees of the Institute for Sex Research quickly made it clear that their important work would continue, with Pomeroy and Gebhard to serve as codirectors.[71] Indeed, in two years, the institute published *Pregnancy, Birth, and Abortion*, its first book since Kinsey's death. Unlike the first two reports, however, this book fell well short of the best-seller lists, suggesting that an era had ended. "The curiosity of the general public seems to have been satiated," Gebhard remarked soon after the new book was published, thinking America's fascination with the science of sex may well be over. More conservative students at the university and local citizens were no longer protesting the work being done at the institute, another sign the cultural phenomenon had run its course. Funding was also becoming increasingly difficult to obtain, and this problem was compounded by the loss of the charismatic Kinsey. Now in the red, the institute had allowed *McCall's* magazine to publish some of the more interesting findings of the new book before its official release, something Alfred Kinsey never permitted.[72]

While *Pregnancy, Birth, and Abortion* was certainly informative, the lukewarm reception it received appeared to be justified. The third "Kinsey Report" lacked the fireworks that made the two earlier ones such sensations, although there were some interesting findings. Ten percent of the sample of women studied had accidentally become pregnant, readers learned, and married women had more abortions than single women. Just 3 percent of unmarried women who had abortions permanently gave up sex, and 75 percent of widowed and divorced women continued to have sex. Despite the book's disappointing response, Pomeroy, Gebhard, and Martin (who never flew on a plane together, as it was only they who knew the code to the raw research data) had no intention of shutting down the institute. Next on the institute's agenda was a book on convicted sex offenders, with volumes on homosexuality, prostitution, marriage, and sex in art to follow, just as Kinsey had intended. Kinsey's legacy could be found in other ways two years after his death. Couples who "parked" on campus had nicknamed a favorite spot "Kinsey's

Hollow," his name fittingly linked to the activity that made him famous.[73] Happily, work at the Kinsey Institute continues to this day, its mission to "advance sexual health and knowledge worldwide" very much consistent with the vision its leader had when he founded it in 1947. As the nation looked to the 1960s, however, a new frontier was forming, one that would serve as a perfect breeding ground for America's "sexidemic."

# 2

# Easy Rider

What the hell is wrong with freedom? That's what it's all about.

—*Billy (Dennis Hopper) in the 1969 film* Easy Rider

In December 1966, UCLA psychiatrist Ralph Greenson weighed in on what he described as a rising tension and even hostility between men and women. "It is my definite impression that women are becoming sexually more assertive and demanding, and men are more indifferent and lethargic," he told the American Medical Association (AMA), believing this held true for both young adults and the middle-aged. Women were thus responsible for this escalating war between the sexes, Greenson felt, with their growing independence making men feel more timid, especially in the bedroom. Married women were no longer submitting passively to passionless sex with their husbands as they used to, he explained, while single women were showing all signs of enjoying sex without romantic love, just like men. "Apparently, as they have gained greater freedom, they feel entitled to equal sexual satisfaction along with their other equal rights," Greenson informed his AMA colleagues; women's greater awareness of their femininity was having a direct and deleterious effect on men's masculinity.[1]

Greenson's take on gender relations in the mid-1960s represented just a small piece of the ever-growing "sexidemic" in America. One's sexuality was seen as a way to express one's identity in the increasingly balkanized society of the 1960s, which was part of a rise of individualism and new attention to the "self." What would become known as the sexual revolution could thus be seen as reflective of a mass existential crisis sweeping the country as traditional ties to family, community, the government, and religion fractured. This was especially true for younger, middle-class women who were actively searching for meaning and purpose in their lives beyond that of suburban mother.[2] Sexuality (and arguably society as a whole) transitioned more in the 1960s than in any other decade in American history as attitudes and behavior attached to the counterculture eclipsed those of the postwar way of life. Breakthroughs in sex research, the widespread adoption of sex-ed programs in public schools, the struggle for sexual freedom on college campuses, an explosion of erotic pop culture, and, last but not least, the introduction of the birth control pill all irrevocably altered the landscape of sex in America. By the end of the decade, Americans had a serious case of cultural vertigo, much of it due to the whirling universe of sexuality.

## AN ADEQUATE BODY OF SEXUAL INFORMATION

Even with the promise of a "new frontier," however, few people in 1960 could predict the social and sexual turbulence that was around the corner for the nation. The arena of sex looked backward more than forward at the beginning of the decade, the domestic orientation of the postwar American Way of Life very much in play. Marriage courses at universities remained a common way for young adults to learn about sex, for example—these not all that different from the ones GIs had taken after they returned from the war. An estimated one hundred thousand American college students in 1960 were taking one of about one thousand marriage courses, which filled a large gap in many young people's educational experience. One of the better-known ones was taught by James Peterson, whose "Education for Marriage" course at the University of Southern California was one of the most popular on campus. Peterson was the host of a show on CBS called *For Better or Worse*, in fact, and he used his television skills to make the subject less intimidating than it might have been. Still, Peterson spoke frankly about the biological and psychological aspects of sexual intercourse—exactly what the students wanted. Four-fifths of the two hundred students attending his class were women, many of them learning about the course at sorority "hen parties." "In college, almost all students are looking forward to marriage, yet they run into the sexual tensions of courtship," Peterson said; he felt his class was a "teachable moment to do a great deal of good." Women would sometimes refer their dates to the course, and those engaged to a fellow student strongly encouraged them to attend as well. "If she's gonna learn all that baloney, I'd better be up on it, too," a male student reasoned, reluctantly conceding that he should be as knowledgeable in the subject as his future wife.[3]

While helpful, such courses did not provide nearly enough information about the intricacies of sexuality for many with wedding plans. Some couples planning to get hitched in the early 1960s went to a marriage counselor for sexual advice, but many more read one of the plethora of "marriage manuals" still being published. (The library at the Kinsey Institute for Sex Research held no fewer than 1,400 of them.) One of the most popular remained the Stones' *Marriage Manual*, which had first been published in 1935 and was revised in 1951. It could be reasonably stated that the book had a significant impact on Americans' sex lives for a quarter century, with both men and women using it to better negotiate their way around the bedroom. The kind of information provided in this and other marriage manuals was, however, primitive at best. One might learn the route the male sperm took to reach the female egg, for example, or that the best time for a woman to get pregnant was the two or so days in which she was ovulating. Impotent men should advise their future wives about their condition, *A Marriage Manual* also made clear, with plenty of other mostly biological information provided in the book. Companionship, intimacy, and sympathy were emphasized, and the various methods of contraception were explained. Lessons in what was termed "The Art of Marriage" were also offered, one of which was for husbands to give their wives a generous amount of foreplay before intercourse. Given that 60 percent of women rarely or never reached a sexual climax, according to studies cited in the book, such advice was well warranted.[4]

Although *A Marriage Manual* and similar books were certainly better than nothing, it was clear that "marriage manuals" fell well short of what Americans could and should know about sex in the 1960s. It was thus not surprising that William Masters and Virginia Johnson's 1966 *Human Sexual Response* redefined the landscape of sexuality in the United States by offering readers a completely new and different understanding of the physical dynamics of sex. *Human Sexual Response* was hardly the only book to be purchased that year with a heavy dose of sex (John Cleland's infamous *Fanny Hill* was doing very well in paperback, as was Richard von Krafft-Ebing's English translation of *Psychopathia Sexualis* and the works of Marquis de Sade), but its scientific foundation set itself apart from all others. The book had almost as big an impact as Kinsey's 1948 *Sexual Behavior in the Human Male* despite its overtly clinical language and frequently unintelligible syntax.[5]

Based on eleven years of research (and about seven hundred subjects experiencing a reported ten thousand orgasms), *Human Sexual Response* offered detailed measurements of all kinds of sexual activity; nothing like it had ever been published. While Kinsey had produced his books based on interviews, questionnaires, and statistics, Masters and Johnson focused on what people did rather than what they said. Readers found the goings-on at the team's "live sex lab" fascinating, a clear deviation from the accepted view of sexuality as an intimate, private affair. (The lab included not just electrocardiographs and electroencephalographs but also floodlights and color-movie cameras.) Knowledge abounded in many fields, of course, but sexuality largely remained a no-man's-land, requiring Masters and Johnson to push the boundaries of scientific inquiry. And more than most fields, sexuality was a wellspring of misinformation and misunderstanding, which made their effort that much more important. Much misery and anxiety could be eliminated if the facts of sexuality were brought to the surface, the two believed, with no better time and place to do that than 1960s America. Treating sexual problems was the logical next step, and this was the planned subject of their next book.[6]

For the moment, however, the two doctors (he a gynecologist and she a psychologist) were enjoying the enormous success of *Human Sexual Response*. Although the book cost a whopping $10 (*Valley of the Dolls*, the best-selling book of 1966, cost $5.95), it was difficult to find in bookstores, but this only added to its mystique. The book was primarily targeted to professionals, but that did not stop the general public from hunting down a copy.[7] The book's publisher (Little, Brown) had also limited the number of review copies (even *Science* magazine did not receive one), and the jacket carried no endorsements. Some major newspapers, including the *Chicago Tribune*, refused to review the book, with editors seeing it as an odd literary specimen specifically for the medical community. Many ordinary Americans thought otherwise. Mail poured into their Reproductive Biology Research Foundation in St. Louis, much of it from people seeking help for their own sexual problems. (Of the initial one thousand letters received after the book's publication, 70 percent were requests for help while 10 percent were considered "favorable" and 20 percent "hostile."[8]) Many people jokingly asked if they could buy the movie rights for the book, knowing a film as blatantly sexual would do well at the box office. Removing the taboos, repression, and sinfulness surrounding sexuality was to Masters and Johnson a serious business, however, as was the knowledge that their work would result in "saving" many marriages. Now armed with the facts, parents would be better equipped to talk about sexuality with their children, the pair also believed. Judging by the book's success, it did indeed appear that the general public was more than ready to embrace what Masters referred to as "an adequate body of sexual information." Only the instinct for survival or self-preservation was stronger than that of sexuality, they and many others were convinced, and this was the underlying basis that made their work so essential.[9]

The broad interest in Masters and Johnson's work was all the more surprising given that the team had faced considerable difficulty finding any major institution willing to support their research. (Telling a CEO, dean, or government official in the mid-1950s that one wanted to observe individuals and couples having sex was not the best way to acquire funding.) While the general public was fascinated by their research, some critics found the duo's approach as cold as the paper on an examination table. Masters and Johnson had proved that sex had "lost its vitality as a human experience," wrote the Freudian-trained psychiatrist Leslie Farber in *Commentary*, while Malcolm Muggeridge of the *New Statesman* sneered that, with the realization of the "cult of the orgasm, the American Dream [was] at last fulfilled." Given the criticism and hardships that Kinsey had faced while pursuing his work, it was amazing that anyone would want to venture into the still largely hostile territory of sex research.[10] Just as they had hoped, however, Masters and Johnson's work helped to jump-start new studies in sex research and added legitimacy to those already in progress. Columbia University's medical school was now planning to launch a program in human reproduction with the assistance of a Ford grant, and researchers at the University of Minnesota's sex clinic were applying the couple's findings to their own. "We feel for the first time that we are working with the support of public opinion, not against it," said Johnson immediately after the publication of *Human Sexual Response*, hoping the taboos surrounding the scientific study of sex were finally disappearing.[11]

Two years after its publication, *Human Sexual Response* was still selling two to three thousand copies a month and was available in ten different languages. Perhaps the biggest sign of the authors' success was that their work was spoofed in two recent novels, *The Experiment* and *Venus Examined*. After a busy and lengthy book tour, Masters and Johnson were happy to be back home in St. Louis but were excited to be working with a group of Japanese researchers to set up their own sex lab. A lucrative consulting business was next for the team, with no shortage of couples seeking personal help for their impotence, frigidity, or premature ejaculation problem. Many Freudians continued to gripe that Masters and Johnson's focus on symptoms and behavior was superficial and did not address the deeper underlying causes of such problems, but the pair's high success rate spoke for itself. The majority of couples experiencing a sexual problem were cured through their techniques, the doctors claimed, something that for the moment kept criticism directed toward them to more of a murmur than a shout.[12]

## A TAILOR-MADE SETUP FOR BIG TROUBLE

Other researchers of sexuality were more interested in its sociology than its physiology. In his 1960 *Premarital Sexual Standards in America*, for example, Ira Reiss went into the field to learn more about young people's attitudes and behavior regarding sex, a rapidly growing area of exploration. Reiss, a professor of sociology at Bard College, interviewed hundreds of people in their late teens and early twenties, finding that there were five major groups with respect to premarital sex. The first was "Total Abstainers," those who did not engage in any kind of sexual activity (a declining number, Reiss found). The second group was "Petters," those who engaged in a variety of sexual activities except intercourse, thereby retaining their virginity, and the third was "Equalitarians," those who did "go all the way" but were monogamous. The fourth group Reiss identified was "Double Standard Bearers," those who believed it was acceptable for a man to be sexually active but not the woman, since she was believed to have less sexual desire. Reiss called the final group "One-and-a-Half Standard Bearers," young people who subscribed to the "double standard" but made an exception for women who were engaged or "in love." Interestingly, Reiss found quite a few women who publicly subscribed to the "double standard" but who discreetly had sex with men they met while on spring break in Florida, showing that social norms and personal desires were two very different things.[13]

As in the 1950s, experts of all stripes offered thoughts on how to keep young people's sexual desire in check. Ann Landers, whose advice column appeared in more than four hundred newspapers in the early 1960s, had firm opinions regarding teenage sexuality that she compiled in her 1961 book *Since You Ask Me*. For Landers (whose real name was Eppie Lederer), it was the now-easily-had automobile that served as the literal vehicle of teen sexuality (the same had been said to be true in the 1920s). The car, according to Landers, was both "a portable bedroom" and the means by which boys could find willing girls outside their own neighborhood. ("Cheap" girls were apparently more likely to live out of town.) The parked car, especially one at a drive-in theater, was a hotbed of youthful lust, and the opportunity to "neck" was almost too great to resist. "Add to this a full moon and a few cans of beer or a pint of bourbon which just happens to be in the glove compartment and you have a tailor-made setup for big trouble," Landers wrote, a double date with a more experienced couple adding even more fuel to the fire.[14]

For Landers and many other adults, it was vital that teenagers keep their sexuality under control, lest they feel guilty and ashamed, had their reputations ruined, or, in her words, "break [their] parents' hearts." A girl could get pregnant, of course, but authority figures like Landers had no intention of advising young people of what precautions to take to avoid that from happening beyond abstaining from sex. Landers even advised teens not to go steady, of the mind that spending a lot of time with one person was a recipe for disaster. Keeping busy—preferably with outside activities—was the best thing for young people to do, since idle hands were the devil's workshop. If teens must neck, a well-lit living room was the best place for it to take place, with at least one parent required to be home. Setting a time limit—no more than thirty minutes—in advance was also a good idea to keep things from going too far. Petting presented even more risks than necking, as it was likely to lead to feet leaving the floor and, thus, a reclining position. It was boys who were the real problem, Landers made clear, as their biological drives made them do whatever it took to talk a girl into going as far as possible. Controlling such drives "distinguishes men from beasts," she wrote, making her case for a civilized society in which people, especially teenagers, were not slaves to their natural impulses.[15] Arnold Toynbee, the British intellectual, saw things not much differently than Landers, oddly enough. Toynbee believed that the postponement of adolescents' sexual awakening allowed them to acquire knowledge, which was vital to the West's leadership position.[16]

With such standard advice both outdated and ineffective, it was becoming increasingly clear that a different model of sex education for young people was required. It was readily apparent to both students and teachers that there was a gap between standards and practices with regard to sex in the early 1960s; in other words, what young people were expected (or, more likely, were not expected) to do and what they actually did was often quite different. More and more educators were deciding it was time to see if anything could be done about it, and they got together to discuss the possible options. Deans, guidance counselors, and clergymen from across the country gathered at Columbia University's Teachers College in 1963 to discuss sexuality among both high school and college students, for example, hoping a two-week conference dedicated to the subject would provide some answers. These authorities admitted to not knowing what to tell students about sex but felt that some direction was needed, since the idea of unregulated sexuality among America's youth was unacceptable. Opinions at the "Work Conference on Sex Mores among Young People" varied, not surprisingly, with some thinking that students having sex was fine as long as it was part of "successful interpersonal relations" and "meaningful living" while others were not so sure. All agreed that sexual attitudes had not kept up with the times, however, with lingering postwar conservatism putting the brakes on forming a clear understanding of and opinion about the realities of youthful sexuality. There was a need for "an 'ethics of transition' to hold us over until morals catch up with real life," suggested Isadore Rubin, managing editor of the monthly magazine *Sexology*, as few were able at this point to recognize that a full-scale sexual revolution was bubbling.[17]

The profound interest in sexual activity among students on the part of university officials and other adults—something that may seem strange today—was a function of a number of factors. A half century ago, educators viewed their role as not just intellectual but also moral, shaping students' sexual behavior as part of the process of molding responsible adults who would contribute to society. Similarly, because college students represented a significant part of the next generation of adults, what they believed and how they acted today was perceived as the foundation for the dominant values of tomorrow. The fate of the nation thus rested upon young people's future sex lives, one might venture to say, making their education in the subject that much more important. American adults' undue concern for young people's sexual behavior was nothing new, of course, but took special resonance as major cracks began to appear in the postwar consensus rooted in traditional family life and gender roles.[18]

Rather disturbingly to many adults, it had become abundantly clear by the mid-1960s that a high percentage of college students had every intention of being sexually active. Both administrators and students were gradually adopting the view that this was acceptable as long as the couple was in a committed relationship. This had little to do with the "free love" movement of the latter part of the decade, which represented the outer limits of the sexual revolution. Still, premarital sex on campus was generally an exciting, somewhat risky proposition, with all kinds of social and cultural codes developing around it. A sexual relationship was often referred to as an "affair," a much more pleasant use of the word than when used as a euphemism for adultery. Automobiles and cheap motels were still used for sex, but such trysts were seen as anachronistic and a last resort now that one did not have to leave campus. At Yale, a necktie on a dormitory door handle meant "Do Not Disturb," while students at other universities used an array of other signals to prevent *dormus interruptus*. Deans tended to limit evening visiting hours during the week to try to prevent on-campus sexual activity, not realizing that twenty-year-olds were equally content having sex in the middle of the day (and could undress, copulate, and get dressed in a half hour or less). At Michigan State, "grassers" involved some goings-on in the great outdoors, while undergraduate men at the University of Georgia were in literal hot pursuit of "first-nighters," women who consented on the first date. Getting a coed drunk to make her more willing—something quite common in previous decades—was now considered bad form. Sleeping with "townies" was also deemed less than dignified now that perfectly respectable coeds were game. Dating two women—one "nice" and one less than nice—had also become largely unnecessary with the advent of the best-of-both-worlds, liberated female college student.[19]

Midsixties college students interested in having sex were fortunate to have a number of things working in their favor. Elements of Freudian psychology helped their cause, for one thing, with popular psychoanalytic theory heavily based around the notion that repressed sexuality was a dangerous thing. Finding a proper outlet for one's desires was thus healthy for mind and body, as anyone taking Psychology 101 would have learned, and this theory was intellectual ammunition should an adult question one's behavior. (Psychoanalyst Erich Fromm's prosexual *Art of Loving* was a best seller at many campus bookstores.) While half-century-old Freudian ideas retained considerable currency, the social stigma of marrying a nonvirgin was fading fast and helped to pave the way for premarital sex. As well, having grown up in what was then believed to be a sexually permissive climate (the dancing, dating, and driving of the 1950s), it was considered not overly surprising that college students of the 1960s were taking sex to the next level.[20]

More practically, many doctors in big cities were not hesitant to fit women for diaphragms if asked to do so, especially if the patient included a prefix of "Mrs." before their (fictitious) names. It was very unusual for university health clinics to prescribe the birth control pill in the midsixties, as doing so was viewed as condoning premarital sex. A rare exception was the University of Chicago, which did provide the pill (Enovid) to unmarried female students (while requesting that they have a consultation at the school's mental-health clinic). "I have no statistical proof, but from what I heard I'm convinced there's more premarital sex today than in the early '50s when Kinsey published his study," said Gael Greene after interviewing over six hundred students on some one hundred campuses to write her book *Sex and the College Girl*. Experts like Greene were split on whether premarital sex within the context of a meaningful relationship was a good or a bad thing. Monogamous sexuality among college students boded well for marriage, some believed, while others argued that married couples that had not waited would eventually find their sex lives boring. For many, the latter proved to be an accurate prediction.[21]

## A FOURTH R

While university officials grudgingly accepted the fact that students would figure out a way to have premarital sex, those in charge of adolescents' education had no intention of making such a concession. It was clear in the mid-1960s that the American school system was grappling with the issue of sex education, with no one sure exactly what to teach and when. New York City was still ignoring the subject, but other big cities, notably Los Angeles and Washington, D.C., were offering courses in sex ed. What was being taught varied considerably, with some school districts limiting curriculum to biology and physiology and others addressing intercourse and other sexual acts. The likelihood of pregnancy was a common theme in sex ed at this time, with a strong undercurrent of abstinence running through most programs. If pressed, teachers might bring up the option of contraceptives, but these were usually for "married people" and presented as highly unreliable. One film for pubescent boys making the rounds defined masturbation as "a careless habit that leads to unhappy thinking," a supposition that no doubt triggered more questions than answers. Homosexuals were "not behaving in a normal and decent way and you must avoid them," boys were also told in a commonly shown film; sex education at this time had zero tolerance for any activity outside that between a married man and woman.[22]

Based on what kids did and did not know about human sexuality in those days, it was easy to make a case for some kind of sex education. Some teenage girls believed that it was physically impossible for them to get pregnant if they were not married, a good example of the confusion surrounding the "facts of life." Other girls were buying a single birth control pill from prescription drug dealers after being told it would prevent conception from a one-nighter.[23] Adolescents in Europe, notably Sweden and Norway, were better informed about sexuality; the teaching of the subject in public schools there was not nearly as controversial.[24] American students were eager to learn about sex, however, knowing full well that one day, perhaps soon, they would find the information useful. (The most common age for women to marry in the mid-1960s was eighteen, while the most common age for men was twenty-one.)[25] Most parents also were in favor of schools taking on the tough subject of sex, knowing that even having the awkward "birds and the bees" talk would probably not do much good. "Community and family pressures are gradually forcing the schools to accept reproduction as a fourth R," noted *Time* in 1965, although human sexuality was "a harder topic to handle than space orbits."[26]

Given that many adults had trouble understanding the birds and the bees, it was unsurprising that teaching the subject to children was more difficult than rocket science. Many younger boys were bothered by the fact that most sperm died in the female body, while younger girls were equally concerned by the (false) possibility that sperm could stay alive in the ovum for as much as a year to fertilize an egg. Why more than one sperm did not fertilize an egg was understandably confusing to many children as well. How the penis ended up in the vagina to begin with was perhaps the most challenging question for teachers to answer. That boys showed considerable interest in the subject was a reflection of the family focus of sex-education programs. Sex was presented as, more than anything else, part of family life, in part a means to discourage premarital intercourse. Not just teachers but also clergy and doctors typically offered input in the development of a sex-ed curriculum, a process that took years to complete. Once launched, a program was examined and reexamined, with virtually every aspect of the courses scrutinized to work out any bugs. Parents in some school districts had the annual opportunity to preview all materials used in classes, a smart way to gain community support and defuse protests. Parents were also sometimes provided with vocabulary lists of words used in sex-ed classes. (After being asked by a parent over the family dinner what they learned in school today, more than one preteen had been known to casually say things like, "About the penis.") Students tended to take the content taught in sex-ed classes in stride, with parents (and sometimes teachers) being far more anxious about the subject matter.[27]

Teachers in this relatively early period of sex ed viewed their mission as a grand one, seeing the subject as significantly more important than any particular field of academic study. Gender and marital status were not criteria in choosing instructors—a refreshingly open-minded decision, all things considered. The ability to say words like "masturbate" in front of a room of children was a key criterion for the job, however, as was the ability to engage young people in an honest conversation about such a sensitive topic. Teachers were convinced the potential rewards of delivering this kind of information to the younger generation were well worth the challenge. Society at large would benefit from sexually well-adjusted adults, those selected to teach the subject believed, since all students would grow up to be sexual beings. That the subject of human sexuality was so emotionally charged and controversial made this mission that much grander, with teachers in these heady days of sex ed embarking on a journey perhaps equivalent to astronauts exploring, as a popular television show of the time expressed it, "the final frontier." No one could say how effective sex ed was—there was no objective data in the field— but teachers were confident that their efforts would pay off big dividends over the long term.[28]

As the push for sex education picked up speed, most of the nation's schools had some kind of dedicated program by the latter part of the decade. The rush toward sex ed was so fast in fact that there was a lack of qualified teachers for the subject, and what exactly should be taught was still a major problem. Opposition to any sex ed remained an issue, however, with some schools requiring children to get permission from their parents to attend the courses. The year 1967 was a tipping point for sex ed in America, with New York City, Chicago, and many other cities adopting a program for the first time. The federal government was also showing interest and intended to play a significant role in children learning about sexuality by offering grants to local communities through the Department of Health, Education and Welfare. Even the Roman Catholic Church made it clear it was going to have a say about what children of its faith knew about sex. The New York Archdiocese had developed a "Program of Family Life Education" for its four hundred parishes, and Catholic-based Fordham University was offering students lectures and discussions about sex. Demand for sex education in the late sixties now exceeded supply, a reversal of what had held true since the subject emerged in the early part of the twentieth century. (Organizations such as the YWCA, Child Study Association, and American Purity Alliance had pushed for sex education before World War I, to no avail.)[29] Parents were generally leading the charge for sex ed, realizing that they could use some help in this area as the sexual revolution rolled on. Cases of venereal disease, unwed pregnancies, and illegal abortions among teenagers were all up significantly over the past decade, and the "generation gap" of the times made it difficult for parents to warn their children about such dangers.[30]

Frightening facts about sexual activity among young people made the need for some form of sex ed that much clearer. In 1966, for example, the Connecticut State Department of Health predicted that based on present rates one thirteen-year-old girl of every six in that state would become pregnant out of wedlock before her twentieth birthday, a statistic that raised considerable alarm. Some believed the forecast was too high and some, too low, but all agreed that if it was close to accurate there was plenty to worry about when it came to teenage sexuality. Out-of-wedlock pregnancies in Connecticut were representative of the national average and served as solid evidence that adolescents were (1) having sex and (2) not taking proper precautions. One gynecologist estimated that two additional girls were having premarital intercourse for every one that became pregnant, which made educators, ministers, parents, and teenagers themselves only that much more concerned. Apart from the moral issues, having an abortion was no easy matter in most states in these pre–Roe v. Wade days. A twelve-year-old victim of rape or incest in Connecticut could not have a legal abortion without medical justification, for example, making some girls go to extreme measures. Those girls whose parents could afford it were often sent to Puerto Rico, Europe, or Japan to have a legal abortion, others got hastily married, and still others were sent off to visit "Aunt Sally" for a few months. Poor and, especially, black girls were at a severe disadvantage should they get pregnant, since their options were even more limited than those of wealthier, white girls.[31]

## PSYCHOLOGICAL VD

Despite the obvious need for teens to learn how not to get pregnant, sex education was not living up to its grand mission. Sex ed in the sixties often had to do less with sexuality than with health, biology, and some basic physiology ("plumbing," to professionals), with some psychologists thinking much more information would make kids confused or anxious. "It's hard to go from sex back to math," observed Rhoda Lorand, a psychologist and author of *Love, Sex and the Teenager*; she and many of her colleagues argued that sex in grade school would do more damage than good.[32] Most educators, however, now believed it was never too early for children to start learning about sex. Elementary school children were sometimes given clay model representations of male and female genitals, or shown anatomically correct manikins. In emergencies, that is, when a child asked specifically about fertilization, a cartoon called "Fertility and Birth" that depicted sexual intercourse (and the delivery of a baby in a hospital) was at times shown. Some teachers and staff members recognized the need for something more than the "father places the seed in the mother" or "joyous miracle" stories, the beginnings of what could be considered legitimate sex ed. Programs in Evanston, Illinois, and Palo Alto, California, were known for their forthrightness; the fact that two of the country's elite universities were based there was not a coincidence.[33] Interestingly, the school system of Anaheim, California, was also considered one of the most progressive in the country when it came to teaching kids about sexuality, with seventh graders learning about masturbation and ninth graders about premarital intercourse. Even the Anaheim program did not address contraception, however; America was still not ready to face the fact that teenagers would be having sex regardless of what adults told or did not tell them about it.[34]

Down the road in San Diego, five "social-health teacher-counselors" were making the high school rounds, their mission to instill "wholesome attitudes toward boy-girl relationships and respect for family life." The counselors (two men and three women) used literature, charts, models, tapes, and films to get their message across, with 99 percent of the students electing to attend the program. Boys and girls were taught separately, something that did not hold true for many programs. Sex education in San Diego began in sixth grade, when kids were taught the mechanics of reproduction. In ninth grade, they learned about a full range of sex-related topics including sex outside marriage and "deviations," with these covered in more depth again in the twelfth grade. San Diego's sex-ed program had started during World War II, while most communities across the country had started theirs in just the last couple of years. "America seems to have suddenly discovered an urgent need for universal sex education—from kindergarten through high school," wrote John Kobler in the *Saturday Evening Post* in 1968, "and is galloping off in all directions at once to meet it." Not bound to district standards, private schools were adopting innovative ways to teach students about different aspects of sexuality. At Cincinnati's prestigious Hillsdale School, for example, a teacher in the English Department was examining the implications of extramarital sex via the novel *The Scarlet Letter*, while a teacher at Shady Hill day school in Cambridge, Massachusetts, was using her own pregnancy to discuss the process of reproduction.[35]

Although abstinence was the underlying if not overtly expressed message, sex ed had become by the late 1960s the most contentious issue in elementary education. Political conservatives tried to stop school districts from teaching the subject, believing the subject was at best a waste of taxpayer money. Opponents of sex education would often show up at PTA meetings, accusing administrators and faculty of being Communist sympathizers and of indoctrinating students with "psychological VD." Critics of sex ed made their voices heard at the 1969 annual convention of the National Education Association but were disappointed when the organization passed a resolution that reaffirmed its support for the courses. The opposition was hardly ready to concede, however, urging local elected officials to take their cause to state legislatures. Three boards of education in California had already been sued for "invasion of privacy," in fact, a backdoor approach to getting the courses thrown out of schools. A series of twenty-minute films called *Time of Your Life* was largely responsible for triggering the backlash against sex ed in California, as some parents were shocked to learn what their children were learning (the male and female anatomy, the mechanics of erection and ejaculation, and the role of the clitoris in sexual pleasure, specifically).[36] In Tennessee, it was now a misdemeanor for instructors to teach the subject without first getting approval from both the state government and the local school district. Legislators in six other states were debating whether any mention of sex belonged in public schools, with New York governor Nelson Rockefeller approving a law that withheld funds targeted to sex-ed curriculum. Congress was considering a similar bill, and the battle lines were drawn between proponents of sex education and those vehemently against it.[37]

America's war over sex ed could be said to have officially begun in the fall of 1968 with the publication of a pamphlet called "Is the School House the Proper Place to Teach Raw Sex"? Produced by the Christian Crusade of Tulsa, a right-wing, anti-Communist organization led by Billy James Hargis, a fundamentalist preacher, the booklet named the Sex Information and Education Council of the United States (SIECUS) as the main enemy. The controversial nonprofit health organization advising schools on sex-ed curriculum was "tossing God aside . . . to teach American youth a new sex morality independent of church and state," the pamphlet stated, informing students of "their right to enjoy premarital intercourse . . . if they so desire." The John Birch Society agreed that sex education was a "filthy Communist plot" (as was fluoride in the drinking water, it maintained), and this triggered a widespread movement against teaching the courses in public schools. Dozens of parents' organizations including Sanity of Sex (SOS), Parents against Universal Sex Education (PAUSE), and Movement to Restore Decency (MO-TOREDE) sprung up across the country protesting sex ed; some of them were aligned with Christian Crusade and the John Birch Society, and others were comprised simply of "concerned citizens." The specific charges made by these groups ranged from the clearly absurd (teachers wanted to train youth in the ways of immorality) to the somewhat sensible (sex ed made students overly interested in sexuality) and the entirely reasonable (the subject belonged more in the home or church than in the school).[38]

Although opponents of sex ed were more vociferous than proponents, they were in the minority. Seventy-one percent of adult Americans were in favor of sex education in general, according to a recent Gallup poll, probably for the same reasons cited by Mary S. Calderone, the director of SIECUS. "Sex is so intrusive and our culture is so permeated with sexual messages that planned and relevant sex-education programs are vital now," she explained, believing that children were exposed to this part of life "from the time of birth." Schools had not created the sexual revolution, defenders of sex ed made clear; they were, rather, trying to help students better manage its consequences. The coursework in such classes was useful in teens' transition to adults, they added, with studies showing how many Americans in their twenties and thirties often lacked the most basic information about human sexuality. This all made sense, but supporters of sex education could have done a better job of describing what these classes actually consisted of. Sex was just one part of sex ed, with curriculum typically covering everything from family life to stages of growth, hygiene, reproduction, and even responsible social behavior. Allowing all children to opt out of the classes at their parents' request, as some schools already did, was another way to lessen the intensity of the fight over sex education.[39] But like religion and politics, sex remained a topic that should just not be discussed in public, more conservative folks believed, and teaching sex to children was an especially perilous proposition.

## I'M WILLING IF YOU ARE

Despite the best efforts by secondary school teachers and "experts" to persuade teens not to have sex, there was little adults could do once they got to college. Still, some college officials were determined to try to keep the lid on the sexual revolution as it fermented on campuses in the mid-1960s. Vassar president Sarah Blanding made news when she announced that nonvirgins were not wanted at her college, for example, an extreme example of anti-premarital sex sentiment. (Many pointed out that, should her proclamation be carried out, Vassar's campus would look like a ghost town, and the school should be renamed the Poughkeepsie Victorian Seminary for Young Virgins.) Other colleges and universities, such as Harvard and Columbia, were attempting to slow encroaching "immorality" by limiting visiting privileges by members of the opposite sex in dorm rooms. Doors were being closed too frequently, administrators had learned, and the solution to the college campus sex problem was believed to be a literal open-door policy.[40] It was in fact typical for many colleges and universities to have various rules outlawing contact between male and female students. In one college, couples had to have three feet touching the floor at all times, allow six inches between their heads while sitting, and leave a dorm-room door ajar if together, apparently subscribing to the Ann Landers school of sex advice.[41]

Such rules were increasingly being thrown out of college and university regulations, however, as administrators recognized that students should have greater sexual rights as they demanded. Keeping men out of women's dorm rooms and women out of men's dorm rooms might make things more inconvenient for students wanting to have sex, but even deans who had never heard the Rolling Stone's "Let's Spend the Night Together" were aware that it was not going to prevent them from having sex. Americans, especially young adults, were viewing sexuality in a new and different light in the mid-1960s; this shift in attitudes toward sex was just one part of the counterculture movement beginning to sweep the nation. "All of us, college students and adults, have become captives of the attitudes we have created," wrote Lester Kirkendall in the *Nation* in 1964, believing this new paradigm of sexuality was a serious problem. (Kirkendall was a professor of family life at Oregon State University and author of *Premarital Intercourse and Interpersonal Relations.*) This generation of young adults was really not much different than their parents or grandparents, Kirkendall explained, believing it was more the times that had dramatically changed. Even Kirkendall was flummoxed about how to solve what he and most authority figures saw as the problem of intensifying sexuality on campus, conceding there was little people like he could do to stop the sexual revolution in its tracks.[42]

Indeed, over the next couple of years, groups of students at a number of universities around the country took the offensive in promoting what they defined as sexual freedom. Student committees at Stanford, the University of Texas, and UCLA made it known to their respective administrations that sex was a private matter and should thus not be regulated while, somewhat paradoxically, also demanding that college health services make available contraceptives to all female enrollees. Only married women (and, occasionally, brides-to-be with a note confirming as much from their minister) had access to birth control pills at many colleges, a policy seen by these committees as a moral judgment on premarital intercourse.[43] "In giving the pills [to unmarried women], we would be implicitly condoning the use they would subsequently make of them," admitted a staff member at a university health clinic, which was precisely what sexual freedom groups were complaining about.[44]

The University of California at Berkeley's Sexual Freedom Forum was, not surprisingly, the most extreme of these student-run organizations. Members of the group could often be seen sitting behind tables on campus where they gave out literature on birth control, abortion, and venereal disease, and sold buttons with sayings like "TAKE IT OFF" and "I'M WILLING IF YOU ARE." Members had also given lectures on these subjects with university approval, but the administration had turned down the group's request to screen a pornographic movie. That did not stop the organization from expressing their sexual freedom off campus, however, holding a number of parties at a student's apartment in which all the guests were naked. Students did the watusi, the jerk, and other popular dances of the day while completely nude, with some couples retreating to the bedroom to take their freedom to the next level. Berkeley's Sexual Freedom Forum insisted its cause was as much intellectual and philosophical as sensual, however, and its mission was to not allow society to dictate how individuals should or should not express their sexuality.[45]

Knowing that the university health clinic would not prescribe birth control pills to them, unmarried women pursuing their personal sexual freedom had to find another source. The family doctor was not a good option; he and the other patients in the waiting room were literally too close to home. Seeing a local gynecologist near the college was thus the best bet, especially because they were known to be lenient about prescribing the pill to single coeds. These same gynecologists were often the first person unmarried pregnant women went to for medical counsel, which was why they were more apt to write the prescription. "If you had seen as much grief as I have, you wouldn't hesitate to exercise that power," said one of them, fully aware of the potential consequences of refusing a young woman's request. Critics felt, however, that the pill undermined traditional moral codes because it circumvented the standard ritual surrounding sex between unmarried people. For decades, planning and supplies had been required for sex to take place on a date, and such preparations kept sexuality in check. The man with the condom in his wallet was in effect the seducer, with the woman either resisting or succumbing to the man's advances. But now it was the woman who had prepared for sex by being on the pill, turning the dynamics of the mating dance completely upside down. Sexually independent women were frightening to many men, as feminists pointed out at the time, and this was the underlying basis of the fear and paranoia surrounding the birth control pill in the 1960s.[46]

Although the prospect of the nation's young women being turned into an army of nymphomaniacs because of easy access to the pill caused considerable concern (and probably some excitement) to many Americans, the truth was much less dramatic. "They are pairing off, going steady, getting pinned, and entering into semiformal alliances at earlier and earlier ages," noted Andrew Hacker in the *New York Times Magazine* in 1965, speaking of sexually active college students. The vast majority of unmarried women on the pill had no interest in promiscuity, in other words; their sexuality was limited to one partner who, more often than not, eventually became their husband. Most were "one-boy girls, and all but an insignificant handful are one-boy-at-a-time girls," according to Hacker who, as a professor at Cornell, was doing informal research among his students to reach his conclusions. Besides that, why should college women who did not want to rush into marriage not enjoy a sex life as men had always done? Hacker asked. The "double standard" was thus playing a role in the controversy over the pill and women's sexuality in general—traditional gender roles and relationships were not about to be redefined overnight.[47]

## THE ARRANGEMENT

If college students having premarital sex in dorm rooms made many adults uncomfortable, the idea of them doing it in a shared apartment or house drove them nearly crazy. Parents who were aware of the situation hoped the end of the school year would mean the end of their child's "cohabitating," but these parents were frequently disappointed (especially as they wrote out the monthly rent check). Living together (or "love leasing," "super going steady," or "light housekeeping") offered student couples what they often referred to as an "unstructured relationship," that is, the benefits of domestic life without the commitment of marriage. "I have the image of marriage as a contractual, nonromantic relationship in which nothing happens," said one Berkeley student, thinking cohabitation allowed one to feel young and not tied down. Just around 1 percent of college students in 1966 were believed to be living together, a good indication of how daring it was at the time. Landlords were sometimes in the dark about what was going on in their rented houses or apartments and would not have been happy to learn the truth. Anyone could see that cohabitating would become increasingly popular in the years ahead, however. "Stable, open nonmarital relationships are pushing the border of what society is going to face in ten years," predicted David Powelson, a psychiatrist at Berkeley, and this aspect of the sexual revolution was to be seen as not so revolutionary in the near future.[48]

The gap between actual sexual behavior and prevailing morality could be clearly detected when two unmarried students were discovered to be "shacking up." In 1968, a female student at Barnard College living with a male student from Columbia University was found to be in violation of school regulations, for example, something that entailed an appearance before the Judicial Council when its members found out about it. The members of the council voted to ban the female student from the snack bar, a token gesture that signaled the greater tolerance among college administrators for unmarried couples living together. Cases like this one were increasingly popping up across American campuses (a twenty-seven-year-old graduate student at Cornell had been expelled for living with a woman off campus a few years earlier), with the general public expressing a keen interest in what was sometimes referred to as "The Arrangement." The Arrangement was seen as one of the more telling expressions of the decade's sexual revolution, as was the decision by more institutional authorities to now allow it. State laws forbidding "lewd and lascivious" cohabitation and fornication between unmarried couples were also being ignored, another sign that the times they had a'changed.[49]

All kinds of changes regarding student sexuality were taking place on American campuses in the late 1960s. Visiting hours for dates in dorms and fraternity and sorority houses were being extended, overnight leaves were being increasingly allowed, and off-campus residency requirements were relaxed. The dorm mother—an institution at colleges and universities for decades—was gradually being eliminated, much to the delight of many students saying good night to each other. (She was often nicknamed the "necker checker.") Coed dorms were being built at the University of Texas in Austin, something that would have been considered shocking a decade earlier. At UCLA, students were fleeing the dorms once school officials made living on campus optional. "Splitting the rent and sharing pad, bed and shopping cart in an all-American-style live-in" was the thing to do among an increasing number of students, *Life* observed in 1968, and this was all part of what the magazine considered "the new morality." Despite the popularity of the Arrangement, most couples were not ready to tell their parents about it, sometimes going to extreme lengths to cover up what their folks would interpret as "living in sin."[50]

Interestingly, the sexual revolution as played out on college campuses was a matter more of attitudes shifting rather than of behavior changing. Some of the day's top researchers in the field including Ira Reiss (now at the University of Iowa), William Simon and John Gagnon of Indiana University's Institute for Sex Research, and Joseph Katz of Stanford's Institute for the Study of Human Problems confirmed that the "revolution" did not involve sexual promiscuity among young people, as many assumed. Versus previous generations of college students, those of the 1960s were more open and felt less guilty about sexuality, something quite different than how the "free love" movement was commonly perceived (then and now). And while the percentage of female students having premarital intercourse had gone up dramatically over the past couple of decades, sexual activity among male students had hardly changed. Experts thus agreed that there had indeed been a sexual revolution, but it was mostly about a shedding of inhibitions and change of moral standards within the context of a monogamous relationship. In fact, a good argument could be made that male college students, at least, were less promiscuous than their fathers and grandfathers had been as they did not have to go to prostitutes to have sex now that many "nice girls" were receptive to the idea. (Friends now felt sorry for the unfortunate fellow who had to go to a prostitute for sex.) The view that the birth control pill had made young people promiscuous or that they were being sexually active in order to rebel against the establishment were thus mythologies, the counterculture perhaps not as "counter" as popularly believed.[51]

The sex lives of college students (especially those of women) was of so much interest to social critics in the 1960s that none other than Vance Packard, author of the number 1 best sellers *The Hidden Persuaders* and *The Status Seekers*, decided to write a book on the subject. In his 1968 *Sexual Wilderness*, Packard reported on studies showing that the percentage of "coeds" who had sex before they married had indeed risen quite a bit over the past twenty years. Kinsey had put the number at 27 percent in the 1940s while Packard's research indicated it was now at 43 percent, a jump of nearly 60 percent. (British, German, and Norwegian college women were, however, even more experienced.) Packard suspected there would be regional differences regarding this particular statistic, which turned out to be true. Premarital intercourse among women was far more common on the East and West coasts than in the South and Midwest, leading Packard to conclude that the decision to have sex before marriage was directly linked to eroded traditional values. The fact that more American women attended college in the 1960s than the 1940s played a significant role in this shift in attitudes and behavior, of course, as a university setting was likely to encourage independent thinking and the opportunity to find a desirable sexual partner.[52]

Margaret Mead, the renowned anthropologist, also believed that Americans' focus on the behavioral component of the sexual revolution was largely missing the point. Throughout history, there had always been swings between sexual restraint and liberty, making the relative freedoms of the late 1960s not unique or particularly important. For Mead, it was overpopulation—a major concern at the time—that represented the most significant dimension of the sexual revolution. Because of the threat of overpopulation, there was the real possibility of reproduction no longer being viewed as women's primary role, something that posed huge implications for society. Freeing women from the responsibility of producing children was a much bigger story than whether Americans were currently having more sex with more people, in other words, an observation that could only come from someone with a broad, cross-cultural perspective. The scenario of women being perceived simply as people was exciting to Mead, viewing it as an evolutionary change equal to the discovery of nuclear energy. "All this talk about who is sleeping with whom where is of relatively less importance," she grumbled; our obsession with sex was making us unable to see the forest for the trees.[53]

## ONE OF THE WORST FEATURES OF OUR WESTERN CIVILIZATION

Who was sleeping with whom was precisely the point for other critics of the sexual revolution, however. For some, like British author J. B. Priestley, "the new morality" had blurred the lines between appropriate and inappropriate sexuality, both in popular culture and in people's lives. "Our society would be healthier and happier, I believe, if we were not so dangerously confused about eroticism and sex and love," wrote Priestley in 1963, believing many people were not drawing a proper distinction among those three very different words. Of the three, eroticism was the real problem, Priestley argued, its commercialization "one of the worst features of our Western civilization." In addition to striptease bars, movie stars like Brigitte Bardot and Marilyn Monroe were prime examples of commercial eroticism, since their only role was to titillate the male viewer (unlike stars of the past like Greta Garbo, who was to Priestley "a symbolic figure of mysterious, exotic sex"). Unlike sex and love, eroticism was impersonal, purely a sensation rather than something of meaning and value. Most concerning, eroticism was damaging relationships between men and women, Priestley felt, and mistaking it for sex or love was a disturbing sign of the times.[54]

Many found the eroticization of Western culture in the sixties truly alarming. "It sometimes seems that all America is one big Orgone Box," *Time* observed in 1964, speaking of Wilhelm Reich's famous device designed to capture and stimulate one's libido. Sex had recently invaded popular and consumer culture with a vengeance, leading the magazine to conclude that the country was "undergoing a revolution of mores and an erosion of morals." This was the nation's second sexual revolution, it was generally agreed, the first one taking place after World War I when youth culture rejected Victorian-era propriety for Jazz Age hedonism. This second revolution went significantly further than the one forty years earlier, however; the then shocking sexual behavior of young people was now considered quite tame. In fact, sex itself was no longer considered particularly shocking, which made this revolution so socially (and historically) significant. Detaching sexuality from moral judgment was perhaps the most interesting occurrence of the 1960s sexual revolution, as well as its most disturbing element to traditionalists (especially the religious). "The Puritan ethic, so long the dominant moral force in the U.S., is widely considered to be dying, if not dead, and there are few mourners," noted *Time*; the privatization of morality and uncoupling of sex and sin was a major cultural shift. The Supreme Court's 1957 blessing of sexual material (except that which was considered obscene, i.e., violated "contemporary community standards," appealed to "prurient interest," and had no "redeeming social value") obfuscated the division between the high and the low, and served to open the floodgates to a sea of pornographic books and films. Producers of such material were actually getting quite worried about the future of their businesses, wondering how to continue to attract readers and viewers after describing or presenting sexuality as far as it seemingly could go.[55]

The modern art world's embrace of eroticism was a good example of the shifting sands of morality in the mid-1960s. In 1966, Sidney Janis's gallery in New York hosted an exhibition called "Erotic Art 66" that lived up to its title. The thirty works by nineteen artists (including Andy Warhol, Jim Dine, James Rosenquist, George Segal, and Larry Rivers) in the show were all erotic in nature, leading Janis to call the genre "cop" art (blending "op" and "pop" art with "copulation"). Erotic art was nothing new, of course (ancient Greek sculpture could get pretty racy, as could works by Old World masters like Titian, Rubens, and Rembrandt), but branding it as such was a clever way to capitalize on America's current obsession with all things sexual.[56] A couple of years later, "The First International Exhibition of Erotic Art," which consisted of no fewer than one thousand works, was a big hit in Sweden, proof that Americans were not the only ones intrigued by "cop" art.[57]

By the summer of love, the consensus was that the nation was experiencing a rebirth of sorts, with sex being a key dimension of America's reinvention. "The old taboos are dead or dying," pronounced *Newsweek* in 1967, reporting that "a new, more permissive society is taking shape." Sexuality was rampant in not just art but also film, novels, theater, music, fashion, advertising, and even dance, the magazine told readers who were no doubt already aware that America was a different place than it had been just a year or two earlier. Recently accepted standards of conduct, language, and manners had been overturned, with no agreement now what should be seen and heard. Many Americans were bewildered by this transformation in morality, not sure if it was an extension of our freedoms or, rather, a breakdown of society. The most conservative social commentators could not help but compare counterculture America to the decline and fall of Rome, each civilization steeped in decadence and hedonism. Liberal thinkers, particularly those in the arts, thought otherwise, seeing the fuller expression of sexuality as a welcome break from our repressive past. Regardless of one's view, it seemed clear that there was no going back to the old ways. "This new freedom of expression is unlikely to reverse itself because the forces that have produced it are a permanent and irresistible part of modern life," *Newsweek* observed, seeing it as "part of a larger disintegration of moral consensus in America."[58]

Judging by how some described the state of the nation in 1967, comparisons between contemporary United States and ancient Rome were not completely far-fetched. "All America seems to be engaged in one vast, all-pervading, all-permissive, Sexological Spree," William I. Nichols, publisher of *This Week* magazine, told the Economic Club of Detroit that year. Nichols found three alternative reactions to this sexplosion. Some were taking advantage of the libertine times by joining in the fun, others were outraged by it, and still others seemed dazed by it, not sure what to think or do.[59] Some observers believed the so-called sexual revolution was a myth, however, created by the media because it made a good story. Americans' actual sexuality had hardly budged over the last decade, this contingent claimed, claiming that neither the birth control pill nor countercultural values had affected what individuals did in the bedroom to any significant degree. Because sex was so woven into the fabric of society, cataclysmic change was unlikely if not impossible, they insisted, making this revolution more smoke than fire. Even the first sexual revolution of the 1920s was less of a revolution than a moderate shift in attitudes, people like Arno Karlen argued, and the same thing was happening four decades later. "Four-letter words and mini-skirts don't mean people act very differently in bed," he wrote in the *Saturday Evening Post* in 1968; morality is one thing, but behavior is quite another.[60]

There was significant evidence that Americans were indeed acting quite differently in bed, however. Reliable data on the number of Americans having extramarital affairs was understandably difficult to obtain, for example, but there was no doubt that standards regarding adultery had changed. Once cause for considerable anxiety and guilt (and, of course, grounds for divorce), more Americans were viewing cheating on one's spouse as an acceptable, if not ideal, part of married life. Psychiatrists were reporting that those straying saw their actions as a healthy way to keep their marriages happy, a positive thing rather than the dastardly act it had long been perceived as. Jealousy within a marriage also appeared to be waning, professionals agreed at the 1969 American Psychiatric Association annual meeting; some wives were not particularly upset to learn that their husband was having an affair. This could partly be explained by the fact that wives themselves were more often taking a lover, and the birth control pill and economic independence were named as principal factors for this development. "Just a few years ago, I believed that a woman could not be casual about her own extramarital relations," Penn State sociologist Jessie Bernard told her colleagues, finding that "now a new kind of woman is emerging who can accept the sex-as-fun point of view without conflict." Sexual exclusivity was less important than keeping a marriage going, more couples were thinking, something Americans of generations past would have found absurd and appalling.[61]

## THE NEW WHITE-COLLAR OBSESSION

Not everyone was ready to join in on the sexological spree, of course. Americans were deeply divided on "the new morality" (also referred to as "the new permissiveness," "the new eroticism," and "the new freedom"), some seeing it as a welcome, long overdue liberation from lingering Victorian-era priggishness and others seeing it as the end of civilization as we knew it. The battle between those taking full advantage of the rights guaranteed by the First Amendment and those arguing that discarding established values and standards was ruining the country was a heated one in the late sixties. Interestingly, those falling into the latter group were more bothered by the proliferation of sex in popular culture than what people were actually doing sexually. Many of the erotic movies, books, and plays being produced were designed primarily to shock audiences to bring commercial success, but many found them decadent, salacious, and disturbing rather than some kind of artistic breakthrough.[62]

That the spread of graphically sexual arts and literature happened in such a short period of time made this conflict that much more jarring. By the end of the decade, sex had become what *Time* called a "spectator sport," with American popular culture offering the opportunity to see, hear, and read things that only recently would have been considered wholly unacceptable. "From stage and screen, printed page and folk-rock jukeboxes, society is bombarded with coital themes," the magazine said in 1969; yesterday's taboos were now considered not just acceptable but also stylish.[63] "There are more explicitly erotic films, more blunt-spoken novels, more nudity on stage, more appeals to the libido in advertising than ever before," echoed *Newsweek*, seeing an "anarchic increase in sexual outspokenness." Judging by the response of its readers, the proliferation of sexuality in pop culture was "a matter of national concern," according to the magazine, an "explosive scene" that threatened the country's moral equilibrium.[64]

For those willing to face some condemnation and possibly the long arm of the law, however, "coital themes" or simply nudity could help turn a creative product into a big hit. Just six months after debuting off Broadway, *Hair* (subtitled *The American Tribal Love-Rock Musical*) opened on Broadway in April

1968, and the rest, as they say, is history. The show's language and treatment of drugs were controversial enough, but it was the nude scene that turned it into a cultural phenomenon. Within a year, *Hair* was playing in five American cities and six abroad, reason enough for other shows to feature naked bodies onstage (some inviting audience participation). With a scene featuring what appeared to be actual intercourse and another depicting an ape raping a nun, the off-off-Broadway play *Che!* made *Hair* look like a church service. (After one of the performances, the entire cast was jailed on charges of public lewdness and sodomy.)[65] *Oh! Calcutta!* opened off Broadway in 1969, it too packing houses with extensive nudity and kinky sketches. Playwrights and producers could easily justify having cast members appear unclothed on stage because it was considered artistic and "natural," but the knowledge that audiences would likely flock to the theater to experience it was even more reason to go the nude route.[66]

Nude theater was surely attention grabbing, but underground cinema and "sexploitation" movies were probably the most visible symbol of the new eroticism. Andy Warhol's *Blue Movie* (which contained forty-five minutes of simulated copulation) and Russ Meyer's *Vixen* certainly made some waves, but it was *I Am Curious (Yellow)* that really got people's attention.[67] The censorship battle that preceded the release of the Swedish film actually helped it find an audience (although the movie was promoted by its distributor as being "not about sex"). It was true that the sexual component of the 1967 film (released in the United States in 1969) represented a relatively small portion of its total running time, but those minutes included cunnilingus, fellatio, and intercourse in a variety of positions and settings. That the protagonist showed all signs of being a nymphomaniac also suggested that the film really was about sex despite its publicity campaign, something Americans of course already knew based on the buzz surrounding it. (The lead character "has only to be touched in a sensitive spot and immediately she begins to wave her legs in the air like an octopus seeking its prey," wrote Robert Hatch of the *Nation* in his less than glowing review of the film.) For weeks after *I Am Curious* opened, a long line extended down Fifty-seventh Street in New York City to buy tickets at the Cinema 57 Theater—90 percent of the crowd was male, according to Hatch. The film was equally popular in Washington, D.C., quite ironic given how hard Congress had tried to prevent it from getting into the country. Theater owners across the country were clamoring for the rights to show the film, knowing that they could make millions of dollars with a multiscreen run.[68] That an even sexier sequel called *I Am Curious (Blue)* had been made was even more exciting to some Americans genuinely curious about the Swedes' famous reputation for uninhibited sexuality.[69]

It was rare that a novel, even a best seller, crossed over from literature to become a cultural sensation, but Philip Roth's *Portnoy's Complaint* did just that, largely as a result of its sexual content. The book became the fastest-selling hardcover novel in history and was often sold out at bookstores. (The Miami public library system ordered 159 copies, but that was not nearly enough to meet the demand. There was a long waiting list for the book, despite a recent "Rally for Decency" at the Orange Bowl.)[70] The release of the book in February 1969 had been much anticipated, with some critics calling it an American masterpiece even before it was officially published. (Excerpts had appeared in various literary magazines.) The book's protagonist, Alexander Portnoy, was what *Life* magazine called the "sexually obsessed modern man" who was seething underneath the surface of a Nice Jewish Boy. The book became all the rage among the sophisticated set; its language and primary themes—masturbation, sexual fantasies, pursuit of true eroticism, and the struggle with the moral code of monogamy and fidelity  became the stuff of conversation at swanky dinner parties. Comics like Lenny Bruce, Mort Sahl, and Nichols and May and other novelists such as Saul Bellow and Joseph Heller had covered some of this same territory, but arguably no one had previously approached sex with as much candor (and humor) as Roth.[71]

Indeed, most of the sexually oriented creative output of the late 1960s was decidedly more middlebrow or lowbrow than *Portnoy's Complaint*. Following up on her phenomenally successful and quite steamy *Valley of the Dolls*, Jacqueline Susann produced *The Love Machine*, a novel clearly designed to exploit the current view of sex as spectator sport. ("Sweaters are always being ripped open in Miss Susann's books. Pants are always being frantically unzipped. And everyone is always *wanting* everyone else," wrote Nora Ephron in her review of the book in the *New York Times*.) If that was still too brainy, there was always *Screw*, a fifty-cent tabloid that came close to delivering its first issue's promise to "uncover the entire world of sex." "We will be the *Consumer Reports* of sex, testing new products such as dildoes [sic], rubbers, and artificial vaginas," declared Al Goldstein and Jim Buckley, who had each put up $175 to launch the publication. The pair had big dreams, envisioning a giant, penis-shaped skyscraper called "The Screw Building" to house its vast world of sex.[72]

Writing for the *Nation*, Desmond Smith observed how what he called "pop pornography" had become big business in America. "Pop pornography, which is the slick version of what once was called 'smut,' has become the bluest of the blue chips," he wrote, the profit margins on sex-based books, magazines, films, and merchandise attracting more and more players. Pornography had been around forever, but now it was openly marketed to the middle class as part of a new "pleasure ethic," a historic breakthrough of sorts. "Pop pornography is the new white-collar obsession," Smith declared, and the mainstream media was also surfing the trend. Excerpts of Susann's *The Love Machine* appeared in *Ladies' Home Journal*, the magazine's editors fully aware that suburban housewives would much rather read about clothes being torn off in the heat of passion than another article about Lady Bird Johnson. "Pornography, in a few brief years, has moved from an under-the-counter item to an open-market commodity," Smith remarked, seeing it now as "part of the capitalist system."[73]

The tentacles of "pop pornography" could indeed be found throughout the media universe. Novelists Irving Wallace and Harold Robbins were also satisfying the demand for white-collar erotica, as were women's magazines like *Cosmopolitan* and *Mademoiselle*, whose editorial formats were geared around sex. *Playboy*'s empire had grown considerably since 1953, and the father of "pop pornography" fully exploited the demise of the Puritan ethic over the last decade and a half. Not only were there many more readers of the magazine, but also the brand now included nineteen clubs and resorts around the world, a film division, and a syndicated television show called *Playboy after Dark*. One of the most popular television commercials of the time was for Noxzema shaving cream, in which a beautiful blond (the Swedish model Gunilla Knutson) urged male viewers to "Take it off, take it all off." There was little doubt that marketers very familiar with the adage that "sex sells" were consciously packaging the sexual revolution, a genuine social movement appropriated by Big Business. "What we are now observing is a commercial happening, like Father's Day or National Shoe Week," Smith concluded, seeing sexuality-as-merchandising-technique as one of the principal themes in contemporary American culture.[74] The commercialization of sex would soon become seen as an inevitable and relatively harmless phenomenon, however, as the boundaries of American sexuality were pushed to the limit.

# 3

# Carnal Knowledge

Women today are better-hung than the men.

—*Jonathan (Jack Nicholson) in the 1971 film* Carnal Knowledge

Anyone walking through the corridors of UCLA's Neuropsychiatric Institute in 1975 might have smelled something funny in the air. Over the course of three months, twenty men were smoking five medical-grade joints a day in the ward, all of them volunteers for a study to determine the effects of marijuana on sexual performance. Researchers were interested in the study because considerable numbers of Americans were smoking marijuana prior to having sex, finding that the weed enhanced the experience. Men liked pot because they believed it increased their sexual endurance (it could just have been that their sense of time was distorted), while women said it loosened their inhibitions and made the act generally more pleasurable. The UCLA study showed that high levels of marijuana could lower testosterone levels and sperm production among men, however, with impotence and infertility risks for especially heavy users. Interviews with five hundred steady marijuana users confirmed the study's findings, leading the researchers to warn male potheads to take it easy on the weed lest their sex lives become a major bummer.[1]

Worrying that the joint one was smoking could make sex a less groovy affair was just the latest example of the country's sexual troubles. There was no shortage of bigger problems that were continuing to turn sex into a complicated, not very pleasurable part of life for many Americans. What to teach kids about sex remained a controversial issue, one that was compounded by increasing peer pressure for teenagers to lose their virginity and by readily available birth control. Adults were having an equally tough time negotiating the terrain of sexuality in the 1970s. Judging by the demand for sexual therapy at the rapidly growing number of sex clinics opening up for business, problems in the bedroom appeared to be rampant in America. There were also plenty of sex manuals being published, some of them turning out to be best sellers. One could not help but wonder if the feminist movement, which helped to shift the focus of sex research to women's sexuality, was playing some role in the sexual turmoil of the times. Everyone seemed to agree that the sexual revolution of the sixties was in sharp decline or had already ended, and its legacy was now being questioned. Sexual excesses of various stripes were leading many to hope that America was ready to embark on a new and different journey that harked back to an earlier time. In short, carnal knowledge was turning out to be a dangerous thing, and the nation's "sexidemic" was becoming a true crisis.

## ABOUT YOUR SEXUALITY

How much carnal knowledge children should possess was a particularly thorny issue. Sex education remained a flashpoint in American culture, a topic that divided many parents and communities. In typical programs of the early seventies, students would indeed be taught the facts of life, that is, reproduction, pregnancy, and birth, but information regarding sexual intercourse often took a backseat to the challenges involved with raising a family. Still, more conservative parents viewed sex ed as an evil akin to atheism, rock 'n' roll, and, again, Communism. Regardless of their actual content, sex-ed programs inherently condoned homosexuality and endorsed masturbation, critics were convinced, and such perversions were real threats to the family and the American Way of Life. Supporters viewed sex education as a long overdue effort to liberate Americans from their neuroses, however, an opportunity to rid the next generation of our Puritan "hang-ups." Despite their differences, each side wanted teens to preserve their chastity before marriage, disagreeing strongly about what strategy to take but sharing the same objective. Many students, ironically, had more important things on their minds than sex, worrying more about getting drafted or how what was called at the time the "ecology" was being destroyed.[2]

Oddly enough, it was a religious organization that chose the boldest approach to teaching kids about sex in the early 1970s. Nearly half of the 1,100 Sunday schools in the Unitarian Universalist Association had adopted a program called "About Your Sexuality" for twelve- to fourteen-year-olds that could very well have been considered pornography had it not had educational value. The program consisted of filmstrips depicting adults engaged in sexual intercourse, masturbation, and homosexual acts along with tape recordings of teens talking about the first time they had sex. The curriculum also offered information on birth control, human reproduction, venereal disease, menstruation, and seminal emissions, although it was, not surprisingly, the visual component of the course that the adolescents found most intriguing. Students were encouraged to ask any questions they liked and to speak of sexuality in the vernacular, with no language considered too "dirty." Even more remarkable about the program, the Unitarians did not try to impose a particular view of sexuality on the students (i.e., abstinence), keeping with the faith's liberal ethos. Six other Christian denominations, including the Episcopalians and Presbyterians, were taking a look at "About Your Sexuality" to see if it could be adapted for their Sunday school classes, but it seemed highly unlikely that leaders of those faiths would be as open-minded as the Unitarians.[3]

State governments were definitely not as open-minded as the Unitarians. In most states, those under eighteen years old were in the early 1970s not allowed to receive any sex-related medical services, that is, birth control pills or abortions, without their parents' permission. (The law in Utah was particularly draconian; giving contraceptives to unmarried minors would make them "more likely to commit the crime of fornication and to become infected with venereal disease," ruled that state's supreme court.) Some teenagers were fighting for such rights, as were civil liberties groups, claiming that limiting access to contraceptives and abortions was a form of discrimination.[4] In the meantime, however, many high school girls were showing up at Planned Parenthood clinics, thinking (often correctly) that they may be pregnant. Given the evidence that the time between the onset of puberty and when young people began having sex was narrowing, this might have been expected. There was now significant social pressure to lose one's virginity, with some girls finding themselves in a race with their friends to have sex first.

The expectation to embrace the new freedoms to be enjoyed was, ironically, effectively forcing some girls to have sex when they felt they were not quite ready.[5] The waning sexual revolution, based on college campuses a decade earlier, appeared to be trickling down to high schools, an observation borne out by statistics. One study by two Johns Hopkins researchers published in 1977 reported that 25 percent of girls sixteen or younger had had sex, and 40 percent of girls seventeen or younger. These numbers were up sharply from a study done in 1972, proof enough that teenagers were very much a part of the intensified sexual climate of the decade.[6]

Educators were clearly not keeping up with kids when it came to sex. Well into the 1970s, schools were using films produced a decade or two earlier to teach students about the subject. Once a year, a staff member, often the school nurse or a coach, would still usher boys and girls into the gym or auditorium to see films with titles like *Girl to Woman*, *Boy to Man*, and (the Walt Disney–produced) *Story of Menstruation*. A discussion would supposedly follow, although few students had the nerve or inclination to ask a question. It was only after the films were so damaged that they could no longer be shown that administrators, teachers, and parents became sufficiently motivated to create a real sex-education curriculum. With few off-the-shelf programs available, schools typically developed their own curricula from scratch, with a consultant from a university perhaps brought in to help. Instruction tended to focus on the biological component of sexuality, addressing everything from the workings of the endocrine system to the joining of spermatozoa and egg. Framing this process within the context of "family life" was considered extremely important, as was locating sexual reproduction within the orbit of community and society. Programs often omitted or glossed over more controversial topics such as masturbation, homosexuality, venereal disease, contraception, and abortion, however, leaving students with more questions than answers.[7]

American educators were not the only ones doing a poor job facing the realities of sex among young people, it need be said. Premarital sex was strongly discouraged by educators in the Soviet Union, for example, although most teens took part in it. (The country's severe housing shortage, which prevented many couples from being alone, seemed to be more of a deterrent of premarital sex than the state.)[8] In China, premarital sex was considered during Chairman Mao's three-decade regime contrary to the interests of the nation and a selfish, immoral, and unpatriotic act. Romance, love, and sex were all viewed as a waste of time for teenagers, and young minds were better spent thinking about how to, as Mao's motto went, "serve the people."[9] Masturbation too "sap[ped] the revolutionary will," according to Communist dogma. With the passing of Mao in 1976 and rise to power of Chairman Hua Kuo-feng, however, many things in China began to change, including sexual attitudes and behavior. "It is normal for healthy youths to join in the bedroom once or twice a week," went a piece of advice from a booklet published in China in 1978, something that would not have happened during Mao's rule.[10]

## HUMAN SEXUAL INADEQUACY

While kids in America were left largely in the dark about sex in the early 1970s, adults remained equally puzzled about what to do when they experienced some kind of sexual problem. Couples having sex problems often went first to their minister, hoping he or she would know how to remedy the situation. Completely unequipped to do so, ministers typically referred couples to their family doctor, who more often than not had little (or no) more knowledge of the subject. (Only a third of the country's medical schools offered a course in the nonphysical aspects of sex, and one frequently used text recommended men find a hobby or take a cold shower to control their sex drive.)[11] Physicians would in turn suggest to couples they seek out one of the country's few sex clinics, the best-known one being the Reproductive Biology Research Foundation in St. Louis headed up by William Masters and Virginia Johnson. At the discreetly named Central Medical Building, couples (both spouses had to take part) would meet with the famous sex therapists themselves, with all interviews taped (purportedly so a stenographer would not have to be in the room to take notes). No sexual activity was allowed while in treatment until advised otherwise, something that typically took two weeks. By 1970, about eight hundred couples had made such a trip to St. Louis to get treated for some type of sexual dysfunction since the clinic had opened in 1959. Masters and Johnson used many of these cases to write their new book, *Human Sexual Inadequacy*, which quickly became a best seller much like their 1966 *Human Sexual Response*. "They are the most important explorers since Alfred Kinsey into the most mysterious, misunderstood and rewarding of human functions," *Time* magazine wrote of the pair, with *Newsweek* seeing them as pioneering "shamans" of the underdeveloped field of sex research.[12]

As their new book confirmed, both the greatest asset and the greatest liability of Masters and Johnson was their scientific approach to studying sexuality. A couple was for the pair a "marital unit," while making love was a "coital opportunity." The pair was often depicted in the media wearing white lab coats, only adding to their clinical persona. Sex was at its most basic level a biological function like respiration or digestion, they firmly believed, an idea that could be easily detected in their immensely popular books. While their jargon (e.g., "erective incompetence," "ejaculatory dysfunction," and "orgasmic return") helped position the team (who got married in 1971) as experts of the first degree, it also made their books virtually useless for readers hoping to solve sexual problems on their own. (This was reportedly intentional; the pair wanted the medical profession to become familiar with and test their techniques before the general public did.)[13] Masters and Johnson now claimed that 80 percent of couples they treated personally overcame their problems, however, an amazing record of success if true. After initial interviews, a physical exam, and series of meetings, couples proceeded to the physical part of therapy, beginning with "sensate focus" exercises. Back in their hotel room, couples engaged in mutual "pleasuring," touching and stroking each other to free themselves from inhibitions and to intensify the sensual dimension of sex. From there, the program concentrated on the specific "inadequacy" that brought the couple to St. Louis, most often premature ejaculation and impotence for men and "frigidity" for women. After men learned the "squeeze technique," how not to be a "spectator" during sex, or what made their partner feel good, couples usually left St. Louis a lot happier than when they arrived.[14]

Part of the profound interest in Masters and Johnson among the general public was simply due to the fact that they were a male and female team, something that was unusual at the time. The couple themselves viewed their "dual-sex therapy team" concept as a key asset not only because of gender differences with regard to sexuality but also because it helped patients feel more comfortable talking about such intimate matters. The grand mission of the two doctors was to relocate sexual inadequacy from other fields, notably psychology, social work, religion, and even the law, to medicine. Despite attacks from critics for their technical approach, Americans were in dire need of such a clinical treatment of sexual dysfunction, Masters and Johnson believed. Sexual problems were a major cause of divorce, not a surprise given that perhaps as many as half of the nation's married couples were in some way sexually incompatible. The lack of knowledge about human sexuality among some Americans was indeed truly startling. Many grown men in the 1970s still believed that masturbation was harmful to their body or mind, or that it really would grow hair on one's palms. Other men were obsessed with the size of their penises, believing theirs were smaller than average and thus less effective. Some women, meanwhile, thought that men had permanent erections, this perhaps understandable because they had never seen one. Masters and Johnson thus saw a big part of their job as to dispel the variety of myths that pervaded sexuality, for example, that men with bigger penises made better lovers, that baldness was a sign of virility, that old people could not and should not have sex, and that there was a physiological difference between a clitoral orgasm and a vaginal one. (Some women experiencing only the latter had taken to saying they were having "the wrong kind" of orgasms.)[15] The two also rejected the idea that simultaneous orgasm or joint climax should be the goal of sexual intercourse, seeing the event as "just a beautiful coincidence."[16]

As the superstars of their field, Masters and Johnson were the "go-to" sex therapists of the 1970s, often called upon by the media to offer insights on all things sexual. In the world of sports, for example, it was popularly believed that having sex before a "big game" was a bad idea, because the activity was seen as so strenuous that it would hurt the player's performance the following day. When news got out that Baltimore Colts coach Don McCafferty had banned players' wives from staying with their husbands before the 1971 Super Bowl, Masters got the call. "I can't imagine a morning-after effect for a conditioned athlete," he told the science newsletter *Behavior Today*, estimating the average energy spent having intercourse as equivalent to running just fifty yards. (Loss of sleep was a different matter, he made clear.) Masters's medical opinion was backed up by someone having real experience in the matter—New York Jets quarterback Joe Namath. The Casanova of professional football admitted he had slept with a woman on the eve of the 1969 Super Bowl, and it certainly had not affected his great performance. "It loosens you up good for the game," Broadway Joe explained, challenging commonly accepted wisdom in sports.[17]

## THE NEW SEX THERAPY

Masters and Johnson's brand of "new sex therapy," as it was popularly called, became nothing short of a global phenomenon after the publication of *Human*

*Sexual Inadequacy.* Hospitals were fast opening sex clinics to meet consumer demand, most of them staffed with disciples of the famous duo. Physicians and psychiatrists trained at the Reproductive Biology Research Foundation in St. Louis were offering their own programs not just in big cities but also in smaller ones like Milwaukee, New Haven, Ann Arbor, Durham, and Chevy Chase. Masters and Johnson–style sex clinics could also be found in London, Geneva, Stockholm, Hamburg, and Amsterdam, proof that Americans did not have a monopoly on impotence, frigidity, and premature ejaculation. Much of the appeal of the "new sex therapy" resided in its ability not only to improve individuals' sex lives but also, as a result, to save couples' marriages. A husband's becoming impotent could lead to his wife believing she was no longer attractive, for example, the beginning of a chain reaction often leading to divorce. Men began to worry that their wives would seek out sexual gratification elsewhere, the problem frequently not even discussed because of its sensitivity. Husbands were suddenly spending a lot of time working late to avoid the issue, and their wives were equally busy with social activities and volunteering. The elephant in the room had a way of creeping into time spent outside the home, however, with no apparent escape from the sex-challenged marriage. Making an appointment at a sex clinic was thus an act of both desperation and courage, as the couple was finally ready to acknowledge and hopefully resolve the thing that was ruining their marriage and lives.[18]

Although psychoanalysts tended to think this literally hands-on kind of sex therapy did not resolve underlying issues ("Rub there is not going to change people," said one), it was precisely because it involved more than talking that supporters believed it worked. Talk therapy alone ignored the fact that sex was physical, but this new therapy suggested that the body as well as the mind should be involved in treatment. By the early 1970s, many Americans were ready to take on such an intimate challenge, something that likely could not have been said of previous generations. Most sex clinics had two- to four-month waiting lists, evidence that the sexual revolution had made Americans more receptive to discussing such a personal issue with strangers. The percentage of Americans with sexual problems had perhaps not changed, but the counterculture, the feminist movement, the birth control pill, and legalized abortion had encouraged a climate in which it was permissible to openly and directly address them. Performance anxiety had largely replaced guilt as the leading cause of problems in the bedroom, experts agreed; although the psychology of sexual dysfunction was quite different than in decades past, the symptoms were much the same.[19]

While Masters and Johnson were the most famous sex therapists, they along with their loyal disciples were hardly the only ones doling out advice to Americans having some kind of problem in the bedroom. One New York psychiatrist was using nude encounter sessions to treat patients, the kicker being that he personally participated in them (but not in the intercourse phase, which took place in private).[20] A much easier and more affordable potential solution was to pick up one of the growing number of sex manuals at the local bookstore. David Reuben's *Everything You Always Wanted to Know About Sex—But Were Afraid to Ask* seemed to be everywhere in the early 1970s, and the best seller was considered by some to be the most popular nonfiction book of its time. (The Woody Allen movie of 1972 very loosely based on the book made it even more of a cultural phenomenon.) Other sex guides such as Ruth Dickson's *Now That You've Got Me Here, What Are We Going to Do?* made *Everything You Always Wanted to Know* seem almost scholarly, however. "Don't forget that the lips are home base," went one bit of advice in the fluffy how-to, the author reminding readers to "come back up every once in a while for a little mouth-to-mouth resuscitation."[21]

As the next generation of "marriage manuals," sex manuals emerged as a legitimate literary segment in the early seventies. Many bookstores created entire sections devoted to the subject just as they recently had with organic food and gardening and "women's lib." The sex book aisle was almost always conveniently located near the "Women" and "Psychology" sections, making it easy for the curious browser to peruse a few titles as if it were just another intellectual exercise. Men could frequently be found thumbing through another wildly popular book, Joan Garrity's *The Sensuous Woman*, hoping to get some pointers. Other men planted themselves in the aisle for hours, thinking it was an ideal place to meet a sexually adventurous woman. Some books, notably Alex Comfort's equally sensational *Joy of Sex*, were kept near the cash register, because too many copies were ruined by customers flipping through the pages.[22]

The writing style and tone of sex manuals varied considerably. Some were lighthearted and fun; others, serious and technical; and still others, descriptive and erotic. Writing for the *New York Times Magazine* in 1973, Mopsy Strange Kennedy divided sex manuals into two categories: the "No-Nonsense" school and the "Give Me Back My Nonsense" school. The former told readers how they should be having sex, while the approach to the latter was to, in the parlance of the times, "do your own thing." There was no right or wrong in the dark, the authors of these less didactic books insisted, seeing sex not as a subject to be mastered but rather as a pleasure to be enjoyed. Perhaps as a response to Masters and Johnson's extremely "No-Nonsense" approach, quite a few best sellers fell into Kennedy's "Give Me Back" school. *The Sensuous Woman* and Xavier Hollander's *The Happy Hooker: My Own Story* fit into the category—Kennedy credited those two memoirs with helping to put sexiness back into sex. Such frankness was refreshing, she believed, preferring it to both the sterility of physicians' sex manuals and the wink-and-a-nod approach of postwar how-tos.[23]

The demand for answers to sex-related questions appeared to be insatiable, however, and even the spate of books on the subject apparently did not address individuals' specific issues. In New York, for example, a nurse-psychologist named Ann Welbourne set up a Community Sex Information and Education Service that was proving to be very popular. More than 150 people were anonymously calling the telephone hotline every day to get answers to their questions from staffers with training in psychology and sociology. Areas of interest included premature ejaculation, anatomy, masturbation, birth control, venereal disease, menopause, and abortion. A surprising number of callers were from married men, their questions most often relating to how to "turn a woman on." Dozens of other communities across the country were keen on setting up similar hotlines, since Americans were as confused as ever about the intricacies of human sexuality.[24]

## A NEW BONDAGE

Doubts about the importance of a primary symbol of the sexual revolution— the birth control pill—had also recently emerged. Eight million American women were regularly taking oral contraceptives in 1970, yet there had been precious little research done on the relationship between the pill and sexual behavior. It was generally accepted that the birth control pill had served as the spark that lit the fire of the sexual revolution by allowing women to be sexually active without the fear of becoming pregnant. That the popularity of the pill coincided with the counterculture reinforced this belief, a symbiotic coupling of a genuine scientific wonder and young peoples' desire for "free love." Many experts began to question this conventional wisdom, however, beginning to think that the impact of the pill on sexual activity was overstated. Women would have had sex with their respective partner whether or not oral contraceptives had come along, sex researchers were now coming to believe, and the link between the pill and promiscuity was a particularly weak one. "Most people in my field have the impression that the pill hasn't changed sex behavior," said Harold Lief, director of the Division of Family Study at the University of Pennsylvania; his experience was that "the vast majority of girls who ask for contraceptives are not virgins." While the pill certainly reduced worry after sex, it did not act as an aphrodisiac before sex, in other words, an important distinction. On a social level, then, the pill was thus not much different than two earlier birth control devices, the condom and the diaphragm; none of them turned America into a sex-crazed nation.[25]

Rethinking the role of the birth control pill within American culture could be seen as part of a new wave of attention being paid to female sexuality in the 1970s. Masters and Johnson had of course addressed certain elements of female sexuality, notably the "clitoral versus vaginal orgasm" issue, in their *Human Sexual Response*, but it was the feminist movement that really raised awareness of women's sexual experience. Books written about women by women challenged much of the commonly accepted wisdom about human sexuality which, considering how little research had been done in the field, was likely not as wise as many believed. In her 1972 *Nature and Evolution of Female Sexuality*, for example, psychiatrist Mary Jane Sherfey turned classical views of human sexuality upside down by dispelling a host of popular myths regarding gender. Human embryos were essentially female for the first six weeks of life, it was now known, meaning the development of male genitals was a biological deviation, not the other way around. The idea that the clitoris was basically a small penis was thus all wrong, as was Freud's celebrated theory about women's envy of the male anatomy. The notion that women were naturally monogamous also was not correct if anthropology was a fair judge, Sherfey pointed out. Some female primates displayed extremely sexually aggressive behavior, a biological impulse designed to maximize the chances of reproduction. This same drive existed in human females, but it had, over thousands of years, been suppressed; virtually all societies were intolerant of unrestrained sexuality among women. Other recently published books about women's sexuality included Barbara Seaman's *Free and Female: The Sex Life of the Contemporary Woman* and Natalie Gittelson's *Erotic Life of the American Wife*, these too bringing much-needed feminist thought into the phallocentric field.[26]

Now that the sexual revolution appeared to be over (some argue it never really ended), all facets of sex in America were open to question. The sexual revolution itself was increasingly being reassessed, as was all the expert advice on the subject that had sprung out of it. "The much-vaunted sexual freedom that the sex researchers and their disciples insist we share is turning out to be a new bondage," thought Derek Wright, author of *The Psychology of Moral Behavior*, believing that the new openness toward sexuality was coming at a high price. Because our social mores had changed, there was now a greater pressure to be sexually active, Wright argued, something that was not necessarily a good thing for everyone. All experts seemingly agreed that not releasing one's sexual energy was going against the forces of nature, a complete reversal of what had been held to be true for hundreds or thousands of years (especially among the religious). More disturbing to Wright was that partners were increasingly grading each other's performance based on standards sex experts were prescribing, seeking approval from one another. Sex was becoming not unlike a competitive sport, an activity in which one felt the need to achieve and succeed rather than something to simply enjoy. Anyone not up to snuff was quickly labeled impotent or frigid, which could cause much greater anxiety and other psychic trauma. Human sexual behavior was a diverse and primarily learned activity, Wright reminded "sexologists"; categorizing and classifying sex was a potentially dangerous thing.[27]

Wright's concerns did little to stop the parade of "sexologists" from offering advice to those reporting sexual problems of some kind. More couples, especially older ones, who would never have sought such advice before the sexual revolution, were now consulting with therapists. Group sex therapy was becoming increasingly popular in the midseventies, as a cheaper alternative for those willing to discuss issues like premature ejaculation, impotency, and frigidity among as many as forty strangers (albeit with similar problems). Group sex therapists often showed pornographic films to clients (the term "patient" was not used), the counselors believing that they reduced anxiety about sexuality and illustrated the options available. As another exercise, groups were divided along gender lines, with the women discussing female sexuality while the men listened and watched in another room via closed-circuit television. (The process was then reversed.) Besides the benefit of clients learning that others shared similar troubles, group sex therapy was much more affordable than private couples therapy. Ten sessions of the former ran around $600–$700, much less than the $2,500 Masters and Johnson charged for a two-week stay at their clinic in St. Louis.[28]

For roughly Masters and Johnson's fee, one could also get help at the Berkeley Sex Therapy Group, which took a different approach to treating sexual dysfunction. The five Bay Area psychologists there used "sex surrogates" for their male patients, that is, women who were paid to have sex with men suffering from impotency or premature ejaculation ($50 for a two-and-a-half-hour session). One of Berkeley's surrogates was in 1972 juggling five clients (a clinical psychologist, an IBM executive, an attorney, and two college students), hosting them at her apartment decorated with an incense burner and a heated waterbed.[29] (Masters and Johnson had employed this kind of therapy for dozens of unmarried males until 1970, when they got sued by a very angry husband of a surrogate.) At least thirty psychologists and psychiatrists in Los Angeles were now using surrogates, as were a few in New York. The women helped men overcome "performance anxiety" by helping them reach a state of enhanced body awareness. (Initial sessions involved just touching, but later ones progressed to intercourse.) Although ethically questionable, the therapy seemed to work. Masters and Johnson had found it very effective for treating impotence, in fact, and were disappointed that they had to give it up for legal reasons.[30]

With their new book, however, Masters and Johnson were quite pleased to rid themselves of some of their image as what *Time* called "the high priests of sex-as-mechanics." Both *Human Sexual Response* and *Human Sexual Inadequacy* had reinforced this image, each book's heavily scientific approach to sexuality only adding to many readers' "performance anxiety." *The Pleasure Bond*, cowritten with Robert J. Levin, an editor of *Redbook*, was based on hundreds of conversations Masters and Johnson had with couples and was an attempt to take sexuality out of the lab and into the bedroom. Still, some critics found the big ideas of the book—that more and better communication led to better sex, that sex should be viewed as pleasure rather than work, and that sexuality was ideally a state of being rather than an act—rather unoriginal and obviously informed by the time's rampant self-help babble.[31] Much more original was Jerry Gillies's *Transcendental Sex: A Meditative Approach to Increasing Sensual Pleasure*, one of a number of sex guides inspired by the time's keen interest in all things Eastern. Gillies combined East with West by marrying meditation with sex, making a case that the act should ideally be not just a pleasurable one but also a spiritual and even transcendent one.[32]

Any kind of sex advice was a good thing for those suffering from a serious problem, most would agree, but the greater openness about sexuality was also making some think they were "dysfunctional" when they were probably not. Americans were a competitive people and were thus naturally inclined to view sex as one more activity at which they wished to excel. This was borne out not just by anecdotal evidence but also by research studies in the field. In a 1978 University of Pittsburgh survey of one hundred couples "who believed their marriages were working well," for example, the incidence of sexual problems were "strikingly high," according to the researchers. Although the vast majority of the couples said their overall marital and sexual relations were happy and satisfying, half the men and three-quarters of the women reported a wide variety of sex-related "difficulties." Even among happily married people, sex was good but not good enough, in other words, and higher expectations likely led to dissatisfaction in the bedroom.[33]

That almost two-thirds of the happily married wives in the University of Pittsburgh study reported having problems achieving arousal or orgasm revealed how widespread sexual "dysfunction" was among American women.[34] In her 1976 *The Hite Report: A Nationwide Study on Female Sexuality*, Shere Hite reported the findings of her research involving more than 1,800 women that perhaps explained the larger problem. Critics had a field day with her methodology, but Hite offered a compelling thesis: more women experienced orgasm from direct clitoral stimulation than from intercourse, suggesting that standard sex was not very well suited for female sexuality. It was up to women to change the commonly accepted view that intercourse was the ultimate sexual act, Hite argued, an ambitious but worthy effort if they were to enjoy sex as much as men.[35] Many men did not like what they read in *The Hite Report*, finding her thesis decidedly anti-male and just not true.[36] As soon as the ink was dry on her best seller, however, Hite was hard at work on the sequel, a report on male sexuality. With her whopping $300,000-plus advance, Hite had sent out thousands of questionnaires to men, hoping the answers would be the foundation for an argument as provocative as in her first book.[37]

## RESPECTABLE MIDDLE-CLASS PORN

While many ordinary Americans were sexually unsatisfied, those in the business of sex could hardly have been happier. Despite the deep recession of the early 1970s, the nation's porn industry was enjoying very good times, a function perhaps of America's sexual woes. Law enforcement officials estimated annual sales of erotic books, films, and paraphernalia to be $500 million in 1970, although others put the figure closer to $2 billion. Peep-show emporiums in New York City's Time Square (where viewers paid a quarter to watch a two-minute segment of a pornographic film) were alone generating $5 million in revenue, enough money for the mob to take over the business. Full-length films or "blue movies" (shown in theaters in these pre-VCR days, of course) accounted for the biggest profits. Many amateur-made "sexploitation" films costing thousands to produce raked in millions at the box office, such a return on investment attracting big-time investors. (To get around possible obscenity charges, filmmakers often defined them as sex-education movies or documentaries.)[38] Long dominated by European (especially Danish) imports, the American porn business was now more than holding its own domestically and even exporting some films across the pond. Much of the appeal of pornographic movies from an investment perspective had to do with the cheap cost of talent. Men typically made no money at all for starring in a "skin flick" (free sex was enough incentive to take part), while women usually earned just $25–$35. Processing film, especially color, could be costly, but the likelihood of wide distribution almost guaranteed that a blue movie would turn a profit.[39]

Pornographic paperback novels, sold in adult bookstores, were also very popular in the early 1970s, as were "dirty magazines." Total nudity was now legally allowed in such magazines, which cost anywhere from $3.50 to $15 at retail. (The tabloid newspaper *Screw*, however, cost just fifty cents.) One of the best-selling "action" magazines was rather humorously titled *The Illustrated Presidential Report of the Commission on Obscenity and Pornography* and contained not just the full text of the report but also a generous selection of photographs supposedly used as evidence by the commission. In Manhattan, Los Angeles, and San Francisco, live sex shows, in which naked couples performed for viewers, were the latest trend, this too turning out to be quite a profitable venture for entrepreneurs.[40] In Miami, one could get a topless shoeshine for $2, while in Los Angeles one could rent a camera and make one's own porn movie at a "modeling studio" for $25 an hour.[41]

That the courts (including the Supreme Court) had deemed most pornography as a form of free speech protected by the First Amendment did not mean that all Americans were happy to see it flourish. Lyndon B. Johnson had in 1967 appointed a congressional committee to determine the social consequences of pornography ("the most extensive research into erotica and its effects ever undertaken," according to the *Nation*), with President Nixon urging what he called a "citizen's crusade" against it while the study was being completed.[42] When operators of movie theaters in smaller towns, knowing there was big money to be made, decided to screen pornographic films, a firestorm often ensued. Local committees to preserve "decency" were quickly formed, the battle lines drawn between citizens convinced such films would have a negative impact on family and community life and entrepreneurs simply seeing a great business opportunity.[43] The war was also waged on a national level, with more conservative critics and media outlets making it clear that, just because "smut" was legal, did not mean it was good for America and Americans. In 1970, for example, *Life* magazine took a firm stance against the "go[ing] public" of pornography, reporting in one of its classic photo essays how the industry was a blight upon the land:

> We've done it at last! We have succeeded in supersaturating our frazzled poor selves in sex of every kind and variety. On our screens, in our bookstores, clogging our mails and our minds now is every conceivable manner of biological union: heterosexual, homosexual, monosexual, and, for the truly jaded, a whole zoological garden of bestiality.[44]

Much to the chagrin of the city's "morals squad," New York was a veritable "pornocopia," with no shortage of opportunities to partake of sexual entertainment. In 1970, the police believed there to be fifty-five "dirty" bookstores, sixteen "skin houses" (movie theaters), six peep-show emporiums, six burlesque houses, eight "figure modeling" studios, one live peep show, and five live sex shows. While New York was especially bountiful in pornography, sexual material of some kind could be found in most other cities across the country. There were an estimated 2,250 adult bookstores in America, the pornography commission had found, and a fair number of blue movie theaters were also liberally sprinkled around the country. No fewer than twenty-seven adult bookstores and movie houses were operating within a seven-block radius of the White House, in fact, something that was no doubt driving its current resident crazy. ("The warped and brutal portrayal of sex in books, plays, magazines and movies, if not halted or reversed, could poison the wellsprings of American and Western culture and civilization," President Nixon had recently said.) But with obscenity difficult to define, courts clogged with more important cases, and lawyers well versed in working the system, the Justice Department and local law enforcement could do little to stop the flood of pornography in America.[45]

When hard-core porn invaded Bible Belt towns like Waterloo, Iowa, however, many locals were willing to do whatever they could to stop what they saw as depraved as Communism or atheism. That's exactly what happened in Waterloo in 1970 when a Des Moines movie-chain operator decided to screen 16 mm pornographic films in a theater on Commercial Street, right in the middle of town. Despite the Supreme Court's anticensorship ruling, the mayor of the town tried to stop the showing of what he called "Triple-X" movies by citing a 1939 ordinance banning "any exhibition, amusement or entertainment . . . detrimental to the public health, morals or safety." A state district judge ruled the mayor's action unconstitutional, however, and soon movies such as *The Divorcee, Motel Confidential, Night of the Vibrator*, and *The Female Frenzy of Dr. Studley* were playing to mostly full houses. Farmers, traveling salesmen, students from the University of Northern Iowa, and some locals were happy to pay $3 ($5 a couple) to see the films, with Waterloo seemingly none the worse since porn came to town.[46]

Even in progressive San Francisco, however, many locals were not happy about all the pornography that was now in their backyard and being produced there. In 1970, Dianne Feinstein, then president of the city's board of supervisors, took a tour of the city's porn shops and movie houses along with a group of concerned citizens. "What we found was total degradation of the human spirit, a terrifying look into the darkest recesses of the sick mind," wrote Merla Z. Goerner in her society page column of the *Chronicle*, her colleagues equally appalled at what they had seen. Feinstein herself admitted that San Francisco was "the smut capital of the United States," the city's pornographic movie industry rivaling the notorious one based in Copenhagen. While Goerner and other residents remembering "old San Francisco" would prefer it if all the shops and theaters were shut down, Feinstein thought they should be regulated and perhaps contained to one area of the city. Those familiar with the history of the city were not surprised that San Francisco had earned its dubious title as the epicenter of pornography in America. All kinds of vice soon followed the Gold Rush of '49, which was the foundation for the city's famous tolerance for alternative lifestyles.[47]

Still, many civic leaders felt things had gone too far after the utopian summer of love in 1967. In addition to all the bookstores and theaters, commercial sex seemed to be everywhere in the city. Teenage prostitutes, both male and female, had set up shop not just in the sketchier parts of the city but also in the heart of downtown and directly in front of fancy hotels like the St. Francis. Sexually themed newspapers, comic books, and other ephemera published by the city's thriving underground press was ubiquitous, and bars in the heavily visited North Beach and Tenderloin districts regularly featured nude dancing (along with risqué marquees, explicit window displays, and sidewalk barkers). Concerned citizens found the city's live sex shows (both simulated and real) and a new transvestite group called the Cockettes (some of the men had beards and mustaches) especially disturbing and worried that out-of-towners would also be put off by such sordid entertainment. "Just walking around the city can give the casual visitor the impression that porn, not tourism, is San Francisco's leading industry," thought William Murray after he took a look around to write a piece for the *New York Times Magazine.*[48]

As the case of Waterloo, Iowa, illustrated, one did not have to be in San Francisco or any other major American city to view some form of hard-core pornography in a public setting in the early seventies. Some pornographic films were crossing over into mainstream theaters, causing quite a ruckus in many communities. One film in particular, *Deep Throat*, tested the boundaries of obscenity, the criteria still being whether it appealed primarily to "prurient interests," went substantially beyond community standards, and had absolutely no "redeeming social value." Courts around the country held trials through 1972 and 1973 to determine if "Throat," as it was sometimes referred to, was obscene and should thus not be shown publicly; the film served as a test case for pornography in general. (Fifteen sexual acts, including seven of fellatio and four of cunnilingus, were featured in the seventy-minute film, leading *Screw* magazine to nominate it as "the very best film ever made.") Regardless of or because of the legal issues, *Deep Throat* was turning out to be the most commercially successful pornographic movie ever made. Between June 1972 and January 1973, the film was shown in seventy-three American cities and grossed almost $3 million. Young, hip, upper-middle-class Americans, many of them women, were lining up to see the film that was credited with sparking the (brief) "porn chic" trend.[49]

Even in normally sexually tolerant Manhattan such a trial was held, with all kinds of experts weighing in on whether the movie (about a woman whose clitoris was located in her throat) contributed to society in any meaningful way. New York City officials believed that if the courts judged *Deep Throat* to be obscene, they could finally begin to clean up Times Square, with its many X-rated movie theaters, prostitutes, massage parlors, and live sex shows. The trial held in Manhattan Criminal Court illustrated how difficult it was to define obscenity. "This is one of the first sexploitation films to show sympathy for the idea that a woman's sexual gratification is as important as a man's," Arthur Knight, a professor at the University of Southern California and film critic for *Saturday Review*, told the judge. A number of psychiatrists also offered testimony, some concurring with Knight's view that the film had social value and others arguing that it had few, if any, merits. Perhaps the most interesting observation came from the judge, Joel J. Tyler. After Knight noted that the sexual activity in the film did indeed go beyond the "missionary position," Tyler asked what that meant. Told that the missionary position involved a woman being supine while a man was prone on top of her, the judge quipped, "It's worthwhile to me, if nothing else happens, to have gotten this education." Judge Tyler determined the movie was obscene, not too surprising given his apparent lack of familiarity with some of the more basic dimensions of human sexuality.[50]

With hard-core pornography flourishing, less graphic media were put in a precarious competitive situation. Around now for two decades, *Playboy* had lost much of the sheer excitement that had surrounded the publication of each issue and, of course, its centerfold. The wholesome, girl-next-door quality of Playmates was wearing a bit thin, especially when viewed against women featured in other magazines that had followed in *Playboy*'s wake. "It's respectable middle-class porn," M. J. Sobran of the *National Review* described *Playboy* in 1976, "tame stuff compared with most of the skin mags at any newsstand." The circulation of *Playboy* had dropped, much in part to a competitor that had appeared on the American scene in 1969. *Penthouse* (which was first published in the UK in 1965) was giving *Playboy* a run for its money by means of its raunchier photos and editorial that appealed to a new generation of male readers. Versus *Playboy*'s pseudo-virgins, *Penthouse* models "come across as grad school nymphomaniacs," Sobran thought, just the look more sophisticated consumers of porn found attractive in the 1970s. Photos of genitalia could be found in *Penthouse*, something that *Playboy* had always shied away from. It was clear that the sexual revolution had raised the bar of mass-market pornography; what played well in the 1950s and early 1960s now looked as dated as a Studebaker.[51]

The new, more brazen sexual landscape of the 1970s made the editors of *Playboy* unsure of which path to take. Should it go down the more revealing (some would say vulgar) road and compete head-on with *Penthouse* and the growing number of similar magazines? After initially flirting with *Penthouse*-esque images, Hugh Hefner decided to stay true to the *Playboy* brand (large breasts, basically). Given the kind of images to be found in the number 3 magazine in the category, Hefner's decision made sense. With its close-ups of vaginas, *Hustler* made even *Penthouse* look innocent. Despite the industry trend, Sobran, and surely many others, found this more anatomical approach decidedly nonerotic. "The more pornographic they become, the less they can be called *sexual*," he wrote of the photos in *Hustler*, thinking they were not only in bad taste but also crossed the line of the freedoms protected by the Constitution. The authors of the First Amendment were certainly brilliant visionaries, but even they could not anticipate the likes of *Hustler, Oui, Gallery*, and *Swank*.[52]

## THE AMERICAN WAY OF SWINGING

The kudzu-like spreading of pornography was not the only thing critics blamed on the excesses of the sexual revolution. Swinging (or mate swapping or group sex) had probably always been around to some extent in America, but the wild west of sexuality in the 1970s was the ideal climate for it to thrive. In his 1971 *Group Sex: A Scientist's Eyewitness Report on the American Way of Swinging*, Gilbert D. Bartell took what was probably the most in-depth look at swinging culture published to date. Over the course of three years, Bartell, a professor of anthropology at Northern Illinois University, along with his wife Ann, met with hundreds of swingers (defined as people interested in "having sexual relations as a couple with at least one other individual"). Finding such people was easy. Bartell simply placed a number of ads in *Kindred Spirits*, one of dozens of magazines catering to swingers (others included *Ecstasy*, *Swinger's Life*, *National Registry*, and *Select*), and the responses poured in. From there, the protocol was generally standard. Two couples would arrange an informal meeting and, if all went well, plan a much more intimate second encounter. As many as two dozen couples converged at swinging parties, some of them involving literal group sex and others in which twosomes retreated to separate rooms. Candles or mood lighting often set the scene, with "stag films" sometimes shown on projectors to break the ice. For sexually adventuresome people, swingers could be initially surprisingly shy; strong drinks were often required to get participants to relax, and frequently no one seemed eager to make the first move. Swingers were also, rather oddly, obsessed with personal cleanliness, the Bartells found in their research (in which they did not actively take part). At one of their parties, swingers could be found in the bathtub or shower just as often as they could be found in bed; a generous supply of soap and towels was an essential element of such get-togethers.[53]

Swingers could be said to be conservative in other ways. Outside the big caveat that one was sleeping with someone other than one's spouse, sex was typically conventional. Two women might pair off, but two men rarely did, as swinging culture was distinct from the gay scene. (Not only homosexuals but also blacks were typically not welcome at early seventies swinging parties.) Interestingly, expressing affection for a partner was considered bad form; the brief relationship was understood as being purely about sex. The general rule was to swing once, and only once, with a particular couple so that the activity would not cause marital discord or breakups. ("The couple that swings together stays together," went the group's motto.) Swingers were, demographically speaking, also quite "normal." Of the estimated one to two million American swingers, most were middle-class suburbanites, according to Bartell's study. A whopping 42 percent of the male swingers the Bartells encountered were salesmen, with a fair number of the rest being professionals of some sort. More than three-fourths of the female swingers he met were stay-at-home housewives, most of them with kids. Contrary to what some critics believed, swingers also tended to be antidrug and "antihippie," not at all aligned with the ideals or lifestyle of the counterculture. Swinging was something quite different from the "free love" of the sexual revolution, in other words; its advocates wanted to have little to do with rebellious, antiestablishment youth culture.[54]

Club 101, based in California's San Fernando Valley, was one of the better-known swinger organizations in the early 1970s. Every weekend, about twenty couples met at a mansion as if it were any other party, the only difference being that in about an hour the strangers would all be having sex with each other. Club 101 was a much larger gathering than most swinger get-togethers, however, with two to six couples as the norm. Bartell estimated there to be more than eight thousand couples regularly swinging in greater Chicago and about four thousand in the Atlanta area. Although most swingers found each other through classified ads ("Groovy couples wanted. Nothing way out. Photo appreciated. Can travel," went one ad in *Select*), New Yorkers could connect in person at the Captain Kidd bar and Los Angelenos at the Swing bar.[55]

Some group sex activity was, of course, more spontaneous. Party games like strip poker and spin-the-bottle were known to lead to more intimate recreation, and après ski soirees could get pretty wild after some fondue and a few bottles of Almaden or Blue Nun wine. Sexually restless husbands almost always were the instigators in a couple's decision to swing, although Bartell found that initially reluctant wives were soon more than happy to have joined the party.[56] Some women who had been married for some time became interested in swinging because it offered them assurance that men other than their husbands still found them attractive. Threesomes consisting of two women and a man were a popular choice, although husbands often took special delight in watching their wives have sex with other men. Couples typically found the anticipation of a swinging occasion as exciting as the event itself, the debriefing afterward also a source of considerable titillation. Interestingly, spouses viewed swinging as a marriage-friendly alternative to cheating, that is, a way to be sexually adventurous while remaining, paradoxically, faithful.[57]

By the mid-1970s, however, swinging was in decline in America; much of its novelty was gone for even its most enthusiastic participants. As with its close cousin, open marriages, couples were finding that having sex with other people was affecting their relationships despite the no-emotional-attachment rule. Nena and George O'Neill, coauthors of the 1972 best seller *Open Marriage*, were retreating from their position, recommending in their new book *Shifting Gears* that couples seek "change and growth" in their marriage versus swinging. The only place that swinging appeared to be growing was Atlanta, where the phenomenon was relatively new. The porn industry also was retrenching, with sales of "dirty" books and magazines down considerably.[58] Los Angeles had imposed a moratorium on new pornographic movie theaters and bookstores, and a number of cities were passing ordnances to bar such businesses from operating within a designated distance from a residential area, school, church, or park. The courts too appeared to be tilting back toward a more conservative position regarding sexual content. Larry Flynt, the publisher of *Hustler*, was ordered to stand trial in Atlanta for disseminating obscene material and had already been convicted of the same charge in Cincinnati. "After an era of revolution, is a counterrevolution under way?" asked *Time* in 1977, as the sexual mood in America was showing all signs of reversing course.[59]

Even college students were becoming more conservative in their sexual ways, research showed. Students' view that marriage was an obsolete institution had peaked in 1971 and was still declining, according to researcher Daniel Yankelovich, and the trend now was toward stable, committed relationships on campus. Behavior only recently considered old-fashioned—falling in love and fidelity—was on the rebound, a response to the loneliness and hurt many felt when promiscuity was the norm. Both marriage and cohabitation were "in," many college students were reporting, and "free love" was more associated with the days of Woodstock than with Watergate. "There's no doubt that all the experimentation and kinkiness are declining," said Ellen Frankfort, author of *Vaginal Politics*, thinking Americans were more interested in connectedness than experimentation. "People found that instant sex was about as satisfying as a sneeze," explained Joyce Brothers, the populist psychologist who believed the sheer logistics of having a handful of lovers was too much work.[60] One of the few voices still preaching "avant-garde" sexuality was Comfort, author of the megahit *The Joy of Sex*. In his new book *More Joy*, Comfort predicted that group sex and bisexuality would become mainstream activities within ten years, a forecast that seemed highly anachronistic in these more sober days.[61]

## A SOCIOLOGICAL PHENOMENON

Comfort was dead wrong about group sex becoming as American as apple pie, but bisexuality was indeed losing much of its stigma. Kinsey had argued that human sexuality consisted of a range between heterosexual and homosexual, an idea that gained currency in the more tolerant 1970s. Bisexuality (a term Kinsey did not like because in biology it referred to something quite different) was, rather suddenly, considered quite stylish, a symbol of sophistication and confidence. As gays did a decade or so earlier, bisexuals were "coming out" en masse in the midseventies, no longer assigned to the margins of society. "It has become very fashionable in elite and artistically creative subgroups to be intrigued by the notion of bisexuality," said Norman Fisk, a psychiatrist at Stanford University, thinking it could very well be "a sociological phenomenon." The feminist movement was no doubt playing a role in the increasing popularity of bisexuality, as was the greater recognition of the "clitoral orgasm." Widespread use of the birth control pill had also helped to propel bisexuality by encouraging a climate of recreational (versus procreational) sex, one more legacy of the sexual revolution.[62]

Popular and consumer culture both reflected and helped to shape what was commonly called "bisexual chic." Bisexuality was viewed as two different things: a sexual attraction to men and women and androgyny. Each could be easily detected in the hipper pockets of American culture, with bisexuality now shorthand for au courant style. Threesomes could be found in *Vogue* fashion spreads, for example, while more trend-forward cosmetic marketers featured young women and men wearing makeup in their ads. Pop song lyrics occasionally referenced bisexuality, and some celebrities were not shy in pronouncing they enjoyed the company of both men and women. "Bisexuality is in bloom," announced *Newsweek* in 1974, thinking its flowering was likely inevitable given the recent overlapping of gender identities. With both style and social roles blending along gender lines, "the only thing left to swap was sex itself," the magazine observed, and a new ethos of "anyone goes" was taking hold among the creative set. On some college campuses, the prom queen's date was turning out to be another prom queen, while the prom king was showing up wearing eye shadow. Rock stars like Mick Jagger and David Bowie were serving as inspiration for some men to get in touch with their feminine side, and hipper clubs like Max's Kansas City in New York and the Bistro in Chicago were hotbeds of androgyny. Some bisexuals saw themselves as neither entirely male nor entirely female, a new and different "breed" of human. With all kinds of sexual permutations popping up, the owner of Le Jardin, a trendy discotheque in New York, joked that "trisexuals" could be found at his club, not too much of an exaggeration.[63]

Although many bisexuals were delighted that their "best of both worlds" lifestyle was now being celebrated, there were problems with having sex with both men and women. Relationships with friends of the same gender often changed when someone announced he or she was bisexual, the dimension of sexuality now added to the dynamic. The homosexual community was not entirely receptive to bisexuals, with some gays feeling the latter felt superior to them. Others gays were skeptical about the entire concept of bisexuality and thought it was simply a stepping-stone to coming out as one of them. Many lesbians did not entirely trust bisexuals, thinking they would prefer to be with a man if the opportunity presented itself. The general consensus was that bisexuals were typically sexually capricious, pursuing relationships with each gender with little apparent emotional involvement. Psychologists saw deep meaning in bisexuals' fickleness, thinking they were developmentally challenged and were likely to lead lives of instability and chaos. Bisexuals argued that having more options was the whole point, however and that limiting oneself to just one-half of the population did not make much sense.[64]

The popularity of bisexuality in the 1970s illustrated the degree to which sexuality in America had changed over the course of a generation. While sexual frivolity was in descent, it was clear that Americans had in general broadened their horizons when it came to sex. Billed as the most ambitious survey of American sexuality since the Kinsey studies of 1948 (male) and 1953 (female), a new study was published in 1973 by the Playboy Foundation, a nonprofit operating under the aegis of its parent magazine. Playboy reportedly spent $125,000 on the study, using the findings in a series of articles that celebrated the magazine's guiding philosophy, which was grounded in the freedoms and pleasures promised by the sexual revolution. Hugh Hefner was no doubt happy to see that there was quantitative evidence showing that Americans had come a long way sexually since the publication of the first issue of *Playboy* in 1953; further, Hefner felt his magazine very likely played a prominent role in the cultural sea change. Over the past twenty-five years, "there have been dramatic increases in the frequency with which most Americans engage in various sexual activities and in the number of persons who include formerly rare or forbidden techniques in their sexual repertoires," read the report that was conducted by the Chicago-based Research Guild and based on a survey of some two thousand people. (Kinsey had done over twelve thousand interviews.)[65]

The details of the study, which were published in a book called *Sexual Behavior in the 1970s* the following year, confirmed that sex in America had indeed changed in a number of significant ways over the past quarter century. Premarital sex took place both more frequently and earlier than it did in the late 1940s and early 1950s, especially among women. Single women also reported having more orgasms than their sisters of a generation earlier (three times as many, in fact), and young wives were far more likely to have extramarital affairs. Perhaps most indicative that Americans had become more sexually adventuresome was that both oral sex and heterosexual anal intercourse were each much more popular. Fifty percent more Americans took part in the former than those in Kinsey's day, while about a quarter of Playboy's sample had experienced the latter at least once (Kinsey's numbers of anal sex were too low to even report). Interestingly, the statistics on homosexuality had hardly changed between the two studies, suggesting that gay culture had become much more visible but not more common in terms of actual activity.[66]

Findings from an exhaustive poll conducted by a much different kind of magazine in 1975 confirmed that Playboy had not cooked the books to serve its own cause. Redbook asked more than eighteen thousand women about their sexual attitudes and practices, finding that sex in America was indeed quite different than during the Truman and Eisenhower years. Eighty percent of the women (most of them young, white, middle-class mothers, reflecting the readership of the magazine) said they had had premarital intercourse, with an even higher number (90 percent) of women under twenty-five reporting premarital sex. Eighty-nine percent of the women had experienced oral sex, and close to a third of those married had had extramarital affairs. (Half of working women had strayed, suggesting that some hanky-panky was going on at the office.) Less than 4 percent had taken part in swinging, but almost a quarter said they wanted to, another indication that women of the mid-1970s were considerably more "liberated" than their mothers were at the same age. Perhaps the biggest surprise of Redbook's study was that "strongly religious" women reported being more sexually satisfied than their "fairly religious" and "nonreligious" sisters. The devout had more orgasms than the nonpious, something the editors of the magazine mulled over for some time. Current thinking among the clergy that sexual pleasure helped make a good marriage explained this particular finding, the editors proposed, as religious men apparently took this message to heart.[67]

Some observers of the scene were less sanguine about the direction sex in America had taken, however. "We are now living in a time in America . . . where there seems to be no ground rules to sexual love," wrote author Willie Morris for *Newsweek* in 1974, believing that the nation's "structure, principles, [and] inhibitions" had disappeared. The much-celebrated sexual revolution had by the midseventies left Americans culturally adrift, Morris argued, and relationships between men and women were none the better because of it. Three out of four marriages were ending in divorce among middle-aged Americans living on the East Coast, just one sign of the social wreckage taking place. The contract of marriage was hardly perfect, Morris admitted, but "the rhythms and expectations of love now have entered a wholly uncharted terrain," he felt, "far out at another extreme." Shuttling from one sexual relationship to another was an aimless pursuit, Morris was convinced; whatever those doing it were looking for was simply not obtainable. Liberation had ultimately led to distrust among many, he added, and the knowledge that another brief encounter was waiting in the wings was almost guaranteed to ruin one's current relationship.[68]

Other writers were happy to say good riddance to the once important and exciting movement that had overstayed its welcome. "The concept of a loosened, public, open sexuality has become part of mainstream American life," declared Bob Greene, columnist for *Newsweek*, "and with it the death knell has sounded for the daring revolution that it once was." The sexual revolution had lost much of its energy and power some time ago as it became absorbed into everyday life, Greene argued. Indeed, seeing male prostitutes as guests on daytime talk shows was not particularly shocking, condoms and vibrators were being openly advertised, and paperback copies of *The Joy of Sex* could be found near the cash registers of grocery stores. Swapping and swinging, words that once had to be whispered in most suburban homes, were now not mentioned out of apathy. Even Hugh Hefner was looking less and less the playboy than, according to Greene, "everyone's kindly and slightly bewildered uncle." Films much racier than the images found in his magazine were playing in theaters on Main Street, USA, much of the postwar naughtiness of comely centerfolds gone for good. "Shacking up," a daring enterprise a decade earlier, no longer caused parents and clergy much distress, especially since it was now justified as much for economic reasons as for sexual ones.

With the sexual revolution in the country's rearview mirror, Greene predicted values like faithfulness, fidelity, and selectivity would soon be in vogue and that America was on the brink of a new era in romance and relationships.[69]

## THIS SAVAGE, TROUBLED TIME

Greene would be proven right, but American popular culture showed no signs of embracing values like faithfulness, fidelity, and selectivity. What *Time* referred to as "sex rock" could be heard all over AM radio in the mid-1970s, for example, an intensifying of rock 'n' roll's never-ending love affair with sexuality. The lyrics to songs such as People's Choice's "Do It Any Way You Wanna," the Staple Singers' "Let's Do It Again," KC and the Sunshine Band's "That's the Way (I Like It)," and Leon Haywood's "I Want'a Do Something Freaky to You" were overtly, unapologetically sexual (as were the titles alone). With its grunts, groans, and moans, however, it was Donna Summer's big hit "Love to Love You Baby" that made listeners turn up (or down) the volume. Over the course of the sixteen-minute song (it took up a whole side of the album of the same name), Summer simulated what the BBC counted as twenty-three orgasms; nothing like it had ever been played on the radio. (Summer, who was actually quite reserved, laid on the floor of the recording studio in the dark to record it.) This wave of "sex rock" was a new phenomenon that illustrated how far America had evolved (or devolved) in terms of commercial sexual content. In 1966, the Rolling Stones had considerable trouble getting their much more innocent song "Let's Spend the Night Together" on the air and famously caused quite a row for singing the titular lyrics on *The Ed Sullivan Show*. The Federal Communications Commission (FCC) was vigilant about preventing songs with lyrics referencing drug use to be aired on the radio but admittedly had no clue how to address the more subjective area of sex. A reverend in Florida was, meanwhile, deciding to take matters into his own hands, setting fire to $2,000's worth of record albums after learning that almost all unmarried girls in North Florida who got pregnant were reportedly listening to rock 'n' roll at the time.[70]

Film too was becoming increasingly sexual even as Americans gradually adopted more conservative values. The 1970s certainly had its share of sexually controversial movies (*A Clockwork Orange*, *Fritz the Cat*, *Last Tango in Paris*, *Pink Flamingos*, *Caligula*, *Midnight Cowboy*, *Born Innocent*, and *Bob, Carol, Ted, and Alice*, to name some), but it was *Looking for Mr. Goodbar* that was perhaps the most disturbing. Although the novel on which it was based had been a best seller, many viewers of *Looking for Mr. Goodbar* were nonetheless shocked, especially during the last fifteen, very violent minutes of the 1977 film. The film and novel were based on a true story of a woman who was brutally murdered by one of the men she had picked up in a bar. Jack Kroll of *Newsweek* considered *Looking for Mr. Goodbar* to be "the most powerfully explicit American film on sexuality so far" and believed the protagonist's addiction to sex was "a fact of our time." "The movie breaks new ground in its depiction of the sheer pleasure of sex," he continued, thinking the film was a fitting, if extreme, reflection of "this savage, troubled time."[71]

Television of the late 1970s was also venturing into new sexual territory. (The lead character of *Maude* having an abortion in a 1972 episode was a prime example of the boundary pushing.) The medium was not nearly as sexual as movies, but one would not know that judging by the number of complaints about it. There was, of course, no sex on television at the time, literally speaking, but there was a certain degree of kissing and embracing and plenty of innuendo. Still, both critics and viewers consistently griped about how sexual (and violent) television had become and that it was damaging the "moral fiber" of the nation. Network executives believed this was unjustified and pointed to the fact that commercial television was the most conservative of mass media when it came to sex. Pre–Hays Code movies of the 1920s and early 1930s were arguably bawdier than late 1970s television, but the intrusive nature of the latter made it a visible and vulnerable target. Programmers also argued that television was just keeping up with the times, reflecting the changes that had taken place over the years with regard to sexuality. As well, a variety of forces—broadcast standards, management, producers, affiliates, and advertisers—kept sexuality and all other controversial subjects in check, they maintained, and the brouhaha about sex on television was much ado about nothing.[72]

Your average American family sitting on their Naugahyde couch in front of their Zenith or Magnavox Console TV set might have had a different opinion. The ABC series *Three's Company* could have been conceived only in the late seventies, for example, when a show consisting almost entirely of one-liners and double entendres about sex was considered good entertainment. Conceding to pressure to lower the violence in their shows, the networks ratcheted up the sex and were pleased to find that shows like *Three's*

*Company* got high ratings. *Soap*, also on ABC, was another show that would never have made it on the air even a few years before it did in 1977. Besides having a lot of sexual innuendo, *Soap* included Jodie, a homosexual played by Billy Crystal, who turned out to be perhaps the sanest character in the show. *Charlie's Angels* was widely acknowledged as a terribly written show, even within the industry, but that did not stop viewers from tuning in to see what the three buxom, skimpily clad ladies were up to that week. *Love Boat* could get also pretty racy for the times, especially when the Spanish American actress Charo (of "cuchi-cuchi" fame) made an appearance (on no fewer than eight occasions).[73]

Producers and writers were fully aware of the ratings bump a particular episode could get by including a plot device having something to do with sex. Rape and lesbianism were featured in episodes of *All in the Family* and male prostitution in *Baretta*, for example, the medium slowly closing the "sex gap" between itself and mainstream movies. As a result, viewer complaints to the FCC about what was known in the trade as "jiggly" television were way up, a sign of the country's big divide when it came to sexuality. Despite the fact that one could simply change the channel (or turn the set off), some religious groups and parents were highly sensitive about what came into their homes and were not reluctant to try to get what they saw as "immoral" programming off the air. Television executives were mulling over a ratings system similar to that used for movies so that viewers would know ahead of time about potentially objectionable content.[74] Such matters would in the not-so-distant future be seen as trivial, however, as the nation's "sexidemic" took a much more serious turn.

# 4

# Fatal Attraction

I guess you thought you'd get away with it. Well, you can't.

—*Alex Forrest (Glenn Close) to Dan Gallagher (Michael Douglas) in the 1987 film*
Fatal Attraction

In the summer of 1985, Frank Gannon griped about the state of the union, especially when it came to the emotionally charged subjects of romance and sexuality. "We used to be a romantic people," he bemoaned, longing for an America that once produced works like *This Side of Paradise, Tales of the South Pacific,* and *From Here to Eternity.* Writing for *Saturday Review,* Gannon felt that classic romantic qualities like innocence, ardency, and mystery had disappeared not only from our literature but also from our music, movies, drama, and art as well. After peaking during the "brief, shining moment" of the New Frontier, romance began its long decline with the assassination of John F. Kennedy, he suggested. With its cynicism, drugs, and violence, the mid-1960s to the mid-1970s were a disaster for romance, Gannon believed, and the last ten years were not much better. Along with the demise of romance came an equivalent slide in sexuality, he argued, and the parade of experts offering information and advice on technique took much of the mystique and fun out of it. The prevalence of sex in pop culture also diminished its power and intensity. "Being able to see and read and hear all about it inevitably affects our imaginations as well as our emotions," he wrote; Americans were now paying a heavy price for the expansion of sexuality over the past couple of decades.[1]

There was no doubt that the sexual revolution had irrevocably changed America and Americans in many ways, some for the better and some for the worse. With the revolution now officially defunct, due in part to a more conservative cultural climate, it was becoming clear that the greater opportunity to express one's sexuality would not lead to the erotic paradise once imagined. In fact, more Americans than ever were having, or at least reporting, problems in the bedroom, and the 1980s were to become a golden age of sex therapy. The more open climate to talk about sex, which paid a heavy debt to the still going strong self-help movement, was revealing that things were not at all well in America when it came to sexuality. The pressure to perform like the fictional sexual Olympians in movies, in advertising, and on television made matters only worse. All things sexual would get much more complicated in the 1980s, however, as a new disease turned sex into one of Americans' biggest concerns.

## CHAMPAGNE SEX AT BEER PRICES

Even though the Reagans, with their goal of restoring traditional values to the nation, occupied the White House, Americans were not quite ready to end the decade-and-a-half bacchanal they had enjoyed. For the particularly adventurous, there was Plato's Retreat in New York City, a vestige of the unrestrained sexuality of the 1970s. Having opened its doors in 1977, the "first openly advertised, popularly priced spa for public sex," as Sam Keen called it, was still alive and kicking in the early 1980s. Unlike many countercultural or what would become known as New Age activities or institutions, Plato's Retreat had no ideological, therapeutic, or spiritual ambitions. The club, very simply, offered people the rare opportunity to have sex with or in the presence of others, a twentieth-century version of the ancient Greek orgy (hence the name). "It was the Playboy mansion for the masses, champagne sex at beer prices," wrote Keen for *Psychology Today* in 1980 after visiting the place for research purposes only. (As a reporter, he was required to keep his clothes on and, as the manager made perfectly clear, "look but don't touch.")[2]

Arriving at a quiet residential street on Manhattan's Upper West Side, one certainly would not know one was entering a palace of carnality. After paying the $40 cover and agreeing not to consume drugs or alcohol (a rule routinely violated), patrons could enjoy a swimming pool, dance floor, game room, and buffet stocked with cold cuts and potato salad. It was, however, to the mattress room that most visitors quickly gravitated. In addition to the wall-to-wall mattresses and gymnasium pads, the "mat" room had mirrors on the ceilings and along two walls, allowing greater visibility for spectators and participants. Only (nude) male and female couples could enter the room, after which any heterosexual or lesbian reconfigurations were permitted. Thirty or forty couples were typically active in the mat room on any given night, a sea of moving body parts. (Keen likened it to an aquarium.) Most of the diverse collection of guests remained with the partners with whom they arrived, although swapping was perfectly acceptable if mutually agreeable. The room was surprisingly quiet, given all that was going on, and there was little kissing or touching beyond the ocean of mass copulation. "The atmosphere was reminiscent, not of a gourmet restaurant where each morsel is savored, but rather of a McDonald's," Keen thought, "the sexual equivalent of a standardized menu." And unlike the Playboy mansion, Plato's Retreat was not a haven for the beautiful people, as Keen put it diplomatically, making his visit more instruction manual than erotic experience.[3]

While Plato's Retreats could not be found all over America, another writer also found that the sexual revolution had not yet completely run out of steam. In his extensive research for his 1980 *Thy Neighbor's Wife*, Gay Talese found that some Americans were pursuing sexual freedom with full gusto and were as determined as ever to publish sexually explicit material despite the pressures of censorship. (Hugh Hefner was prominently featured in the book.)[4] Perhaps more remarkable than his findings, however, were the time, energy, and money that Talese put into writing the book. It took Talese nine years and $800,000 in expenses to produce the 230,000-word tome, but it was his field research that proved his commitment to the cause. Consistent with the conventions of "new journalism," Talese went to massage parlors, lived at Sandstone (a Los Angeles sex retreat), and took part in orgies, again reportedly for research purposes only. Married (to Nan Talese, a senior editor at Simon & Schuster) and with two daughters, it was true that Talese risked his marriage to complete the book, especially since he nearly fell in love with a couple of the women with whom he slept. Talese received a $4 million advance for the book, however, making his difficult (some would say dream) assignment well worth it.[5]

One would also not know from watching television that the sexual revolution was over. After reviewing a few of the season's new comedies, Richard Corliss of *Time* concluded that a new television genre had been born: the "smutcom." "Never has the medium more fully deserved its reputation as the boob tube," he quipped, the skimpy outfits on women in shows like *It's a Living* obviously designed to capture men's attention.[6] Harry F. Waters of *Newsweek* felt similarly, singling out ABC for "jiggling into a new season."[7] In terms of sexuality, however, television shows paled in comparison to what viewers were seeing on commercial breaks. A new campaign for Calvin Klein jeans was shocking viewers with its blatant sexuality, especially one commercial featuring a fifteen-year-old Brooke Shields. "You know what comes between me and my Calvins? Nothing," she told viewers, her widely spread legs only adding to the spot's raciness. The fact that the respected photographer Richard Avedon shot the commercial (titled *The Feminist*) did not help it from getting pulled off the air by NBC in New York after many viewers complained. Morality in Media, a New York antipornography group, had also received a large number of letters about the commercial, most of them from people thinking Shields was being exploited. "I never thought that people would be offended," Klein responded to the controversy, "shocked" that there had been such uproar about his jeans campaign.[8]

Given all the free publicity he got from his jeans campaign, however, it was not surprising that Klein continued to use sexually themed advertising to sell his clothing and fragrances through the 1980s. An underwear ad in various fashion magazines in 1985, for example, featured two women and a man sleeping together on a bed, many concluding the image was that of a ménage à trois. Other recent Calvin Klein ads were equally provocative, leading one Madison Avenue executive to proclaim him "the creative leader of the new eroticism" in advertising. More important, at least to Klein, the ads appeared to be working: the company's worldwide retail sales were heading toward $1 billion.[9]

Because they pushed the envelope of public eroticism, Klein's ads were now the most familiar among Americans, ranked ahead of even those featuring the iconic Marlboro Man. Seeing how successful his ads were, other marketers decided that, if you can't beat 'em, join 'em, and sexed up their own advertising. "Erotic advertising is popping up everywhere, promoting everything from after-shave lotions to exercise machines," noted *Newsweek*, this new generation of ads more racy than any produced to date. Advertisers claimed, however, they were just following a trend already evident in television, movies, and magazines. *Sports Illustrated*'s annual swimsuit issue was certainly getting ever-more daring, a good barometer perhaps of the nation's "sex quotient." (It was also getting ever-more popular; the average issue of the magazine sold 250,000 copies while the 1984 swimsuit issue's half million copies sold out. For the 1985 issue, the magazine printed a million copies.)[10] "As a society, we're becoming more accepting of overt sexuality," explained Roy Grace, vice chairman of Doyle Dane Bernbach; the erotic ads were reflective of the sex-obsessed times, at least from a public perspective.[11] Soon Guess and Jordache jeans were following Calvin Klein's lead, their ads yet more explicit in order to capture readers' and viewers' attention.[12]

## CELEBRATION IN THE BEDROOM

Not only was the public arena getting more sexualized but many Americans themselves were actively looking for ways to improve their sex lives. Sexy lingerie parties were becoming a ubiquitous feature of the suburban landscape in the early 1980s, for example; the events were an opportunity for women to spice up their relationships. Over bottles of rosé wine, a dozen or so women from their twenties to their fifties gathered in living rooms at these events to examine, try on, and buy flimsy negligees, nightgowns, panties, and brassieres. All of these garments were intended to get their husbands' or boyfriends' undivided attention, something perhaps more difficult to do given the explosion of sexuality in the media. One company sponsoring such parties was Undercover Wear, its line of revealing clothes cleverly branded with names like French Connection, Flowing Passion, Double Trouble, Fringe Benefits, Jungle Fever, and, almost inevitably, Little Bo Peep. Another company called Just for Play was holding similar parties to sell not just G-strings and pasties but also body creams and erotic devices.[13] What made these get-togethers interesting was less the clothing or paraphernalia than the women, however. Not swingers or cheaters and in committed relationships, these mainstream, middle-class, and by any other measure "normal" suburban women (most of them moms) were keen on exploring their erotic and exotic sides, something unlikely to have happened before the sexual revolution. Safe and, more than anything else, social, the parties were a long way from sleazy sex shops or the Frederick's of Hollywood ads found in the back of pulpish magazines. "This is the natural outgrowth of free and open sexuality reaching into the heartland," observed Bob Greene in *Esquire*; "it is the place where the sexual revolution and the Tupperware party meet."[14]

Berkeley, California, certainly was not the heartland, but a group of women there were exploring their sexuality and, in the process, finding that a lot of people were interested in what was on their naughty minds. At its once-a-month get-togethers at a member's home, the Kensington Ladies' Erotica Society swapped sexual fantasies, the middle-aged, upper-middle-class wives and mothers having quite the vivid imaginations. The women compiled some of their stories into a manuscript, and the Ten Speed Press decided to publish it, expecting just a few thousand copies to be sold. Soon more than one hundred thousand were in print, however; the tales in *Ladies' Home Erotica* apparently resonated with a lot of other women. One fantasy in the book involved its author having sex with the pope, while a few others were about unexpected, brief, and intimate encounters with a stranger (specifically a gardener, truck driver, and ex-convict). Erotic awakenings, kinky games, and the potential role of vegetables in foreplay were the subjects of some of the other stories, illustrating that women's sexual fantasies knew virtually no boundaries.[15]

The tentacles of sexuality continued to spread into the nooks and crannies of everyday life in America in the early 1980s. Evangelical Christians interested in partaking in the pleasures of lovemaking while not violating the scripture had their prayers answered with the publication of a number of Bible-based sex manuals. Both sexual problems and advice did not differ much from that found in mainstream sex manuals, but the evangelical versions looked to the scripture for inspiration, offering an interesting twist on the art of love. In their *Celebration in the Bedroom*, for example, Charlie and Martha Shedd suggested couples (married, of course) get in the mood by reading the Song of Solomon ("Your rounded thighs are like jewels") and other erotic bits of the Bible. In their *The Act of Marriage*, Tim and Beverly LaHaye looked to Proverbs 5:18–19 ("Her breasts satisfy thee at all times; and be thou ravished always with her love") as proof that God approved of foreplay. Because "the Bible comprises the best manual ever written on human behavior," true Christians enjoyed sex more than non-Christians, the LaHayes maintained, something that may have made some take their faith more seriously.[16]

While premarital sex and adultery were the only sexual acts specifically outlawed in the Bible, other authors of such manuals believed couples should limit what they do in bed. In their *Intended for Pleasure*, Ed and Gaye Wheat felt a number of restrictions were in order if one was to remain true to scripture. A woman taking the sexual initiative was a no-no, for example (a wife "must be 100 percent committed to being submissive," according to Saint Paul), and couples should not stray from the missionary position ("Let his left hand be under my head and his right hand embrace me," the Song of Solomon specified). The Bible was silent on the issue of oral sex, but the Wheats had their own views on the act. "Oral-genital sex definitely limits the amount of loving verbal communication that husband and wife can have as they make love," their book stated—peculiar logic perhaps but something difficult to challenge.[17]

It was another book, however, that made sex in the early 1980s water-cooler talk. Women had a dime-sized erogenous zone that, when powerfully stimulated, led to a vaginal orgasm, the three authors of *The G Spot and Other Recent Discoveries About Human Sexuality* claimed, quite a finding if true. The book was based on research done by Ernst Grafenberg (hence the "G"), a German gynecologist, who believed that the spot was essentially a "female prostate gland." Although the authors had found in their own research that stimulation of the G spot produced an orgasm, most American gynecologists had serious doubts about the theory. Still, the book hit a cultural nerve, so to speak, with a first printing of 150,000 copies and six book clubs putting it on its reading lists. Much of the appeal of Grafenberg's theory no doubt had to do with people's desire to search for the mysterious patch of tissue between the vagina and bladder. "A lot of women are going to be upset if they can't find it," observed Midge Wilson, a social psychologist, with marriage counselor Marion Holtzer adding, "It's going to be like the Grail."[18]

Technology was also bringing sexuality into America's heartland. Pornographic movies, mostly shown and viewed in seedy theaters in rough parts of town for the last couple of decades, now could be enjoyed in the comfort of one's own home courtesy of the recently introduced videotape recorder. By the mid-1980s, "adult entertainment" theaters and bookstores were in sharp decline as the X-rated home video market blossomed (a phenomenon wonderfully captured in the 1997 film *Boogie Nights*). The success of the videotape recorder was redefining the pornography industry, allowing for mass distribution and creating films for a new, more upscale audience. Fewer than eight hundred adult movie theaters remained in the United States in

1985 as patrons of the art form took their business instead to the more than fourteen thousand local video stores that rented such films. Some television and appliance retailers, record chains, and even gas stations also carried adult films, the traditional porn subculture (or "rain coat crowd," as one industry executive referred to it) rapidly becoming extinct. People who would never have ventured out to see a "dirty movie" were now stopping in at their clean and friendly video store after work to pick up the latest adult film, some of the shops providing order blanks and pencils for customers too shy to ask for movies with names like *Deep Inside Annie Sprinkle*. Major studios like Cabellero and Cal Vista were catering to this more sophisticated consumer by developing films with more interesting story lines targeted to couples rather than just men and spending as much as $400,000 on a single movie. As well, more actors in such films were becoming stars in their own right, with devoted fans looking forward to their next on-screen performance.[19]

## A SEXUAL COUNTERREVOLUTION

Not everybody, however, was happy to see that free and open sexuality had reached into the heartland. George Leonard, writing in *Esquire* magazine in 1982, believed there was a high cost to the sexual freedoms that had been gained in the late 1960s and early 1970s and continued to percolate. The changes that took place within the arena of sexuality over the course of these ten years were undoubtedly remarkable. A host of activities—talking about sex in mixed company, living together openly without being married, having easy access to erotic films and books, and exploring one's sexual fantasies— were now possible, a clear break from the centuries of repression that had so contained this aspect of life. "Perhaps never before had such a radical shift in mores occurred in so short a time," Leonard noted; a good part of the sexual utopia that had been a major component of the countercultural agenda was now a reality.[20]

Like the counterculture itself, however, the sexual revolution had not led to the utopian paradise many had hoped and believed it would. "As it has turned out," Leonard argued, "the sexual revolution, in slaying some loathsome old dragons, has created some formidable new ones." Masturbation, for example, long a taboo, had rather suddenly become recast as a therapeutic act, something one was almost required to do in order to maintain good physical, emotional, and spiritual heath. As well, sex was now something one "had," the intimate experience commodified and expressed in possessive, acquisitional terms. And worst of all, sex had become detached from both love and procreation, its physical qualities eclipsing its much more important social ones. In short, the radical transformation of sexuality in America had trivialized sex, and all of us were now paying the price for the freedoms we had so desired. Lacking the emotional heft that inherently comes with romance and relationships, "recreational" sex, as the concept was now known, was not just dull but also possibly harmful. The objectifying of humans through passionless, commitment-less sex moved us that much closer to Aldous Huxley's *Brave New World*, Leonard suggested, referring to the 1948 novel that portrayed a society in which sex was obligatory and love forbidden.[21]

Leonard was not the only one to think that the losses associated with the sexual upheaval of the last decade and a half exceeded the gains. A 1980 survey in *Cosmopolitan*, of all magazines, revealed many women felt similarly, saying they were disillusioned and disappointed with "the emotional fruit the sex revolution has borne." A majority of the over one hundred thousand respondents longed for the intimacy that had largely vanished from relationships, leading the editors of the magazine to believe there might be "a sexual counterrevolution" in the works or already underway in the country. Sexual experimentation and open marriages had been a big letdown for a good number of women (and men), the data was now showing, something that could be detected in other, less scientific ways. Sex was wilder than ever in the daytime soaps, but novels were going the other direction, with more characters choosing romance over carnal adventures. Traditional marriage ceremonies were also making a comeback, another sign that the sexual revolution was in the nation's rearview mirror.[22]

Some believed that the cultural sea change taking place in American sexuality was a result of the "broken promises" of the sexual revolution. "We have been liberated from the taboos of the past only to find ourselves imprisoned in a 'freedom' that brings us no closer to our real nature or needs," wrote Peter Marin in *Psychology Today* in 1983; the waning sexual revolution was not delivering the happiness or satisfaction many believed it would. True sexual freedom would not only bring joy but also make people whole emotionally, experts from Freud on had theorized, but no such change had occurred. As well, despite premarital sex going over the course of a couple of decades from something "bad" to something "good," there was no evidence that relationships had improved in any meaningful way. One's choices had certainly increased, but with greater opportunities had come not just more pleasure but also more pain, with no net gain achieved. Repression of sexuality was not the all-encompassing problem we had been told it was, in other words, and solving the problem did not lead to personal fulfillment and a healthier society as promised. Rather, greater choice had complicated things considerably, Marin felt; in fact, the sexual realm was now more of "an alien land" than ever.[23]

Interestingly, Marin traced the formation of the alien landscape of sexuality in America to sex shifting from the private world to the public one. In the postwar years, sex was often part of "alternative" culture, an act of rebellion against the mainstream and its narrow definition of socially approved sexuality. The counterculture had changed all that, as had popularizing and commercializing sex over the past couple of decades. Rather than a means to escape from the public world, sex had become a way to join it, a major transformation in how we perceived and related to sexuality. While completely different from the old, "sinful" concept of sex, this new one was equally bad, Marin believed, and explained why so many Americans were unhappy sexually. "The sexual realm is marred by pretense, desperation, and an immense amount of 'bad faith,' which constitutes a simultaneous betrayal of both the other person and oneself," he argued; thus, the state of sex in America in the early 1980s was not at all good.[24]

Going against the grain, however, Lester A. Kirkendall argued that we were just entering a true sexual revolution. While widely hailed as a sexual revolution, the greater freedom and expression of sexuality in the 1960s and 1970s was nothing really new, historically speaking, as Kirkendall pointed out in the *Humanist* in 1984. Since ancient Rome and probably way before that, sexuality had had its highs and lows, with people's attitudes and behavior related to sex being highly dependent on the values of a particular time and place. Americans were certainly more interested in sex and participated in it more frequently during the counterculture, he explained, but the burgeoning sexual revolution promised a much deeper and more sustainable level of social change. New reproductive techniques (e.g., artificial insemination, sperm banks, surrogate mothering, in vitro fertilization, and frozen embryos), changing gender roles and relationships (e.g., working mothers and "househusbands"), a greater tolerance for sexual diversity (e.g., the gay, lesbian, bisexual, and transgender [GLBT] community), and more consideration to the morality and ethics of sexuality (e.g., the antipornography movement) were all part of this new, more authentic, and more exciting sexual revolution.[25] The androgyny sweeping the United States and the United Kingdom could also be seen as part of a new sexual revolution that generally had little or nothing to do with sex. Michael Jackson, Boy George, and Grace Jones were just a few pop stars blurring gender lines in the 1980s and, in the process, making people rethink what it was to be a man and what it was to be a woman.[26]

Men wearing makeup and muscular women belied a shift back to more traditional gender roles in the 1980s, however, something that related directly to the more conservative sexual climate that was emerging. Because the sexual revolution was more about a change in women's attitudes and behavior than about those of men, as Barbara Ehrenreich, Elizabeth Hess, and Gloria Jacobs argued in their 1986 *Re-making Love: The Feminization of Sex*, the sexual counterrevolution also was centered around women. Specifically, the authors believed the backlash against unrestrained sexuality that had begun a few years back posed a threat to women, and the freedoms won in the 1960s and 1970s were in jeopardy as narrowly defined gender identities made a comeback. The current movement predicated on less promiscuity and more restraint was "a campaign against women and their sex lives," they held, urging feminists to remain sexually liberated by not conceding their right to pleasure for pleasure's sake.[27]

## NO EASY CURE

The reality though was that both men and women were finding it increasingly difficult to realize pleasure for pleasure's sake through sex. Sex therapy boomed in the 1980s, a sign that Americans' individual and collective libido was, after a half century or so of continual growth, on the decline. It was William Masters and Virginia Johnson's 1970 *Human Sexual Inadequacy* that essentially launched the specialty of sex therapy; that book (and their behavioral versus psychoanalytic approach) made what had been a suspect and almost secretive field respectable and even popular. Other clinicians such as Albert Ellis, Arnold Lazarus, Joseph Wolpe, and James Semans had helped people with sex problems (or what Tolstoy called "the tragedy in the bedroom"), but it was Masters and Johnson who became famous for doing so.[28] A decade after they had introduced their new therapy for sexual disorders, Masters and Johnson remained the best-known practitioners in the field. Basing their therapeutic techniques on the physiology of sex rather than on psychological issues, the pair (now married) offered a much more practical approach than what was commonly used to treat sexual problems. Because of the claimed 75 percent success rate of their method, which focused on physical exercises, medical schools had begun teaching sexual therapy and family doctors had begun to practice it; help for problems in the bedroom was now easily found.[29]

The seeds that Masters and Johnson had sown in 1970 had over the course of a decade borne considerable fruit. In addition to the 1,200 certified professionals, a few thousand nonprofessionals had also entered the field, seeing money to be made in the growing field of sex therapy. Few states had passed laws regulating the field, allowing people who had only attended a weekend conference on the subject to hang out their shingle. That qualified therapists were modifying and elaborating on Masters and Johnson's original approach was perfectly fine with them, however, as the two had hoped their research would evolve in new ways. The thousands of new practitioners certainly had their work cut out for them; lack of sexual desire was now the leading problem in the area, and this was more difficult to fix than the previous common issues of premature ejaculation, orgasm difficulties, and painful intercourse. Eliminating negative thoughts that quashed erotic feelings was challenging for even the best therapists, but many Americans were determined to have their sex lives improved by getting professional help.[30]

Another trailblazer of sex therapy was Helen Singer Kaplan, founder-director of the New York Hospital–Cornell Medical Center's Human Sexuality Program. Author of *The New Sex Therapy*, *Disorders of Sexual Desire*, and *The Evaluation of Sexual Disorders*, Kaplan was probably the leading expert in sexual dysfunction in the 1980s. Perhaps Kaplan's biggest contribution was discarding the narrow, all-encompassing labels of "impotent" and "frigid" and instead viewing human sexual response in terms of three phases: desire, excitement, and orgasm. Kaplan also recommended group therapy for most patients, a little unusually, with homework assignments carried out in private. Lowering anxiety and increasing pleasure were the usual goals, with Kaplan claiming success rates as high as those of Masters and Johnson.[31]

Sex therapy met 1980s celebrity culture in the person of Dr. Ruth Westheimer, the German-born, four-foot-seven-inch woman looking more like one's grandmother than an expert in the ways of love. Through her books, videocassettes, live radio show, cable television program, and frequent visits with Phil Donahue and Merv Griffin, Dr. Ruth became a national institution in the mid-1980s, offering sensible advice in a frank but humorous manner. ("There is no one right size for the penis" and "Why don't you do it in the kitchen?" went a couple of her typical bits of wisdom.)[32] Dr. Ruth even had a board game, in which players tried to accumulate "Arousal Points" in pursuit of the ultimate goal—"Mutual Pleasure."[33] Despite all the sexual language and imagery in popular and consumer culture, actual information about sex was hard to find in these pre-Internet days, and this was one of the keys to her phenomenal popularity and success. Versus the "do it if it feels good" sex therapists of the 1960s and 1970s, Dr. Ruth was traditional in every respect; indeed, her conservative views helped shape the times' backlash against unchecked sexuality. Love, commitment, and romance were the keys to good sex, the diminutive one repeatedly made clear, and what you do is a lot less important than with whom. "Relax" and "enjoy" seemed to be Dr. Ruth's favorite words in responding to the thousands of questions she received every week, Americans apparently needing constant reminders that sex was not a contest.[34]

Few people would or could have predicted that one of the outcomes of the sexual revolution would be a flourishing sex therapy business. Despite the new liberties to engage in any assortment of behaviors, Americans seemed to have more problems than ever when it came to sex. Sexual contentment remained an elusive thing, as thousands of therapists equipped with hundreds of treatments could testify, and was something quite separate from any politics or social change attached to the movement. Less inhibition about expressing sexual desires had certainly been a godsend, especially for women, but that was hardly a recipe for happiness, professionals were finding. Likewise, that women were now permitted to initiate sex helped level the playing field but, at the same time, made the process a more complicated affair. The erosion of much of the shame and guilt associated with sex was also a good thing, but sexuality often remained an emotional roller coaster. In fact, for some, particularly teenagers, greater sexual latitude had caused problems they otherwise would not have had because of the social pressure to join the club. As well, the greater number of sexual options was encouraging some to not fully commit to a single relationship, with any kind of bump in the road quickly leading to a breakup.[35]

The portrayal of sex in advertising, television, and movies also seemed to be a contributing factor in Americans' collective performance anxiety in the 1980s. The pressure to be sexy and enjoy sex was pervasive, creating a climate in which eroticism was perceived as something to achieve rather than experience. Greater expectations in sex were ironically leading to more disorders and diminished desire, it appeared; the make-believe worlds of sexuality created by Madison Avenue and Hollywood were having a negative impact on the real one. Unfortunately, Americans' tendency to "work" at something to improve it was not proving to be a good formula when it came to sex. "Sexual response is a natural function, influenced and made functioning by time, place and circumstance, and cannot be forced," Masters and Johnson reminded readers of *Ladies' Home Journal* who were hoping that hard work and determination would lead to sexual bliss.[36]

If the results of one survey could be believed, however, most American women had no intention of working hard to achieve sexual bliss. Almost three-quarters of American women would gladly trade sexual intercourse for some tender loving care, according to a poll done by the columnist Ann Landers in 1984, the findings interesting if not to be taken too seriously. After posing the question "Would you be content to be held close and treated tenderly, and forget about 'the act'?" to her female readers (and asking if they were under or over forty years old), more than ninety thousand letters poured into Landers's office. (Only one other time had a column generated a greater response, when more than one hundred thousand readers used the forum to tell President Reagan they were against nuclear weapons.) Sixty-four thousand of the letter writers answered "yes" to the question, 40 percent of them women under forty years old. "Apparently I had touched a hot button," Landers said after publishing the results of the survey in her column, concluding that the sexual revolution had much to do with how women responded to the question. "Women are anxious," she explained, something to be expected after "reading in *Cosmopolitan* that if they don't have five orgasms a night they're undersexed or freaks."[37] Although her sample was huge (ninety or so times the size of those used by professional researchers like Nielsen or Gallup), it was obviously not representative of all American women. The results of her survey "may be symptomatic of a more general dissatisfaction for which there may be no easy cure," wrote Charles Leerhsen of *Newsweek* in reporting the story, as good a takeaway as any.[38]

Rather than help it as one might think, the fitness craze of the 1980s also appeared to be hampering Americans' sex lives. While some were "feeling the burn" in aerobics classes, others were heeding Nike's advice to "just do it" by running (or "jogging," as it was more often referred to in the seventies and eighties). Wondering if there was some kind of relationship between exercise and frequency of lovemaking, psychologist Srully Blotnick found eighty-three men who had recently started running and asked their wives how often they had sex. Frequency of sex typically went from three times to one time a week after the men began their fitness campaign, with fatigue the primary reason for the drop-off. (Training for a marathon virtually extinguished couples' sex lives.) Aches and pains also accounted for some of the decrease in desire, as did the fear among some men that they might suffer cardiac arrest if they engaged in any additional intense physical activity. In many cases, the only solution to the problem was for the wife to start running, so that she like her husband would be more interested in sleep than sex.[39]

## THE NEW YUPPIE DISEASE

The sexual counterrevolution of the early 1980s, with its more conservative attitudes about sex as well as an apparent loss of desire in and greater number of problems having it, had been at least a decade in the making. For many, in fact, "the joy of sex" had turned into joylessness soon after the best-selling sex manual was first published in 1972. In 1986, Blotnick asked two thousand Americans with a median age of thirty-six whether they regarded casual sex positively or negatively, and then compared the findings to those from similar studies done in 1976 and 1966. Fifty-six percent of men viewed casual sex positively in the new study, while 71 percent had in 1976, and 75 percent in 1966. Only 24 percent of women regarded casual sex positively in 1986, while 42 percent had in 1976, and 40 percent in 1966. Blotnick also found that young people in the mid-1980s did not have high regard for the wanton ways of their counterculture-era parents. Thirty-one percent of college students reported that their parents' generation was too promiscuous, while in 1976 and 1966 only 4 percent and 1 percent respectively had felt so about their parents' generation.[40] Alex P. Keaton, the fictional character in the sitcom *Family Ties* played by Michael J. Fox, was not such an exaggeration, it seemed; this conservative, Republican teenager wanted nothing to do with the liberal lifestyle his ex-hippie parents had enjoyed.

It was tempting to assume that it was Ronald Reagan (or perhaps Jerry Falwell) who was responsible for the sexual conservatism of the 1980s, but some thought it was something much different. "The process at hand had less to do with politics or sociology than with an odd amalgam of biology and psychology," wrote Harry Stein in *Esquire* in 1986; the fact that baby boomers like himself were finally growing up was the biggest factor in the pendulum's swing toward restraint and monogamy.[41] Others felt that it was a switch in focus from play to work that triggered the shift in sexual attitudes and behavior, with the desire to advance one's career now being considered the number 1 priority in many twenty- and thirtysomething's lives. Dating two, three, or more people was certainly fun but was also exhausting, boomers were finding, and going out every night was not conducive to getting up in the morning.

It was difficult to know whether inhibited sexual desire (ISD), as the formal diagnosis was known, was truly on the rise or if more Americans were simply willing to talk about and seek help for it. Either way, psychiatrists and psychologists were seeing more people with the problem, the exact cause of which was not clear. Hormone deficiencies could lead to ISD, but it was more likely emotional issues—depression, stress, or marital friction—that lowered sex drive. As well, "fear of intimacy" had emerged as a defining characteristic of relationships in the 1980s, according to therapists, something that was true even for a good number of married people. Many patients in therapy reported they had no difficulty making love with acquaintances or strangers but often said "not tonight, dear" to their spouse, suggesting there was a clear link between ISD and intimacy. Although they were fictional, the sexual exploits of actors on television and in the movies were making some feel they could not compete, while some men felt intimidated by women's greater independence and aggressiveness. One professional considered ISD "the new yuppie disease" and thought the lack of spark in the bedroom was an unfortunate cost of business for the busy two-career couple.[42] More extreme than ISD was impotence, another sexual disorder that was getting more attention. Exact numbers on how many American men were impotent were difficult to find (a 1973 survey estimated one in ten), but more research was showing that physical problems, particularly diabetes and heart disease, were a contributing factor. In 1982, the first Impotents Anonymous was founded, and five years later there were one hundred chapters worldwide. Hospitals looking for new sources of revenue were opening up impotence centers to treat men, and the leading cure in these pre-Viagra days was implanting a prosthesis.[43]

While too little desire was a common sexual disorder, some people had way too much desire. First diagnosed in the late 1970s by a group of researchers led by Masters and Johnson, sexual addiction (which used to be called nymphomania or "Don Juanism") had become in the 1980s a legitimate and recognizable area of therapy. After the term "sex addict" originally appeared in an article in the *Journal of Addiction* around the same time, a movement based on the twelve-step Alcoholics Anonymous was soon spreading. By 1988, thousands of members belonged to hundreds of sex addict clubs in the United States, all of them subscribing to the "one day at a time" ethos of addictive therapy. Fourteen percent of the members were women, but their number was rising as sexual addiction became seen as analogous to other compulsive and harmful behaviors, such as alcohol or drug abuse. And like other addictions, sex addicts often kept their behavior hidden, living in constant fear that their secret would be discovered by friends and family. Sex addicts typically experienced neglect and abuse as children and as adults felt empty inside—classic traits of addiction.[44]

For addicts, the high that came with a sexual "fix" was like a jolt of adrenaline, something quite different from the pleasure a normal person received from sex. Rather than a healthy, joyous experience, sex was an escape or painkiller for those addicted to it, many of them describing it as a trancelike state. Soon after the high came the crash, however, a nasty combination of emotional pain, hopelessness, and shame. Some researchers believed that sex addiction, like alcohol and drug dependency, was rooted in biochemistry, with each experience releasing a flood of mood-altering hormones and chemicals in the brain. Whether the cause was neurochemical, environmental, or a combination, sex addicts felt compelled to continue their behavior despite the consequences. As in the film *Looking for Mr. Goodbar*, female sex addicts often put themselves in dangerous situations to get their fix, and the hunt was part of the thrill. Through therapy, however, more sex addicts were getting help and finding ways to break their pattern of self-destructive behavior.[45]

Despite the obvious fact that sexuality was a serious problem in real people's everyday lives, the field of sex research was not highly respected by those not working in it. Funding was difficult to get for sex research because the taboos, misconceptions, and general moral atmosphere surrounding sexuality made even scientific studies seem like exercises in perversity. This was especially true in the 1980s, when the religious right and Moral Majority helped set a conservative tone throughout funding agencies.[46] As well, studying human sexuality was fraught with problems that made other scientists prone to question the value and validity of findings. Calling oneself a "sexologist" tended to draw smirks, for one thing, with many thinking there must be a personal versus a professional reason he or she entered the field. The pure complexity of sexuality also made sex research challenging to conduct and difficult to understand. One researcher found, for example, that there were as many as eight different reasons women commonly lost sexual desire; this kind of information was not very easy to digest. That sexual issues were more often psychological rather than biological also complicated matters, since the set of variables involved in the activity were unique and typically highly emotional. Gender dynamics obviously played a big role in sexuality, this too making the field more multidimensional than most. One's values, social background, and, of course, experience entered the sexual equation; that it also happened to be arguably the most intimate thing humans do set sex research apart from all other disciplines.[47]

## HELLO, NEW VICTORIANISM

Much more attention was about to be paid to sex research, however, as the mysterious disease most common among homosexuals rewrote the rules of sexuality in America and around the world. "The apparent association between acquired immune deficiency syndrome (AIDS) and multiple sexual partners has forced many homosexual men to re-examine their lifestyles," Nikki Meredith wrote in *Psychology Today* in January 1984, as the disease that had appeared thee years earlier made some gay men choose monogamy. (AIDS was actually a syndrome rather than a disease, gradually destroying the immune system and thus allowing infections to damage organs and eventually cause death.)[48] Early studies of AIDS victims along with previous surveys revealed how promiscuous many gay men were, the numbers surprising to even those in the scene. The median number of lifetime sexual partners among fifty AIDS victims was 1,100, according to a 1982 study, with a few of the men reporting they had had 20,000 lovers. Those without the disease had had a median number of 550 partners, a parallel study showed; this figure was consistent with a 1978 survey of about seven hundred men in San Francisco. Fifteen percent of this group said they had had between five hundred and one thousand partners, and more than 25 percent had over one thousand, these numbers obviously way above the average for heterosexuals. These kinds of statistics made psychologists (and nonpsychologists alike) wonder why some homosexual men were so promiscuous. Did they suffer from a psychosexual disorder, specifically an Oedipal fixation, as psychoanalysts believed, or was there another, less Freudian explanation?[49]

The sheer availability of sex for gay men in pre-AIDS America partly explained how one's number of sexual partners could reach such astronomical proportions. Living in a city with a large homosexual population like San Francisco, New York, or Los Angeles definitely helped; the former city's Castro District was a mecca for those seeking a one-night (or one-hour or even less) stand. Those reporting having had thousands of partners almost certainly had frequented bathhouses catering to gay men and anonymous sex. Such environmental factors were ideal conditions for the "sociobiological" theory of sexuality to play out. Men and women had genetically different agendas when it came to sex, this theory went: Men desired as many partners as possible to maximize the chances of reproduction. Women had no such desire because there was no reproductive advantage in having multiple partners, so their agenda instead centered around finding a good provider. "In homosexuality, we see male and female sexualities in their pure, uncompromised form," wrote Donald Symons in *The Evolution of Human Sexuality*; this explained how and why gay men could rack up such incredibly high numbers of partners through their lives.[50]

Other theories about gay men's "hypersexuality" circulated as the AIDS crisis escalated. Because homosexuals were a minority group whose lifestyles were in opposition to mainstream values, the "alienation" theory went, sexual identity (and activity) became their defining character. For gays, then, sex was the primary means of expressing who one was, making it natural to seize as many opportunities as possible. Another, related idea (certainly not mine) was that, because they were outsiders, gay men had homophobic feelings themselves, and their socially induced "self-hatred" was the cause of "compulsive" (versus recreational) promiscuity. The more partners, the greater sense of self-worth, this disturbing view went, although joy was notably not part of the equation. Sex was essentially addictive, according to this theory; even thousands of partners was not quite enough.[51]

Regardless of the theory, many gays had changed their behavior as friends and lovers began to get sick or die from AIDS. Attendance at bathhouses was way down by 1984, and once busy cruising spots were nearly deserted. Cases of venereal diseases had fallen significantly, a clear sign that Americans as a whole were having fewer sexual partners. In the gay magazine *The Advocate*, classified ads seeking "sex only" had dropped 25 percent, its publisher reported, and were replaced with ads from men seeking "relationships." Advertising in that magazine for escorts or "models" had comprised an entire section but was now down to a single page, more evidence that a brief encounter had fallen out of favor. Rather than limit themselves to the alcohol, drugs, and sex scene, many men were choosing to socialize in other, healthier ways like sports or chorale. On the Fire Island boardwalk, a popular gathering place for gays, men were simply smiling and saying hello to each other, something that would have been considered odd behavior a few years back. There were some reports, however, that after the initial panic in the early eighties there was a resurgence in sexual promiscuity among gay men. Business was up at the Cauldron, a San Francisco private sex club, for example, although patrons tended to be more cautious and selective. Some gay men had changed their behavior but, usually after a considerable number of drinks, would fall off the wagon and go on a bender, sexually speaking, illustrating how difficult it was to make such a radical change in lifestyle.[52]

The large number of unknowns about AIDS in the mid-1980s made even professional futurists predict worst-case scenarios. "The specter of AIDS will change our lives dramatically in the years ahead," Edward Cornish wrote in an article called "Farewell, Sexual Revolution. Hello, New Victorianism" for the *Futurist* in early 1986, thinking, "It will alter everything from the clothing we wear to the songs we sing." "Schools, offices, restaurants, stores, and every other institution will have to reckon with this scourge," he continued, as AIDS looked like another Black Death looming if medical researchers failed to find a cure. Cornish, president of the World Future Society, envisioned more employees working at home to avoid contracting or spreading the disease, with many also steering clear of public transportation and other places where large numbers of people gathered. Romantic love would also make a comeback (hence the change in our singing preferences), he felt, as might traditional religious practices. Interestingly, no futurist had anticipated the

AIDS epidemic, which was perfectly consistent with professional forecasters' inability to predict major social change.[53]

The spread of AIDS through the eighties naturally made the sexual counterrevolution revolve that much faster. Surveys confirmed that fidelity and romance were "in" and casual sex was "out," with the disease accelerating the trend toward greater sexual conservatism. In a 1988 *Glamour* Women's Views Survey, for example, fewer than half of American women said they supported premarital sex, the first time that had happened in four years. Seventy percent of single women reported they had become more cautious about sex, with 22 percent of them now monogamous and 11 percent choosing celibacy.[54] "Today, it seems, pragmatism has shoved passion aside, and one hears the murmur of new more reserved sexual standards in every segment of the population," wrote Linda Wolfe in *Ladies' Home Journal* in 1987, and the AIDS epidemic was the giant wave that had fully turned the tide. About thirty thousand Americans had died from AIDS since it was first identified in 1981, although the specifics on how it spread and to whom was still somewhat of a mystery.[55]

Despite Cornish's alarmist predictions, there was no going back to Victorian-era or even mid-twentieth-century inhibitions and repressions, but a sea change in sexuality in America had without question taken place. This new era was often described as "realistic" or "sensible," with the wild swings of the past being tempered and moderated. Single people had taken to grilling potential lovers about their sexual history and were choosing to date old friends and acquaintances rather than strangers. Statistics also showed that visits by married men to prostitutes had recently plummeted because of the concern of contracting AIDS. Interestingly, many marriages were suffering because of spouses' new fidelity to each other. With adultery, these spouses were content in their marriages, but now, because they were afraid to have an affair for fear of getting the disease, the relationships were ironically failing.[56]

The fact that cases of AIDS in the late 1980s were very rare among nondrug using, nontransfused heterosexuals (and that more than 90 percent of those who had died from the disease were men) did not prevent many from changing their sexual behavior. Some were opting for hasty marriages, and others were choosing celibacy over the Russian roulette of the dating scene. That it took years for the HIV virus to incubate contributed to the near panic, some no doubt thinking their bodies were a ticking time bomb. It was hard to resist comparing AIDS to European plagues of centuries past, the worst-case scenario of death on a massive scale lurking in the back of many people's minds. Bisexuals, those with a history of taking drugs, or even the somewhat promiscuous were considered to be partners to avoid, many heterosexuals decided, the risk believed to be too great. Some who swore they would never use condoms were grudgingly coming around to the idea of using them, a sad but now necessary fact of life if one was to sleep with a person whose sexual history was uncertain. With AIDS, sexuality in America had, in short, been turned upside down. What used to be good for you, a joyous expression of freedom and life itself, was now potentially dangerous to one's health; sex was never to be quite the same.[57]

## SAFETY FIRST

The media frenzy surrounding AIDS as well as popular culture reinforced fears among heterosexuals that they could and perhaps would catch the disease by having sex with the wrong person. *People*'s cover story "AIDS and the Single Woman" certainly made some straight people think twice about picking up someone or getting picked up. As a topical, controversial subject, the disease also not surprisingly worked its way into television scripts. On the popular show *St. Elsewhere*, for example, Mark Harmon's character, an unmarried, heterosexual doctor, contracted AIDS by sleeping with a prostitute. (That Mark Harmon, who agreed to the plot line because he wanted to get off the show, had recently been named the sexiest man in America by *People* also suggested that, if "he" could get it, anybody could.) Immediately after making love with a woman, some men would vigorously wash their penis and urinate in an attempt to rid themselves of any potential virus. Sleeping with female models, for many men a dream come true, became taboo for some after they reasoned the women often slept with bisexual male models. Women interested in having sex on the first date, again typically a desirable situation for many men, joined the off-limits group for the more cautious. These men wondered, If they will sleep with me on the first date, with how many others had they done the same? For some men, however, the anxiety surrounding and care being taken during sex removed much of its fun. Already having given up smoking and drinking and joined a gym to lose some weight in spirit with the 1980s health craze, these men refused to give up their last vice of having sex with as many women as possible.[58]

Until the facts about AIDS were clearly known, many Americans in the mid-1980s chose the prudent path of "better safe than sorry." "As the AIDS threat grows, the mating call is no longer 'free love,' but 'safety first,'" Barbara Kantrowitz of *Newsweek* observed in 1986; nothing was able to prepare Americans for sex becoming potentially lethal. "The days of carefree, casual sex are over," she announced, and a new era of sexuality was beginning. Condom sales had nearly doubled since 1980, with half of the estimated eight hundred million sold annually purchased by women. Some gay men had taken to wearing large safety pins on their shirts to let others know they practiced safe sex. Anonymous sex in gay bathhouses had not surprisingly dropped dramatically; managers of some baths had put up posters reminding patrons to "be responsible to yourself and others." Although they were hard to find, virgins were now in much demand, since he or she was considered totally safe to sleep with assuming the lucky individual had not had a blood transfusion in the last few years.[59] "Safer sex" was beginning to replace "safe sex" as the recommended course of action in recognition of the fact that 100 percent safety was impossible if one was sexually active. By 1988, forty three thousand Americans a month were going to one of the more than one thousand federally funded public sites to be tested for AIDS, with an estimated three times that many getting tested in private facilities.[60]

Expectedly, some entrepreneurs capitalized on the pronounced fear of AIDS among heterosexuals. Dating services and clubs requiring members to agree to be tested for AIDS and other sexually transmitted diseases were popping up around the country and doing quite the business. Members of California-based SafeDate, for example, carried a picture ID card showing the results of his or her tests, both positive and negative. (A card with a "GH" sticker, for instance, told others the member had genital herpes.) Only those free of ten potentially harmful diseases (including AIDS, syphilis, hepatitis B, and crab lice) were eligible to join Peace of Mind in Detroit, while Ampersand Singles Club in New York guaranteed its members they could have AIDS-free sex by means of its screening process. Many members using such services and joining these clubs justifiably felt that potential lovers did not always tell the truth about their sexual behavior and history, making it worth the investment. (Research by Susan Cochran, an associate psychology professor at California State University in Northridge, found that 35 percent of the men in her sample had lied in some way to a woman in order to have sex with her.)[61] Most people simply did not know if they had been exposed to the virus, and this was another reason to sign up. Still, problems remained for those hoping there was no chance of getting AIDS or another sexually transmitted disease. It often took months for AIDS antibodies to show up in the bloodstream, for one thing, and a member could contract something after being tested by a dating service or club. As well, segregating the population between disease carriers and non–disease carriers raised serious ethical and possibly legal questions (the New York State attorney general was in fact investigating whether such businesses violated civil rights laws barring discrimination). For the moment at least, however, AIDS-free dating was an appealing concept to many and a fair reflection of the intense fear surrounding the disease.[62]

The formal rescinding of the sexual revolution due to AIDS played out in other curious ways. Ironically, the most intimate details of sex were now perfectly legitimate in public discourse, with everything from the mechanics of copulation to the kinds of bodily secretions fair game for discussion. Some could not resist thinking that God was taking vengeance on the promiscuous and homosexuals. AIDS hotlines were deluged with phone calls, many of them from heterosexual women who had had too much to drink the previous night and slept with someone they did not know. (Eighty-five percent of the calls to the Atlanta hotline were from heterosexual men and women although straight people accounted for just 3.8 percent of infected Americans.) More people were heading out to higher class bars, thinking there was less chance of contracting the disease from someone patronizing a fancy club (although a number of wealthy and famous people had died from AIDS). The first straight safe-sex educational film, *Norma and Tony*, was making the rounds on college campuses, but students could not get past the seemingly absurd precautions the characters were taking. During the course of the thirty-minute film, "Norma" and "Tony" slathered themselves with spermicide and donned condoms and latex squares before engaging in intercourse; the act was so clinical it hardly resembled sex at all.[63]

In fact, for all the caution some were taking because of the fear of AIDS, many intelligent people were doing little or nothing to protect themselves from risk. A 1988 national study reported by the Alan Guttmacher Institute found that 60 percent of the single, sexually active women in their poll thought using condoms was a good idea, but just 16 percent actually used them, a classic case of belief not necessarily leading to action. Women determining their lovers were "clean" was one reason they did not ask the men to use condoms; another was the fear that having a conversation about unpleasant diseases would ruin budding relationships. Discussing past sexual histories was also a tricky business in the early stages of a relationship, since each party was usually reluctant to tell all, especially if he or she was part of the pre-AIDS dating scene. And even if each party had been monogamous for years, there was no way to really know if their partners had been faithful, another reason to just go with one's better judgment. Men notoriously disliked using condoms, making some women feel that if they insisted on using them their lover would find someone else with whom to sleep. Some men felt that women who demanded using condoms likely had some sort of disease, yet they still remained in the drawer. Even experts in the field fully aware of the risks involved often did not use condoms, something that made little sense. Leah Allen (not her real name), a freelance writer in New York City who had penned numerous articles about AIDS and other sexually transmitted diseases (STDs) and routinely advised readers to use condoms, admitted she never used them herself. "I know that it was stupid," she confessed in *Mademoiselle* in 1989, explaining why smart women like her "chuck all that sage advice into a dark corner in the back of our minds."[64]

Those sticking their heads in the sand when it came to AIDS were in considerable jeopardy if a few of the top sex experts in the world were right. In their 1988 *Crisis: Heterosexual Behavior in the Age of AIDS*, Masters and Johnson along with co-author Robert Kolodny made the case that the fears of the "wider population" (i.e., heterosexuals and nonintravenous drug users) were well justified. (Another book, Gene Antonio's *The AIDS Cover-Up?* had also argued that "casual transmissions" such as coughing could spread the human immunodeficiency virus, or HIV).[65] Combining their own research with a decidedly negative interpretation of government statistics, the trio argued that AIDS was a significant threat for all sexually active people with multiple partners. Undetected AIDS infections were "now running rampant in the heterosexual community," they wrote in the book, meaning millions of Americans would eventually contract the disease (three million, specifically, or twice the official estimate). The nation's blood supply was at considerable risk as well, they warned, the book's title not at all an exaggeration if true.[66]

Critics immediately attacked the claims the authors made in their book, however, accusing them of using conjecture in their interpretations and fuzzy math in their calculations. Masters and Johnson's sampling technique was "on the order of high schoolers doing a class project," Michael Fumento, an AIDS analyst for the federal government insisted, and their information-gathering process was equally unscientific.[67] That the authors suggested there was a chance, albeit minute, that the virus could be transmitted by food handlers, mosquitoes, and toilet seats was nothing but irresponsible, these same critics (including Surgeon General C. Everett Koop) complained.[68] As well, the "gurus of the American bedroom" and "first couple of sexology," as *Time* magazine called Masters and Johnson, should have published their findings in a scientific journal rather than a mass-market book so their data could be reviewed.[69] Like Shere Hite, whose methodology in estimating the percentage of women who were unhappy in their relationships (84 in 100!) was considered flawed, the authors' claims were dubious at best.[70] The couple may have been great sex therapists, but they were clearly out of their league when it came to predicting the future of the AIDS epidemic, others pointed out, as the field of medicine was much different than helping people get aroused.[71] This was not the first time the St. Louis therapists came under attack, however. "Masters and Johnson's research is so flawed by methodological errors and slipshod reporting that it fails to meet customary standards—and their own—for evaluation," Bernie Zilbergeld and Michael Evans had written in *Psychology Today* back in 1980, thinking the study used to write their landmark *Human Sexual Inadequacy* was, in a word, inadequate. Again the validity of Masters and Johnson's claims was being questioned, and the inability of other sex researchers to replicate the pair's findings was one of the big problems.[72]

## A DYING BREED

For those who had lived and enjoyed the sexual revolution in the late 1960s and 1970s, the state of sex in America in the late 1980s was almost too much to bear. "It seems that hardly anyone has a good word to say about sex any more," remarked Susan Jacoby in the *New York Times Magazine* in 1988; AIDS and the pronounced sexual conservatism of the times "give unembroidered lust a bad name." Casual sex, that is, sex without a long-term commitment, was popularly believed to have led to a variety of problems, making it important that sex occurs within the context of love. Some experts in the subject had changed their tune, with a few of the loudest voices of sexual freedom two decades earlier now embracing caution with equivalent enthusiasm. Once praised for liberating us from centuries of oppression and repression, the sexual revolution, and in particular the birth control pill, was now blamed for bringing on an array of troubles ranging from AIDS to teenage pregnancy.[73]

A clear sign of the times was the closing of the last remaining Playboy Clubs in the United States. The first Playboy Club had opened in 1960 in Chicago, extending the magazine's ethos of the good (and sexual) life beyond the printed word and, of course, photography. By the end of the decade, there were twenty-two such clubs around the world serving 750,000 people (mostly businessmen) happy to have paid the $25 membership fee. The idea of women in bunny outfits became less than chic in the 1970s and 1980s, however, and Playboy Enterprises closed its last company-opened club in 1986. In 1988, the last of the remaining franchised clubs (in Lansing, Michigan, of all places) shut down, leaving just four clubs in Japan and one in Manila. "I guess we're the end of a dying breed," said one of the nine Lansing bunnies about to retire her bow-tied, cotton-tailed rabbit uniform, an icon of America's postwar sexual exuberance now extinct.[74]

No one may have been saying anything good about sex in the late 1980s, but it sure could be seen on the silver screen. Despite or perhaps because of the new conservatism when it came to actually having sex, Hollywood filmmakers were liberally splashing their films with it. *Dirty Dancing, Bull Durham, 9½ Weeks,* and *Blue Velvet* were some of the recent movies featuring a generous dose of sexuality; these were a lot different than the teenagers-fumbling-in-the-dark kind of films that had flourished in the early 1980s. AIDS may have curbed unrestrained sex in the real world, but it had also created a climate in which it was more permissible to talk openly about sexuality and enjoy fictitious expressions of it. Socially sanctioned, perfectly safe sex like that in the movies was thus more in demand, it seemed, with Americans perhaps getting vicarious thrills through the actors' on-screen canoodling. *Fatal Attraction* was another late eighties film with a lot of sex, this one however viscerally illustrating the possible dangers of sleeping with the wrong person. While not about AIDS, the film served as a metaphor of the times, demonstrating that certain kinds of sexual attractions now had the potential of being fatal.[75]

The pornographic film business, already chugging along nicely with the advent of the VCR, also got a further boost from the AIDS crisis. Rather than sleep with lots of partners for the variety and novelty it afforded, considerable numbers of people were choosing to enhance their sex lives within a monogamous relationship. X-rated videos, preferably with some kind of plot, often did the trick, and also served as an educational tool. Just another Saturday night at home became something special with a sexy movie, couples who had been together for some time were finding, as the same old, same old was spiced up by watching another couple (or trio) get it on. These movies, made especially for couples, were a long way from the wham-bam-thank-you-ma'am kind of films typical of the pre-VCR days, with romance emphasized over close-ups. Most psychiatrists and sex therapists blessed the occasional watching of porn, not too surprising given that they themselves often used it in their work.[76]

As what had been arguably the most turbulent decade in American history with regard to sex wound down, a book appeared on the scene that challenged virtually everything people were thinking and saying about sexuality. In their *Burning Desires: Sex in America*, Steve Chapple and David Talbot went into the field much like Talese had to explore the nation's sexual frontier (but, in their case, resisted the temptation to "go native"). A "report from the country's erogenous zones," as the book was described, *Burning Desires* made the case that the sexual revolution was still very much alive, although one had to look a little harder to find it. Interviews with swingers, feminist pornographers, sex-obsessed pregnant women, and teenage groupies all proved that reports of the death of recreational sex in America were highly exaggerated, the authors claimed, with places like Key West and Aspen as sexually hopping as ever. As with *Thy Neighbor's Wife*, however, it was the examples of sexual repression that made more compelling reading in *Burning Desires*. Tipper Gore, antipornography feminists, and the therapeutic war being waged against sex addiction were some of the real problems when it came to sex in America, the authors boldly suggested, our new moral conservatism posing more danger than a little promiscuity or kinkiness.[77] As the last decade of the twentieth century beckoned, the landscape of sexuality would become a battleground, and another chapter of sex in America written.

# 5

# Indecent Proposal

Think of it. A million dollars. A lifetime of security . . . for one night.

—*John Gage (Robert Redford) offering $1 million to sleep with David Murphy's (Woody Harrelson's) wife in the 1993 film* Indecent Proposal

In February 1993, the National Center for Men, a Brooklyn-based organization, issued a "Consensual Sex Contract" for men to protect themselves against false accusations of rape. "Whereas, the parties to this agreement want to be sexually intimate, but also want to avoid the misunderstandings that sometimes occur after sex," the contract (titled "Agreement before Lovemaking") began, followed by a number of declarations for a couple to check off. "By signing this contract, we acknowledge that the anticipated sexual experience will be of mutual consent," the agreement (which was included in a press release to the media) concluded, after the terms of the forthcoming act were laid out clearly as a preventative measure.[1] Administrators at Antioch College in Yellow Springs, Ohio, meanwhile, were especially concerned about sexual encounters that one party considered to be unwanted or inappropriate. "All sexual contact and conduct between any two people must be consensual," the college's "Sexual Offense Prevention and Survivors' Advocacy Program" began, with the act requiring a series of verbal consents as it became more intimate. "If one person wants to initiate moving to a higher level of sexual intimacy in an interaction, that person is responsible for getting the verbal consent of the other person(s) involved before moving to that level," the rule specified; a student almost had to be a prelaw major to understand the required sequence of the act.[2]

As the title of *Indecent Proposal*, a movie that came out precisely when consensual sex agreements were first making the rounds, suggested, sexuality in America had become an area of society fraught with moral and possibly legal hazards. The sexual revolution of a generation earlier seemed like a distant memory as an array of social and political events reshaped the landscape of sex in America. AIDS had much to do with this new, more defensive view of sex, of course, as the death of thousands of Americans from the disease over the past decade imbued sexuality with a palpable sense of danger. The 1990s would clearly demonstrate Americans' ambiguous feelings toward sex as many struggled with how to negotiate desire within a climate of fear and distrust. A series of sex scandals in the late nineties, one involving the most powerful man in the world, illustrated that the rich and powerful were hardly immune to this struggle. The battle over sex education also would show how contentious the issue of sexuality was, especially with regard to young people. Sexual dysfunction would rise from already high levels to what some experts considered to be a "pandemic," making the introduction of a little blue pill nothing short of revolutionary. Another revolution was redrawing the contours of sex, as the personal computer and Internet brought every kind of fantasy imaginable into the privacy and comfort of one's own home. As a new century and millennium approached, Americans' relationship with sex remained complex and problematic, its future as uncertain as ever.

## WOMEN ON TOP

Given the ubiquity of sex in everyday life, especially television and movies, one would think that Americans were experts in or at least had a thorough knowledge of the subject. That was not the case, according to a new survey from the Kinsey Institute. In fact, Americans were largely sexually illiterate, lacking basic knowledge in some of the fundamentals of the subject. Working with the Roper Organization, the Kinsey Institute conducted what it called "the first nationally representative survey of what people know about sex," a different study from most others in that it focused on knowledge versus experience. The Kinsey Institute routinely received letters from people asking all sorts of sex-related questions, leading staff members to wonder if Americans as a whole were as uninformed about sexuality as those who wrote in.[3]

The results of the survey, which included questions about contraception, AIDS, sexual stereotypes, desire, personal sexual health, erections, and beliefs about what other people did in the bedroom, confirmed staff members' suspicions. Fifty-five percent of those asked to take the institute's sex test "flunked," the organization reported in 1990, unable to answer half the questions correctly. One key finding was that Americans tended to underestimate others' sexual behavior. Only 21 percent knew that almost one man in three had had a homosexual experience in their lifetime, for example, while just 18 percent were aware that 60–80 percent of women had masturbated. Rather incredibly, half of those asked believed a person could get AIDS from anal intercourse even if neither partner was infected with HIV; this kind of finding revealed that Americans still did not understand how the disease was spread. Other findings from the survey, which were included in a book called *The Kinsey Institute New Report on Sex: What You Must Know to be Sexually Literate*, were equally surprising. Most men believed that women preferred a larger than average penis, but this was not true, according to the survey. (Women actually complained more often about too large penises rather than too small ones, according to the institute, and men were far more accommodating of small breasts than women believed.) Half of Americans did not know a woman could get pregnant while she was menstruating, so it was no wonder that the nation had the highest teenage pregnancy rate in the Western world. Better sex education was clearly needed in this country, Kinsey's latest research showed, since schools and parents were apparently not doing a very good job when it came to explaining the birds and bees.[4]

Despite Americans' illiteracy when it came to knowledge about sex, they got high marks in experience, other studies showed. The average American in 1991 had sexual intercourse for the first time at age 16, according to the Alan Guttmacher Institute, and more than half of teenage girls were now sexually active (up from 36 percent in 1973). Teens were clearly inspired by their parents, who had not become the neo-Puritans some imagined they would because of the AIDS epidemic. Most adults engaged in oral sex, sociologist Lillian Rubin found, and more than one in four had reportedly taken part in group sex. Another sociologist, Annette Lawson, found in her research that a whopping 66 percent of married men and women had been unfaithful and

that the "seven-year itch" (when partners begin to reevaluate their relationship) had shrunk to five years. Finally, based on their survey published in *The
Day America Told the Truth*, James Patterson and Peter Kim reported that
two-thirds of men and 40 percent of women had had *more* than one affair,
with the Janus Report published the following year reporting similar figures
regarding extramarital encounters.[5]

Although some of these numbers seemed highly suspect, which was all too
typical of sex-related surveys, it was clear that Americans had hardly put sex
into a closet and thrown away the key. Magic Johnson's November 1991 revelation that he had tested HIV positive, and that he had contracted the virus
heterosexually, reinforced fears among straights that one did not have to be
gay or a drug user to get AIDS. About 6 percent of the two hundred thousand
reported cases of AIDS in the United States had resulted from heterosexual
contact, but the number was growing, faster in fact than any other segment.
Cases among homosexuals were leveling off, making many wonder if the
next big wave would strike heterosexuals as it had in Africa and southern and
Southeast Asia. "The question now is how far—and how fast—it will travel
into the rest of the population," wrote Philip Elmer-Dewitt in *Time* a couple
of weeks after Johnson's announcement. The problem was especially bad in
inner cities because of needle sharing. Having a venereal disease, as many in
these other areas of the world had, made it much easier for the virus to be
transmitted, however, making health officials assure Americans there was
no reason to panic. Still, the distribution of free condoms had accelerated,
especially after the basketball star's press conference, and FOX had recently
become the first television network to accept advertising for the product (as
long as the commercials focused on health benefits versus birth control).[6]

As anyone with any contact with the gay community in the 1980s could
tell you, the impact of AIDS was devastating. A decade after the disease was
first identified, about 120,000 Americans had died from AIDS, more than the
U.S. death toll from the Korean and Vietnam wars combined. The worse news
was that experts were predicting that more Americans would die from AIDS
in the next two years than in the last ten, making the argument for safer sex
greater than ever. (It was estimated that about one million Americans were
infected with HIV, most of them unknowingly.) The antiviral drugs AZT
and ddI could slow down the advance of HIV, but for the moment at least,
AIDS was incurable and always lethal. Twelve million Americans contracted

another, much less lethal sexually transmitted disease like syphilis, gonorrhea, or chlamydia every year, another reason wearing condoms was so important.[7]

The trend toward monogamy because of the fear of AIDS continued to make some couples look for opportunities to enhance their sex lives. Just as more couples rented erotic films in the 1980s as the VCR became a standard appliance in Americans' homes, more twosomes had begun to make such films in the early 1990s. As the cost of a home video camera dropped, some were deciding to become amateur pornographers, filming themselves having sex with their partner. (Rob Lowe had famously done the same in 1988, starring in the first of what would be a long line of celebrity sex tapes.) Like many things, however, a good erotic film looked easier to make than it really was. Poor lighting and wrong camera angles made amateur films difficult to watch, even by the stars themselves. Couples also found the adage that "the camera adds ten pounds" to be all too true; even the less-than-gorgeous actors in professional porn flicks looked better on screen. Still, psychologists generally approved of homemade erotica, seeing the making of such films as a safe but exciting fantasy for more adventurous couples.[8]

Because the brain was the most powerful erogenous zone, however, a good imagination remained the best resource to have an exciting sex life. Americans, especially women, had quite a range of sexual fantasies, according to a new book. In her 1973 *My Secret Garden* and 1975 *Forbidden Flowers*, Nancy Friday documented women's sexual fantasies, many of them involving being overpowered by a male stranger. In researching her 1991 *Women on Top*, however, Friday found that women were often the initiators of sex in their erotic daydreams, a reflection of the change in gender roles that had occurred between these years. Sex with other women was another common theme in current fantasies, this too a sign of their greater independence and fewer inhibitions. Friday's methodology in selecting the contributors who described their fantasies was especially shaky, but her book did shed some light on what was going through women's minds when it came to sex.[9]

## THE SEX GENIE

Having sex for money was something more women were choosing not to do in the early 1990s. Prostitution had been hit hard by the AIDS crisis, with Rock Hudson's death in 1985 especially damaging to the business. Not only were there fewer customers, but also fewer young women wanted to enter the field given the much greater health risks. "There's a dearth of fresh Midwestern college girls," lamented Bob Richter, publisher of the *Climax Times*, *New York Sex Guide*, and the *American Sex Scene*, all of these used by men interesting in finding a prostitute. The circulation of his magazines was up but only because it was safer to read about prostitution than to engage in it, another way vicarious forms of sex were thriving as riskier expressions of the real thing suffered. The 1970s had been one of the heydays of prostitution in America, when entrepreneurs opened up chains of brothels and swingers clubs across the country much like those who were investing in fast food or oil change businesses. By the end of the decade, however, the good times for prostitution were ending as consumers' tastes evolved and as the political and moral landscape of the country changed. "Even before AIDS," Michael Gross wrote in *New York* in 1992, "the baby-boom generation grew up and got tired, jaded, and Reaganized, and discovered that actions have consequences and parties do end."[10]

For those who believed that recreational sex had completely disappeared in the early nineties, however, Gross had other news. "There's more going on—straight and gay, safe and unsafe—than you'd think," he reported after exploring Manhattan's edgy club scene, with things certainly not at pre-AIDS levels but quite lively all the same. After almost a decade of restraint, the subculture whose lives revolved principally around sex was again enjoying their favorite pastime, with gay men leading the way as usual. "The sex genie cannot be put back in the bottle," Gross observed; the idea of chastity or anything close to it was "untenable." Most significant, sex was now back out in the open, with New York City's nightlife offering a potpourri of sexual diversions for anyone in the market for one. Swingers were now finding each other at Le Trapeze, a clear knockoff of the long-closed Plato's Retreat. "The place looks like a nudist Steak & Ale," Gross thought; the crowd (mostly aging baby boomers) was drawn to the free buffet, Roman tub, mat room, and upstairs room where "anything goes."[11]

While Le Trapeze was certainly at the far end of the spectrum, a bubbling up of sexuality was apparent all over American popular and consumer culture in the early nineties. Madonna, the country's top pop music act, was a one-woman circus of sex, both personally and professionally. Another artist named LaTour currently had a big dance hit with a song called "People Are Still Having Sex." ("Lust keeps on lurking / Nothing makes them stop / this

AIDS thing's not working," went some of the lyrics.) Phone sex had displaced much of the prostitution business, and ads for such were in the back of many publications and plastered across many larger cities. (There was also something called "Voyeurvision," a televisual form of phone sex, on New York City cable.) Gay magazines, notably the *Advocate*, included guides to the sex club scene, and drag culture, that is, transvestism, was liberally splashed across hipper magazines like *Vogue*. Lesbians, meanwhile, had their own sex magazine, *On Our Backs*, which featured ads for clubs like Faster Pussycat in San Francisco and the Clit Club in New York. If the Clit Club was not one's cup of tea, one could walk just a few steps to find Meat (for men) and Jackie 60, which catered to those with pan- or omni-sexual tastes. Across town was Tattooed Love Child, a haven for the sadomasochistic crowd, some of whom wore couture "bondagewear" from designers like Thierry Mugler and Gianni Versace. (Madonna was particularly partial to dog collars.)[12]

There was also no shortage of clubs offering more pedestrian sexual services. Many American cities had at least one strip club, where professional men could find upscale, topless entertainment. (Some believed the trend toward high-class strip clubs was a male response to women's significant gains in the workplace.) Watching women take off their clothes was nothing new, of course, but the lap dance was now drawing men like flies to these joints. A lap dance typically cost $10 for three minutes ($20 for seven minutes), with the unstated or stated purpose for the customer to have an orgasm. Unlike having sex with a woman, however, "performance" was a nonissue, this too explaining the interest in obligation-free (and completely safe) sexual contact. Table dances went for about $20, with some clubs allowing men to rub their faces in the women's breasts. One gay club in New York, billed as an art gallery, offered customers the chance to watch men have sex, the act presented as a form of performance art. As with most sex clubs, condoms and lubricant were freely available for customers inspired by the performance.[13]

As George Chauncey detailed in his *Gay New York*, New York City had had a thriving gay scene since the late nineteenth century, but it was the Stonewall Inn riot in 1969 that sparked the demand for and interest in public spots for sex. Through the 1970s, bathhouses, movie theaters, bookstores, and sex clubs (notably the Mineshaft and Anvil) were popular places for gay men to have sex, most of them shut down by the city as the AIDS crisis unfolded in the 1980s. The closing of Studio 54 in 1986 was one of the more important milestones in the cultural history of sex in America, especially for gay men. (It was not unusual for many frequenters of what Gross called "the last era's sexual supermarket" to know dozens of men who died from AIDS.) By the late eighties, however, "masturbation spaces" such as the Locker Room and Shooting Stars had opened, and gay men began gravitating to "make-out lounges" in clubs like the Rock 'n' Roll Fag Bar. Within a few years, a full resurgence of gay nightlife was underway, with places like Lick It! (a club within a club at Limelight) again packing them in. Public sex was discouraged at Limelight but still occurred regularly (the club had "more nooks and crannies than an English muffin," noted the promoter of Lick It!). Gay men could choose from a dozen or so sex clubs or back rooms in Manhattan in the early nineties, all of them places for patrons to find judgment-free fun and, as important, a community to reaffirm one's identity.[14]

As gay culture made a comeback in the post-AIDS era, lesbians took advantage of the new awareness and openness about homosexuality. "Lipstick lesbians"—women who saw no contradiction between their sexual orientation and "prettiness"—were now part of the scene. Lesbianism had become chic in younger circles and was something in which usually straight women dabbled. Such women occasionally visited lesbian clubs with their friends, their "bicurious" night out consisting of lots of kissing and touching. "Lesbians are a decade behind gay men," stated Susie Bright, author of *Sexual Reality*, thinking the time was ripe for "a democratization of kinkiness." Kinkiness could definitely be found at Pink Pussycat in New York's Greenwich Village, one of many sex toy boutiques that had popped up in recent years. Condomania opened in New York in 1991, the first of what was rapidly becoming a national chain of condom shops. (Sixty percent of the store's customers were women, 15 percent gay men, and the remainder straight men and lesbians.) Another AIDS-related business that was doing well was Check a Mate, a private investigation firm specializing in determining if one's lover was secretly gay or bisexual. "People are afraid to ask questions that might end relationships," said one of the cofounders of Check a Mate; his typical MO was to follow a man on behalf of a female client to see if he frequented gay bars on the "down low."[15]

## ABOUT AS EXCITING AS A PEANUT BUTTER AND JELLY SANDWICH

The resurgence of sexuality in the early 1990s within fringe culture was an extreme version of what was taking place in mainstream circles. "Despite what the media hipsters say, casual sex is alive and well among the twentysome-thing set," wrote Simon Sebag Montefiore for *Psychology Today* in 1992, and the "experts" were out of touch with what was really going on among young adults. Montefiore, a twenty-six-year-old heterosexual male, could not find anyone among his peer group who had formed a serious relationship because of the fear of AIDS and thought that the idea that chastity or virginity was "in" (as a *New York Times* article had recently said) was utter nonsense. Hooking up with someone after knowing him or her for just a few hours still happened, Montefiore informed older people who believed (or wanted to believe) other-wise, and the "sex is dead" narrative was a pure fabrication. Part of the problem was that twentysomethings often did not tell the truth about their sex lives to each other, not admitting they had had a one-nighter or saying they used condoms when they did not. Montefiore felt that "the less likely a person is to catch the [HIV] virus, the more he or she is paranoid about it"; those com-pletely out of the scene were much more fearful about AIDS than those in it.[16]

According to the latest major study of sexuality in America completed by a team of University of Chicago researchers led by Edward Laumann, however, Montefiore might have been overestimating how much sex his peer group was having and how much they were enjoying it. Americans were not the sexual dynamos the media would have one think we were, our sex lives undeniably conservative, predictable, and, perhaps most surprising, fulfilling. Two-thirds of men and women had sex with a partner several times a month or less, *Sex in America: A Definitive Survey* showed, and close to a third of all adults had sex just a few times a year or not at all. Not only were we not doing it like rabbits, but also we were almost always doing it with the same person. More than 80 percent of Americans had no more than one sexual partner in the past year, the study revealed; monogamy was much more often the rule rather than the exception. If that were not enough, the most sexually satisfied people were those who were married or living together, with unat-tached people the least content. The popular image of single people hooking up with someone different every night and loving every minute of it was just not true, the survey indicated, the sheer logistics of sex dictating both atti-tudes and behavior. Having someone you know quite well lying next to you in bed made traditional coupling the best-case scenario for both frequency and satisfaction, it could be said, debunking the idea of America as a land of unbridled lust.[17]

What made *Sex in America* different from other studies, including those done by Kinsey and by Masters and Johnson, was that this one relied on a random sample of people rather than volunteers to provide answers to interviewers' questions. Volunteers for sex studies had higher-than-average sexual appetites, this obviously overinflating the findings of previous researchers. For example, more than three-fourths of married Americans were faithful to their spouses, this study showed, a much higher number than in earlier studies.[18] Watching one's partner undress was ranked ahead of oral sex as "very or somewhat appealing" in *Sex in America*, another finding suggesting that Americans were a lot more old-fashioned than other surveys had found and how the media presented us.[19]

Many were elated to learn that, according to what was called the most scientific survey ever done on American sexuality, most people were not having more adventurous sex than they were. (Another study, claiming to be the first "statistically valid" one of its kind, was completed the previous year, its authors also finding that Americans, specifically men in their twenties and thirties, had rather mundane sex lives.)[20] "The impression that is branded on our collective subconscious is that life in the twilight of the twentieth century is a sexual banquet to which everyone else has been invited," observed Elmer-Dewitt of *Time*, thinking the reality would make a lot of Americans sleep better at night.[21] "You (married, monogamous, straight, once-or-twice-a-week-but-nothing-too-kinky-please) are normal," wrote Katha Pollitt in the *Nation*, good news to those falling into that category who assumed they were not normal because their sex lives did not include a third party or handcuffs.[22]

Garrison Keillor, the author and host of the radio show *A Prairie Home Companion*, was one person happy to hear that "the sex lives of most Americans are about as exciting as a peanut-butter-and-jelly-sandwich," as Elmer-Dewitt put it. Keillor had always believed that Americans had sex on average twice a week and was thus pleased to learn that, if anything, that number was on the high side. It was a burden to think that most other people were having sex much more often and enjoying it more because they had multiple partners, he felt, and the reality was quite a relief and confirmed what he believed all along. "Monogamy is the good life," he wrote in *Time* in 1994, something with which most Americans apparently agreed.[23]

Others were glad to learn that the popular image of Americans as a sex-crazed people appeared to be a mythology. Postfeminist writer Camille Paglia was "delighted to hear that all this talk about rampant infidelity was wildly inflated," and Erica Jong thought the results of the survey were "totally predictable" given that "Americans are more interested in money than sex." Even Hugh Hefner was not surprised by the findings. "Our Puritan roots are deep," went his explanation for our not being a nation of playboys and playgirls. Not everyone thought the study reflected the sex habits of the real America, however. "It doesn't ring true," said Jackie Collins, author of such steamy novels as *The Bitch* and *The Stud*, wondering, "Where are the sex maniacs I see on TV every day"? "Positively, outrageously stupid and unbelievable," opined *Penthouse* publisher Bob Guccione, his experience suggesting that "five partners a year is the average for men." *Cosmopolitan* editor Helen Gurley Brown also disputed the accuracy of the survey. "Two partners?" she asked upon learning that was the median number of lovers a woman had over the course of a lifetime; her extensive experience was that "the correct answer is always three, though there may have been more."[24]

While more scientific than previous surveys, *Sex in America* did not take into account how the personal computer and Internet were steadily expanding the boundaries of sexuality. "Cyberswingers" were finding each other on the "Information Highway" in the mid-1990s, with bulletin boards like KinkNet and ThrobNet being ideal places for those with more exotic sexual tastes to meet. In these prebroadband days and with personal computers snail-like compared to the machines today, however, the experience was less than ideal. "The quality of much cyberporn varies from low to dreadful," thought Barbara Kantrowitz of *Newsweek*, finding that "downloading X-rated pictures takes time and concentration." Adult CD-ROMS were also becoming quite popular, their interactive capabilities a competitive advantage over videotapes.[25]

The mid-1990s technology boom also appeared to be shaping sexual tastes, at least among some women. Scott Adams, the creator of the comic strip "Dilbert," received a lot of e-mails from fans, a considerable number from women telling him they thought the titular character was sexy. Some women said that Dilbert resembled their husband, finding both the illustrated figure and their spouse very attractive and appealing. This might not have been unusual except that Dilbert was a bespectacled electrical engineer who spent most of the time at his desk looking at a computer, not exactly your traditional male sex symbol. Adams believed women's attraction to the nerdy Dilbert was "a

Darwinian thing," his character's technological skills viewed as sexy because in the 1990s that conveyed intelligence and success. For some women, it appeared that a "real man" was now not a hunky actor or an outdoorsy type but rather someone who was fluent in computers, quite a switch in the definition of masculinity. "Information technology has replaced hot cars as the symbol of robust manhood," Adams quipped, that he was himself a glasses-wearing applications engineer for Pacific Bell when not working on his comic strip no doubt shaping his perspective.[26]

## CONTROL YOUR URGIN'

As computer literacy emerged as a main criterion for sex appeal, sexual literacy remained a big problem in America. Not only were adults not very knowledgeable about some of the facts of sexuality, but also they had little idea how to teach the subject to children. Therapists now advised parents not to wait for their child to reach puberty to have "the talk," with no age considered too young to discuss the subject. If the subject of sex came up, parents should not avoid it, they believed, as doing so was likely to make kids think there was something bad or shameful about it. Answering questions honestly was always a good thing, although kids should be reminded there was a proper time and place to discuss certain subjects. As well, there was no need to worry about telling them too much, as children would simply not process any information that was beyond their comprehension. Correct terminology was also important, as using "cute" names for genitals would lead to kids believing those parts were odd or secretive. Kids should never be punished for masturbating (at least in private), most sex educators agreed, quite an amazing thing given how children had been treated in the past for doing such a thing (and no doubt still were in some cases, especially among the very religious). Finally, "playing doctor" was perfectly normal and generally harmless, so there was no need to panic when discovering a couple of kids engaged in the age-old game.[27]

Sex education for older kids was much more difficult and contentious, however. Nine out of ten Americans believed that schools should teach teenagers about sex, but how to do it was a much different story.[28] No clear, consistent message was being given to teens about sex in the early 1990s, and the AIDS phenomenon was making things only more complicated and confusing. Some high schools were handing out free condoms and Planned

Parenthood pamphlets while others were sponsoring sex abstinence groups. Should I just do it or just say no? many teens naturally wondered, the forces of popular culture (especially MTV videos and rap music) definitely pushing the former. (Teenagers saw nearly fourteen thousand sexual encounters on television a year, the Center for Population Options estimated.) Parents and educators tended to be polarized on the issue, as a common ground was difficult to find among the religious right and liberal left. Forty-seven states now formally required or recommended sex education (and all fifty required AIDS education), meaning most kids in America were at least receiving information on the subject. Little beyond the technical and anatomical details was typically presented in sex-ed classes, however; more practical knowledge or the emotional issues involved were left out of the process.[29]

The message at home leaned decidedly toward abstinence. A 1993 *Time* CNN poll of five hundred American teenagers showed that 71 percent had been told by their parents to wait until they were older before having sex. Still, three-quarters of Americans had had sex by the time they were twenty, the statistics showed, suggesting that casual sex among teenagers was the norm. Promiscuity was prized among some boys, while girls tended to award status based on whom one slept with versus how many. Earlier menstruation, later marriages, and a latchkey society were just a few of the larger factors encouraging sex among young people, these too powerful to overcome abstinence proponents' warnings of pregnancy, sexually transmitted disease (STDs), or moral jeopardy.[30] The United States had the highest teenage pregnancy, abortion, and childbirth rates in the West, proof that parents and schools were failing to persuade teens not to have sex.[31]

Schools had four possible options when it came to sex ed. The first option was "Just Say No," in which only abstinence was taught. Teen-Aid was a prochastity program many schools used, with the text *Sex Respect* a popular choice. The second option was "Just Say Nothing," in which schools simply did not get involved in the issue. The third option was known as "Tell It Like It Is," in which abstinence was encouraged while still giving students specific information about birth control and other aspects of sexuality. "Will Power/ Won't Power" and "Taking Care of Business," each run by a company called Girls, Inc., were the best-known programs for this approach. The fourth and final option was "Just Say Wait," in which abstinence was encouraged but specific information about birth control and other aspects of sexuality was typically not given. The best example of the "Just Say Wait" option was a program called "Postponing Sexual Involvement" (PSI), which was created by Marion Howard, a professor at Emory University. PSI relied on older, specially trained teens to role-play as a way to teach younger ones that it was acceptable to say no to sex, a curriculum based on Howard's finding that girls simply did not know how to say no to boys without hurting their feelings. Students learned how to say no (versus "I don't think so") assertively and were prepared with effective counters to likely comebacks. Unlike most other programs, the PSI curriculum worked, delaying seventh and eighth graders' decision to have sex. The key seemed to be Howard's decision to use older teens rather than adults to deliver the message, the former able to speak in the same language as the audience. Teens also understood the kinds of pressure their peers faced, and students found the role-playing approach a lot more tolerable than a didactic lecture.[32]

Despite the success of PSI, more schools in the 1990s were adopting abstinence-only sex-education programs, as well as discouraging or completely ignoring contraception and safer-sex techniques. In addition to the moral or values-based motives for this decision ("Control Your Urgin'/Be a Virgin," went a bumper sticker for the abstinence-only movement), there was a financial incentive as well. Federal funds were available for schools that took an abstinence-only approach, a legacy of the Reagan administration that had essentially underwritten the movement.[33] (The Clinton administration had also demonstrated how conservative it was when it came to sex education by dismissing Surgeon General Joyce Elders for her suggestion that masturbation should possibly be taught.) Many states and local communities were also endorsing abstinence education, encouraged to do so by fundamentalist religious groups like the Christian Coalition and conservative "family values" organizations like Focus on the Family. There was little evidence proving that abstinence education actually worked, however, as statistics showed that adolescents were just as likely to have sex. Teens' just saying no to sex was about as unlikely as them saying no to drugs, in fact, with abstinence-only education as ineffective as the widely ridiculed Drug Abuse Resistance Education (DARE) program. Politics, not facts, were ruling the day in sex education, it seemed, as some felt it was necessary to counter the media's prosex messages with an antisex one.[34]

Kids' education in sex was starting at an increasingly early age thanks largely to television. Exposed to shows like *Baywatch*, *Melrose Place*, and *Beavis and Butt-head* and commercials like one for Pepsi featuring supermodel Cindy Crawford, children as young as nine were becoming conversant in sexuality. Popular sitcoms, even those broadcast at 8:00 p.m., also got steamy occasionally; the escalating sexuality (and violence) on television was the basis for both the V-chip (a computer chip that enabled parents to block objectionable programming) and a ratings system. One episode of *Friends* revolved around a "threesome," for example, another around premature ejaculation. On *Mad About You*, Helen Hunt's character had an intimate encounter with a washing machine—not the kind of thing a previous generation of viewers might see on *The Brady Bunch*.[35] A Gallup poll found that six in ten American parents were often uncomfortable watching television with their kids, since the need to explain a "threesome" or premature ejaculation to a preteen was not something most adults enjoyed, despite experts' advice to tell all.[36] A little knowledge only made kids want to know more, of course, with parents having to decide how to answer all their questions. Being informative and satisfying their curiosity while keeping some of the mystery of sex was a tough line to walk; things had not changed much in this respect when it came to discussing the birds and bees.[37]

## THE MESS ON THE DRESS

Simply watching the news on television would also afford children an education in sex, albeit a not very positive one. As Lewis Lapham noted in *Harper's*, the month of May 1997 was an especially ripe one for sex-related scandals, giving all Americans keeping abreast of current events a lesson in a wide variety of sexual peccadilloes. On May 2, the actor Eddie Murphy was found by law enforcement officials to be in the company of a transvestite prostitute, while eight days later Congressman Joseph P. Kennedy declined to comment on his younger brother Michael's affair with his fourteen-year-old babysitter. On May 20, sportscaster Marv Albert was indicted for biting a woman during some kind of liaison, and two days later there were reports of photographs of fellow sportscaster Frank Gifford frolicking in a New York hotel room with a woman who was not his wife. Kids would no doubt be puzzled by such a string of events, particularly after being told of the need to act responsibly with regard to sex when high-profile, successful people were acting much differently.[38]

A glance at afternoon television only confirmed the range of sexual activities in which Americans were taking part. Any day of the week Montel Williams might be seen talking with a guest about her fondness for S&M; Ricki Lake, chatting up a few cross-dressers; and Sally Jesse Raphael, hosting a threesome who happened to be cousins. On prime-time network shows, depictions of premarital sex far outnumbered sex between married couples, according to a number of studies.[39] Other media were equally sexual in nature. Almost eight thousand new pornographic movies had been released in 1996 (versus 471 Hollywood films), making a trip to the average video store a potential adventure in professional, commercial sexuality. Women's magazines usually featured some aspect of sex on their covers every month, offering young women instruction in the art of love via articles like "How to Give Him the Best Sex of His Life" (*Cosmopolitan*), "Sex Secrets You're Entitled to Know" (*Marie Claire*), or "Is He Your Secret Sexual Soulmate?" (*Glamour*).[40] Given our sexualized media universe and what some adults were up to, was it any wonder that kids just did what they wanted?[41]

The scandal between President Clinton and Monica Lewinsky in 1998 brought sex further into the national conversation. "With such a President, why bother to aspire to an adult code of ethics?" Lapham asked, of the opinion that the most powerful person in the world was not very well versed in the difference between right and wrong.[42] Clinton's approval ratings had not fallen after the news broke about his relationship with the intern, however, illustrating Americans' inclination to be tolerant of other people's sex lives and embrace the notion of "live and let live" when it to came to their private affairs. "Even with a religious revival underway and 'family values' a bipartisan issue, we still feel uncomfortable passing judgment on illegitimacy, adultery and promiscuity," Jonathan Adler wrote in *Newsweek* in March of that year, thinking, "There's nothing more humiliating than to be labeled a prude."[43] As well, many experts in various fields came to Clinton's rescue by offering rational-sounding reasons for why he did what he did. Biologists correlated high levels of testosterone with a need for sex with different people, for example, this possibly explaining the president's risky behavior. Therapists, meanwhile, reported that sexual boredom within a marriage was "pandemic" in America, making Clinton's straying not all that unusual.[44]

More than anything else, however, the Clinton-Lewinsky scandal elevated the public discussion of sex in America, much of it quite bawdy (and funny). Not since the onset of AIDS had there been such a jump in graphic references to sex in the media, with the coverage of "Monicagate" outdoing the Clarence Thomas hearings and rape trials of William Kennedy Smith and Mike Tyson in terms of sheer explicitness. "Oral sex," a term traditionally avoided in the media, no longer was so, giving people greater permission to use it and its less clinical synonym in ordinary banter.[45] Parents found themselves having to define oral sex for an inquisitive child who had heard the term, with experts advising that a brief answer to this particular question was best. Some seniors also did not know the meaning of the term, thinking it perhaps signified a woman being verbally sexually provocative.[46]

Another event of 1998—the introduction of a new drug called Viagra— only added to the louder conversation about sex in the country. "This was the year of talking sexually," thought John Leland of *Newsweek*, reflecting back on 1998. Phrases like the "mess on the dress," as one of the key elements of the Clinton-Lewinsky scandal was sometimes referred to, were now part of Americans' vocabulary. That many Americans were now aware that their president's penis had "distinguishing characteristics" alone suggested that public dialogue about sexuality had reached a tipping point, so to speak. "In this new global locker room, personal details flowed unbidden and unchecked," Leland continued, and Bob Dole's recent declaration that he popped the new diamond-shaped blue pill was a perfect example.[47]

## THE SOUL OF SEX

Talking sexually was getting some men into considerable trouble, however, as the chance of making an "indecent proposal" grew through the hypersensitive 1990s. If medical considerations reshaped the nation's sexual landscape in the 1980s, legal ones were doing the same in the 1990s due to an increasingly litigious society, especially when it came to issues of gender. Political correctness, encouraged by a major jump in sexual harassment and discrimination cases (especially at work), made virtually any kind of romantic advance a potentially risky proposition. "We have made every crude remark and offensive gesture into an occasion for filing lawsuits," R. Emmett Tyrrell Jr. wrote in *American Spectator*; in fact, he had recently been told by a woman that she considered her boss patting her on the shoulder for a job well done sexual

harassment.[48] "Those who can't negotiate the subtle psycho-social-sexual matrix now being constructed for working people are doomed to fail, and quite
painfully too," Stanley Bing observed in *Fortune*, with these folks "probably
ending up standing in the middle of a public square with their pants down
around their ankles."[49]

That sex had become a hot topic within the realm of law was one clear
sign of its increasing secularization and, one could argue, cultural decline.
Allan Bloom, the champion of "Great Books" and author of *The Closing of the
American Mind*, lamented what he considered to be "the death of Eros" as sex
lost all sense of sacredness. "Sex is spoken of coolly and without any remains
of the old puritanical shame," he wrote in an article published posthumously
in 1993; the term was now merely "an incidental aspect of the important
questions of disease and power." Once seen as an indelible part of nature,
sexuality had been reduced to two things: how to get more physical pleasure
or how to protect oneself from another person. The world had become de-
eroticized, Bloom thought, and this was the source of our widespread sexual
discontent. The great forces of modernism—democracy, science, materialism, and the breakdown of religion—had led to the death of Eros, he believed,
as had the recent wave of political correctness in which a remark about someone's beauty could be grounds for a harassment suit. Male lust and treatment
of women was especially viewed with suspicion, a byproduct of radical feminism and academics' reframing of nearly everything into a matter of power
relationships. It was the Kinsey Report that had triggered the beginning of
the end for Eros, Bloom suggested, with Americans thinking clinically and
quantitatively about sex ever since its publication in 1948.[50]

For Thomas Moore, author of the best seller *Care of the Soul* and a number of other books, it was not surprising that the workplace had become a
breeding ground for sexual harassment suits. "Office buildings are the most
sexless places in public life," he wrote for *Mother Jones* in 1997; the modern
workplace was a perfect example of bottled-up, repressed sexuality. Moore
was thinking a lot about sex at the time, as his next book, *The Soul of Sex*, was
an extensive and passionate treatise on Western society's major problems on
all things sexual. Much like Bloom's thesis, Moore's basic argument was that
Americans' bipolar attitudes and behavior toward sex were a function of our
extracting sensuality from public life. This was unnatural and unhealthy, he
proposed, making it not surprising that we were both obsessed and embar-

rassed by sex (often at the same time). As part of his research for *The Soul of Sex*, Moore was reading the Kama Sutra, the ancient Indian guide to sexuality, and could not help but be struck by the profound differences between that culture's relationship with sex and ours. In the Kama Sutra, sexuality was a complex concept, incorporating daily life (dharma), financial security (artha), and the art of love (kama)—a lot different than its predominantly hedonistic role in the United States. The latest articulation of sexuality—Internet pornography—was an apt metaphor for our crude viewpoint on sex, focusing on the body and physical acts. The Indians had even put erotic images on their temples, elevating sexuality to an act of sacredness, while we pushed it into what he called the "gutter," a legacy of our Puritanical shame attached to sex.[51]

With sex relegated to the less attractive margins of society, it made sense to Moore that sexual dysfunction was so prevalent in American society. "Take sex out of the world we live in daily, and it will become a giant, unsettling force in our personal lives," he wrote. The disconnect between public and private sexuality was the cause of much distress. Many of our sexual problems stemmed from the discomfort we felt toward our own bodies, he believed, the intellectual prioritized over the corporal. Moore suggested that if people could have their way they would be completely bodiless; the rise of electronic technologies reflected our desire to deemphasize the physical. The wild popularity of Internet pornography, in which virtual bodies replaced real ones, was perfectly logical, an opportunity to have the pleasure of sex without the deeper emotional sensations we preferred to avoid. Within such a paradigm, issues would eventually and inevitably surface, however, since the bifurcation of body and soul was an untenable concept. "The repression of the body and its main work, sex, wounds the soul immeasurably and deprives us of our humanity," Moore argued, this explaining many Americans' desperate efforts to improve their sex lives. "We have yet to discover that sex is not physical but the love of souls," he maintained, something civilizations thousands of years ago apparently understood quite well.[52]

Our soulless brand of sex played out in various ways, according to Moore (who used to be a psychotherapist). People often had affairs not because their marriages were unhappy but rather because humans had a fundamental, deep need for sex without the heavy morality we attached to it. Extramarital affairs, especially those among coworkers, were "symptomatic of a failure to give sex enough prominence in daily life and in the privacy of a marriage," he felt, and our determination to work as hard and play as hard as possible was contradictory to the pursuit of genuine passion. Friendship, intimacy, and excitement were all too rare in "this cool, gray world," Moore held, explaining why some would risk so much to find them in an affair. Pornography too was an attempt to find something unobtainable in everyday life, and our containment of sex encouraged people to explore their fantasies alone and in private. Finally, by approaching sex education through a biological, secular lens, we were training the next generation for these same kinds of dysfunctions, he warned. The only solution was the merging of soul with sexuality. "Cultivating life as an act of love," as his forthcoming book would be subtitled, was the key to sexual fulfillment, Moore concluded, an idea that was certainly foreign to most Americans.[53]

## KINGDOM OF THE THREE SLIPPERIES

Whether sacred or profane, erotica was a sizable area of America's sexual terrain. Erotica was split sharply by gender, as what appealed to women rarely appealed to men and vice versa. The leading marketer of women's erotica was without a doubt Harlequin Enterprises, which published dozens of romance novels every month under the Harlequin and Silhouette brands. Harlequin's novels were "compelling romances that sweep you away with the promise of love that lasts a lifetime," the company declared, and almost every one was based on the formula Jane Austen had mastered almost two centuries earlier. Although it would take some time for the novel's hero to realize he was in love, he was and would remain a one-woman man, the story would typically go, with monogamy the centerpiece of this presentation of females' sexual fantasies. The top seller of literary erotica targeted to men was *Penthouse*, which offered "letters" from supposed readers in its magazine and various spin-off publications. Words to the effect of "I never thought I'd be writing to *Penthouse* . . ." was how many letters began, the man (often on a business trip) then describing a sequence of activities that went beyond his "wildest dreams." Watching one's wife with someone else was a common fantasy in *Penthouse*, something that would never take place in a book with Fabio on the cover.[54]

In more serious contemporary American literature, erotic fantasies often involved not multiple people but one. In a couple of anthologies of erotic short stories by women, *Slow Hand* and *Fever*, for example, the most memorable passages were about masturbation rather than intercourse, a rather new phenomenon. Nicholson Baker's *Vox* was an almost two-hundred-page-long phone sex conversation, while the protagonist of his *Fermata* fantasized about how he could freeze time so he could have sex with women without their knowing. And in his 1997 novel *Purple America*, Rick Moody included a twelve-page passage ("the single most interesting sex scene in recent American quality lit," Ron Rosenbaum of *Esquire* thought) in which the literal climax was when the man and woman masturbated together. Was this trend toward solitary sex in literature symptomatic of a collective feeling of loneliness and separateness? A longing for control and fear of unpredictability? A desire to avoid any kind of deep connection with others? A reflection of our narcissism and elevation of the self? A sign that we could now only love ourselves? Rosenbaum thought all of the above, but at the same time believed what he called "the going solo trend" was a lot more real than some of the sex scenes written by great writers of the past, notably Ernest Hemingway (*For Whom the Bell Tolls*), Norman Mailer (*The Time of Her Time*), and Harold Brodkey (*Innocence*).[55]

Had the "Bad Sex Award" been around, all three of these famous writers might have been in contention to win the dubious prize. ("My avenger [was] wild with the mania of the madman," Mailer wrote in the 1959 novel.)[56] Since 1993, the UK-based *Literary Review* had been giving out the award for what the editor of the journal (Auberon Waugh, son of Evelyn) considered the worst description of the sexual act in a novel. Even good writers had their hands full when it came to writing about sex, the contest painfully proved, as the fictional event was fraught with the potential of being pretentious, tasteless, or embarrassing. In his novel *The Matter of the Heart*, for example, the 1997 winner, Nicholas Royle, had his female character Yasmin make "a noise somewhere between a beached seal and a police siren" while her male partner Ambrose "punch[ed] smoothly in and out of her like a sewing machine." Erica Jong had been among the finalists that year based on her use of phrases like "jungle flower," "iron stalk," and "kingdom of the three slipperies" (whatever that meant) in her *Of Blessed Memory*. "Liz squeaked like wet rubber" went a line from David Huggins's *Big Kiss*, which alone was bad (good?) enough to win the 1996 award. The 1995 winner, Philip Kerr, had received the prize in part for describing a penis as a "gnomon" (the metal pin on a sundial) in his novel *Gridiron*, while Philip Hook got top honors the year before for describing the deed with phrases like, "They became some mad mobile sculpture" in his *The Stonebreakers*.[57]

Unfortunately, things were not much better when it came to the sexual act in many Americans' actual bedrooms. In a 1999 follow-up study to their *Sex in America* survey, the University of Chicago team headed by Edward Laumann asked nearly three thousand men and women about their sex lives and found that sexual dysfunction was rampant among Americans. Over the past year, 43 percent of American women and 31 percent of men lacked interest in sex for a few months, could not come to an orgasm, climaxed too quickly, felt pain during intercourse, did not find sex pleasurable, had trouble getting aroused, or worried about their performance.[58] As with "the going solo trend," big questions had to be asked. Were Americans' sexual problems the result of our conflicting attitudes on the subject, with our Puritanical roots at odds with our libertarian spirit? Was our hypersexualized society still creating unrealistic expectations, making many feel inadequate? Or was all this dysfunction not culturally based but individual in nature, the result of issues in one's personal or professional life? No one could say for sure, but it appeared that many Americans could qualify for a real-life Bad Sex Award.[59]

Drugs used to treat depression were definitely playing some role in America's pervasive sexual dysfunction. More than half of those taking Prozac and its cousins Paxil and Zoloft lacked interest in sex, were unable to maintain an erection, or had difficulty reaching orgasm, studies showed, so the attempt to solve one problem was causing another. Some (even women) were taking Viagra to counter the side effects of these selective serotonin reuptake inhibitors (SSRIs), an all too common pharmacological ping-ponging. "Have we reached the point where our most intimate activities are governed not by our emotions but by the contents of our medicine cabinets?" asked Miriam Karmel Feldman in the *Utne Reader* in 1999, thinking what she termed "Pharma Sutra" was not a very healthy route to sexual well-being.[60]

It would not be an exaggeration to say that Viagra's ability to radically improve men's sexual performance overnight was a historic breakthrough. Besides taking the shame out of impotence, the little blue pill was also bringing much more attention to women's sexual problems. Although sex therapy had been around now for decades, little was still known about female arousal, and even less about women's sexual dysfunction. More female sexual health clinics were opening, however, and the Viagra phenomenon was making pharmaceutical companies launch an all-out effort to develop a similar pill for women. One-third of women—twice as many as men—sometimes lacked interest in sex, the *Sex in America* survey had shown, with one-quarter not always able to achieve orgasm and one-fifth saying sex was sometimes not pleasurable. Drug company executives naturally wondered if there was a pill, patch, or cream that could solve such problems, and the race for a female (or "pink") Viagra was on. Pfizer was seeing if the pill worked on women, while Zonagan was testing a suppository called Vasofem based on its Vasomax for men. Hormones, specifically testosterone, too could possibly increase women's libido, researchers were thinking (it was actually already being used by some postmenopausal women to increase their sex drive), although everyone working in the field agreed that at this point there were still more unknowns than knowns when it came to female sexuality.[61] "The male erection is understood," said one researcher in 1999, but women's arousal system was a lot more complicated.[62]

Fortunately, a new generation of sex toys specifically made for women's arousal system was readily available at retail stores around the country. "Massagers" had been around for decades, of course, but it was not until the 1970s that the industry was considered respectable. (Norelco, Clairol, Pollenex, Oster, Conair, and Revlon were some well-known companies that extended their expertise in small appliances and personal care to market vibrators.) Sex therapists endorsed the use of such battery-operated gadgets, thinking they were not only good for women to use by themselves but also a great way to add variety to long-term monogamous relationships. For just $15, for example, one could pick up Good Vibration's Crystal Jelly G-Spot; the rubber thing is "a divining rod for the clitoris," thought *Men's Health* (!) in its review of a set of vibrators. Other good choices were Xandria's Little Lady ("curved to tickle the G-spot") and Adam & Eve's Love Wand ("looks like a miniature putter"). "Joy buzzers" were now "more than just a lonely woman's pleasure tool," according to the men's magazine, but also a way to add some literal spark to lovemaking.[63]

## TOUCH HER RIGHT HERE

More hands-on help, one might say, was available for those looking for something more than electronic stimulation. Some couples were attending a weekend retreat called the Sexuality Playshop (later named Retreat for Couples) where participants would "discover a new level of communication and sexuality," according to its brochure. As a more sexually explicit version of the traditional marriage encounter weekend offered by clergy and psychologists, the two-day, $595 Playshop located in northern Georgia taught couples how to "move away from an emphasis on body parts to a greater emphasis on heart and mind." (Other "sex camps" included the Marriage and Family Health Center in Evergreen, Colorado; the Loyola University Sex Therapy Clinic in Maywood, Illinois; Canyon Ranch in Tucson, Arizona; and the Loving Center in Scottsdale, Arizona.) Fifteen or so couples at a time were typically at the Sexuality Playshop, most of them hoping the experience would inject a heavy dose of romance into their relationship. Sex was different than reproduction, explained the leader of the retreat, Jeanne Shaw, and the number of factors required to make a sexual experience a good one was likely to grow the longer couples stayed together. Because normal or "functional" sex was the norm in American society, participants were told, one had to learn how to be erotic, which was the thing missing most often from long-term sexual relationships. Sharing fantasies or "erotic scenarios" was one of the keys to good sex, couples discovered, with women usually having far more vivid imaginations than men. Again, despite the sexual revolution, much about sex remained taboo or "dirty," a legacy of our Puritanical past. Becoming truly erotic, rather than just aroused, thus involved a certain amount of risk, that is, a willingness to do or ask to do something that society might deem immoral or perverse. Likewise, open-mindedness and creativity were the best avenues to eroticism, sex campers took away from the retreat, and the ultimate goal was to develop one's "unique sexual personality."[64]

If sex camp did not bring out one's inner eroticism, a testosterone patch very well might. For men, one of the normal aspects of aging was a drop in testosterone, the hormone largely responsible for libido and sexual performance. (Some researchers, like Theresa Crenshaw, author of *The Alchemy of Love and Lust*, equated these changes with female menopause.) The testosterone patch replaced the hormone that was naturally made by the body, restoring the libido of a sixty-year-old to that of a much younger man. There had been previous ways to deliver testosterone to the body (such as pills, lozenges, and creams), but the patch provided a consistent and correct dosage into the bloodstream, giving men a regular charge to their libidinal battery. Five milligrams a day of Androderm typically worked wonders; moreover, the patch was so effective it was making some men's wives exhausted or late for work. The additional testosterone coursing through men's bodies usually had results beyond a greater desire for sex and harder erections, however. A flattened belly, deeper voice, and more assertive personality were common side effects, all of these welcomed by the patch wearer, who felt younger not just physically but also mentally. While on the patch, most men found themselves with renewed energy, beginning long put-off house repair and maintenance projects or playing competitive sports they had not played in years.[65]

In addition to sexual retreats and tweaking one's body chemistry, a new generation of "sexperts" was helping Americans improve their sex lives. Through the 1990s, Anka Radakovich had advised men on everything from foreplay to fetishes in her "Ask Anka" monthly column in *Details*, frequently drawing on her own extensive experience for material. Although Radakovich's long run in the magazine ended in 1999 ("Men don't need to be told how to perform a triple backflip in bed," said the new editor who killed her column), she had big plans to apply her wealth of knowledge in television and movies. A couple of other, Ivy League–educated women were challenging Radakovich as the queen of the sex advice hill, however. With her masters in sex education from the University of Pennsylvania, Sari Locker certainly had better credentials, at least academically. The twenty-nine-year-old woman used her advanced degree to offer advice on birth control and sexually transmitted diseases in *Teen People* and American Online, and her take was a lot more cautionary than that of Radakovich. Besides Locker ("a Dr. Ruth Westheimer in the body of a Baywatch babe," thought Silvia Sansoni of *Forbes*), there was twenty-six-year-old Amy Sohn, another rising star in sex journalism. The Brown University graduate documented her active dating life in the *New York Press* and had recently published a book, *Run Catch Kiss*, claiming a middle ground between Radakovich and Locker. All were hoping to repeat the success of Candace Bushnell, whose real-life adventures informed *Sex and the City*, the hit HBO series (based on her book of the same name).[66]

Much more conservative on sexual matters was "Dr. Laura," the radio personality doling out advice not much different than Ann Landers and her twin sister Abigail Van Buren did a generation earlier. Xavier Hollander, aka "The Happy Hooker," had been writing a sex advice column in *Penthouse* since 1972, and Dr. Ruth was still plying her more clinical approach to the trade. Women did not have a monopoly on sexual advice in the late nineties, however. Dan Savage was the bad boy of sex journalism, his "Savage Love" syndicated column as blunt and liberal as it could get. "The sexual model that straight people have created doesn't really work" went one of Savage's typical observations, his gayness definitely informing his outside-the-mainstream perspectives. Burning with sexual passion for one's spouse over the course of decades was absurd, he thought, and our culture was setting up much too high expectations for fidelity. Drew Pinsky, aka "Dr. Drew," looked at sexuality much differently as cohost of MTV's "Love Line," consistently praising the virtues of monogamy and intimacy.[67]

Sex advice could also be found in magazines, some of it suggesting that men really were interested in learning things like how to do sexual gymnastics in bed. A third generation of men's magazines was flying off newsstands, making the top contenders of the first generation (*Esquire* and *Playboy*) and second generation (*GQ* and *Men's Health*) look positively stodgy. *Maxim* was the most successful of this new breed, the import from England that focused on drinking, sports, and sex, not necessarily in that order. "Its frat-boy boisterousness (or outright misogyny) would make you think the feminist movement never happened," wrote Richard Turner of *Newsweek*, seeing *Maxim* as a male version of the hypersexual *Cosmopolitan*. "Touch Her Right Here" went a headline on the cover of a 1998 issue, its editors unapologetic about the magazine's blatant crudeness. Given the success of *Maxim*, other "laddie" magazines like *Gear*, *Stuff*, and *FHM* were not surprisingly in the works, a backlash against the pressure men were facing to be political correct, sensitive, and responsible. Laddie magazines were helping men rediscover their "inner swine," as Turner put it, something that had been lost in an age of consensual sex contracts and proposals deemed indecent.[68]

## A RETURN TO MODESTY

Although American popular culture was filled with sexuality, it offered few valuable lessons for those seeking to learn anything really meaningful about this thing called sex. Richard Corliss of *Time* did not like the way sex was being portrayed in the movies, thinking there was precious little eroticism attached to it. Instead, sex had been reduced to a gag (as in *There's Something About Mary*), a vehicle of humiliation (*American Pie*), or an act of violence (*Summer of Sam*), all of these trivializing something that was serious and important. "Lovemaking is a powerful experience, the most convulsive emotional and physical drama in most people's lives," he wrote, "and it warrants as much artful attention from film auteurs as space operas or teen revenge fantasies." Corliss believed some films of the late sixties and early seventies, notably *Midnight Cowboy, Emmanuelle,* and *Last Tango in Paris,* presented sex with the respect it deserved, but the next generation of filmmakers (including Steven Spielberg, George Lucas, and Martin Scorsese) were not interested in romantic sexuality. Corliss loved how sexuality was used in the new film *Eyes Wide Shut,* however, and hoped it would be a hit so other filmmakers would "remember what makes us tick, and tingle, and hurt."[69]

Fin de siècle television also had lots of sex but was not very sexy. MTV's reality show *Undressed* interwove multiple stories centered on sex, but none of the relationships featured were particularly healthy or happy. It was HBO's *Sex and the City* that really had people talking, however, as the show was as good as voyeuristic entertainment could get. In the show, sex columnist Carrie Bradshaw (Sarah Jessica Parker) and her three thirtysomething friends navigate their lives in Manhattan, with much of their time spent talking about and engaging in sex. Critics loved the show, not because it demonstrated how erotic sex was but rather because it showed how mundane and awkward it could be. "It's as real as TV sex has ever been," thought James Poniewozik of *Time*; the show was more real in some ways than "reality" shows like *Undressed.*[70]

For Wendy Shalit, however, *Sex and the City* was precisely what was wrong with sexuality in America, especially with regard to women. Shalit, twenty-three years old in 1999, made a compelling case that her sexy sisters were taking American society down the wrong path; their liberal ways might be good for readers of laddie magazines but not for women themselves. Her just published *A Return to Modesty: Discovering the Lost Virtue* was certainly in the right place at the right time, with the sex scandals of the last couple of years lending credence to her controversial credence. Shalit believed that the sexual revolution had led to women losing power, not gaining it, and argued that the old-fashioned, virtuous ways of the past would be a better platform for their future. "We want our 'feminine mystique' back and with it male honor," she wrote in her book, arguing that modesty was a lot more erotic than random hookups with relative strangers. Even smooching in public was out of bounds, Shalit felt, a good example of how public sexuality had eroded the power of private sexuality. The overexposure of sex and increasing vulgarity of the past few decades was not progressive but regressive, in other words, a neoconservative view that resonated among many. It was hard to disagree that the restraint of the past was a lot more tantalizing than the overt sexuality of the present, as the hidden was always more intriguing than the plainly shown. Most feminists objected heartily to Shalit's thesis, however, claiming that such a simplistic viewpoint did not do justice to women who found their sexual freedom to be overwhelmingly liberating and self-fulfilling.[71]

Shalit was not the only one who thought looking to our sexual past offered the best path for the future. *The Rules*, a self-help book with a decided prefeminist sensibility, had been an unexpected best seller, with a sequel and series of seminars also showing women how to play hard to get. "Rules girls" did not kiss a man on a first date and did not sleep with him for weeks or months; this was one of the ways to catch Mr. Right versus Mr. Just-Wants-to-Have-Sex. Tara McCarthy's 1997 *Been There, Haven't Done That: A Virgin's Memoir* was another manifesto for virtue, as the twenty-five-year-old Harvard graduate made the case that virginity was sexy. New research studies revealed that more conservative values regarding sex were not limited to young women whose views appeared to be shaped primarily by 1950s sitcoms.[72] A 1999 Yankelovich study reported that only 37 percent of Americans thought premarital sex was acceptable, for example, while a UCLA survey found that just 40 percent of college freshmen across the country agreed that "if two people really like each other, it's all right for them to have sex even if they've known each other for a very short time."[73]

End of the century and millennium jitters could be detected beyond the numbers. A number of retro trends were sweeping through American pop culture, in fact, with ballroom and swing dancing considered quite hip among young people, and movies like *Emma* and *The Age of Innocence* praised for their formality, elegance, and grace. Cigars and tattoos were in, these too a throwback to an earlier age of innocence. Would not an equivalent trend in sexuality make sense given the cultural longing for stability and grounding? That too much sex too soon reduced the aphrodisiacal dimension of sexuality, as Shalit (and many others) claimed, was perhaps all the more reason to embrace nineteen-century-century values like innocence, purity, and chasteness. A return to traditional gender roles was a big part of this, of course, and Shalit's "cartel of virtue" among women was another way to bring things back into balance. "Making sex mundane makes for a sexual ethic convenient for male appetites but not for female emotional needs," George Will wrote of Shalit's premise; the conservative Will agreed that things had been out of whack along gender lines since the 1960s.[74]

Was there "a return to modesty" in the ether or were Carrie Bradshaw and her sexed-up gal pals more reflective of the nation's sexual frontier? As the year 2000 approached, predictions about life in the twenty-first century were ubiquitous, with sex included in some experts' forecasts. "Sex will flourish in the twenty-first century as growing openness about sexual matters and new technologies pave the way to new sexual experiences," wrote Kenneth Maxwell in 1997, and virtual sex was just one option we would have in the future. Maxwell, a professor of biology at California State University, Long Beach, and author of *A Sexual Odyssey: From Forbidden Fruit to Cybersex*, believed that sex was finally "emerging tortuously from the dark shadows of secret shame" and that a much bigger sexual revolution than that of the counterculture was on the way. Sex would be no different than other aspects of human behavior like food, clothing, work, or religion, he envisioned, with the taboos attached to it for thousands of years gone. Doctors, rather than sex therapists, would routinely treat sexual problems, he imagined, and the subject would be included in medical schools' basic curricula. Sex toys would be sold openly at the local mall, and prostitution would be decriminalized and regulated by the state.[75]

Maxwell foresaw that it was technology, however, that offered the greatest possibilities for sex to go in new directions and take new forms. "More advanced devices will be able to stimulate the specific pleasure centers of the brain to enhance sensations beyond anything experienced naturally," he predicted, including a noninvasive probing of one's hypothalamus (perhaps by laser) to create a new level of sexual intensity. "The world of sex is at the threshold of trends amounting to a twenty-first-century revolution, bringing about the most dramatic changes in sexual relationships, habits, health, pleasures, pains, and living standards the world has ever seen," he concluded, very optimistic about where sexuality was headed.[76] A new era of sex in America was indeed waiting around the corner, with some changes to take place that even Maxwell could not predict.

# 6

# Ice Age

Things just got a little chillier.

—*Freaky Mammal in the 2002 film* Ice Age

In December 2000, Daphne Merkin of the *New York Times Magazine* mused about the state of sex in America at the turn of the twenty-first century. Many of us suffered from a profound sense of sexual malaise, she believed, for a number of reasons. One of them was our open society in which there were no longer any taboos surrounding sex. "We live in an age in which virtually any type of sexual practice is approved," she wrote, and our knowledge of the erotic lives of celebrities and other strangers was another factor diminishing our personal excitement of sex. Our prevailing ethos of sexual egalitarianism, in which political correctness and showing full respect for one's partner ruled over unbridled lust, was another thing putting a damper on sex. "The narratives of passion that whir in our minds are impervious to the best intentions of both men and women," she suggested; our "compassionate and open formula . . . is morally admirable but ensures dullness in the bedroom." Feminism too had been good for women but bad for sex, she argued. An admittedly nonscientific survey among some of her female friends revealed that a good number of them regularly fantasized about being dominated by an aggressive male, a kind of primal response to the more equal playing field along gender lines. "The politics of erotic desire are essentially undemocratic," it appeared to Merkin, and our elevation of tolerance over the illicit and the public outing of sexual secrets was leading to a more just and transparent society but wreaking havoc on our sex lives. "If you look beneath the kinky surface, you will come upon many more conventional domestic tableaux, in which a lot of us feel left out of the action, resigned as we are to our no longer ardent desires even as our fantasy lives are constantly stoked and stimulated by media images," Merkin concluded, wondering if a more repressive society was more conducive to "private expressions of passion" than the one we had created over the past half century.[1]

Merkin clearly articulated what many Americans were feeling but could not express. The signs of our sexual pathology could be found everywhere. Many Americans were just "not in the mood," according to both research studies and anecdotal evidence; the nation's "sexidemic" was worse than ever if the statistics and cocktail party chatter regarding sexual dysfunction could be believed. Sexless marriages were a regular feature of American life, with many theories proposed and treatments prescribed for such. The still going strong abstinence movement in schools reflected our antisex attitudes, it could be argued, and instilled the idea that sex was dangerous and possibly harmful among a new generation. Despite all this, sex was having its day, as it always does. Americans were pursuing all kinds of sexual experiences in the early 2000s, in fact, attempts to make sex exciting and special. Many were finding that the most pleasurable form of sex was that taking place with and by themselves, however, a sad commentary on our sexually chilly times.

## ONE OF THE GIRLS

If there was any good news about sex in contemporary America, it was that more older people were having it. The graying of the nation's population brought more attention to older folks having sex, something that many believed occurred rarely if at all. The fact was that a good number of septuagenarians and octogenarians were sexually active, with retirement communities an ideal place to find a lover. For decades, doctors had told women to forget about having sex after menopause and that their postreproduction bodies were no longer suited for the activity. This was ridiculous, of course, with many older women finding they were enjoying sex more than ever. Besides being physically pleasurable, sex helped older women remain, in Helen Gurley Brown's words, "functioning females," a way to avoid becoming an "old crone." Brown, the ex-editor-in-chief of *Cosmopolitan* and author of the 1962 *Sex and the Single Girl*, was seventy-eight in 2000 and proud that she and her eighty-three-year-old husband still regularly slept together. "Having somebody make love to us keeps us one of the girls," she wrote in *Newsweek*, believing women of a certain age had to make a conscious effort to remain sexual people. A host of factors—low libido, boredom, marital problems, stress, and, perhaps most important, a shortage of available partners—presented obstacles to having a good sex life after age sixty, she felt, making it necessary to go after it rather than wait for it to appear. But older women frequently had something their younger sisters did not—money—an asset that should be fully exploited to counter their lack of youth. Brown recommended that women take a tip from men by taking a potential lover—especially someone significantly younger—shopping or buying their lover dinner, insisting there was no shame attached to "buying" a sex mate (as long as he delivered). "Women our age should indulge," she declared; sex was a lot more fun and energizing than spoiling grandchildren or baking cookies.[2]

Fortunately for women of a certain age, there appeared to be plenty of opportunities to remain "one of the girls." While the media's obsession with younger women had not changed, many men claimed to favour experience over youth when it came to sex. "Here's to you, Mrs. Robinson," wrote one of them, Paul Theroux, as the play *The Graduate* opened on Broadway in 2002. Even as a teenager, Theroux pined for middle-aged women, with the thought of Ava Gardner in the 1954 film *The Barefoot Contessa* getting him all hot and bothered. Rather than an unstable Lolita, it was the confident, rather domineering Mrs. Robinson or Maria Vargas (Gardner's character) whom Theroux found sexy; knowing what they want was the essence of attractiveness. (Theroux wished Ben had run off with Mrs. Robinson rather than Elaine at the end of the movie.) "Taking charge is the essence of sexual vitality," he declared in *Harper's Bazaar*, considering resourcefulness and independence very desirable traits when it came to pure lust. As well, instead of being focused on the future, as many young women were, most older women had full appreciation for the present, another thing that was very appealing. Similarly, sex was often a means to a particular end—marriage, family, money, or employment—for a young woman, but this was less true for someone older. For a middle-aged or older woman, sex was principally about pleasure, Theroux concluded, making one the ideal choice if seeking out a sexual relationship.[3]

Sex did indeed get better for some women around menopause, but others were not so lucky. Studies showed that a good number of older women had some kind of female sexual dysfunction (FSD), making them less sexually vital. Pharmaceutical companies were no doubt thrilled by the FDA's proposal to make the "morning after" pill available without a prescription, but solving the problem of FSD remained an even bigger business opportunity. Worldwide sales of Viagra were more than $1 billion in 2000, just two years after the drug had been introduced, and the pharmaceutical industry was eager to develop an equivalent drug for women. The facts surrounding Viagra were truly astounding. Four million American men took the pill regularly (4 percent of the total population of Palm Beach County had a prescription for it), and twentysomethings had taken to using it as a party drug. Many believed that Viagra was the beginning of a "second sexual revolution" in which the terms "impotency" and "frigidity" would be permanently retired. A family of drugs dedicated to healing all kinds of sexual problems would soon be on the market, industry insiders promised. This pharmaceutical revolution was equivalent to the counterculture in terms of shaping Americans' attitudes and behavior regarding sex.[4]

It was not for lack of trying that little had been achieved in helping women suffering from low sexual desire or a difficulty becoming aroused. That more women than men reportedly suffered from some kind of sexual dysfunction (43 percent versus 31 percent, according to a well-publicized and often discredited 1999 University of Chicago study) made the medical community that much more intent on developing a "pink Viagra."[5] Hopes for such a drug had been somewhat dashed, however, when it was learned that sildenafil, the active ingredient in Viagra, was no more effective than a placebo in boosting women's arousal. The makers of Cialis believed their drug could work for women, but once again, clinical trials proved disappointing. While men typically became excited through visual cues, emotional connections played a much more significant role in women's sex drive, with no magic pill likely to provide an overall sense of well-being or positive feelings toward a partner. (Freud famously viewed women's sexuality as the "dark continent" of the soul.)[6] "For many women, it seems, the brain also must be involved," observed Allisson Fass of Forbes, as sexual desire for them required something more than just increased blood flow to the genitals.[7]

Until a "desire pill" was developed, all kinds of therapies were being used to treat women with low libido. A company called UroMetrics was trying to market an FDA-approved gadget called the Eros Clitoral Therapy Device, for example, something that harked back to the "pelvis massagers" of the early twentieth century. However, it was a much less complicated form of therapy—testosterone—that was being shown to be particularly effective among women who produced low levels of it naturally.[8] Hundreds of thousands of American men were now taking testosterone for erectile dysfunction and loss of libido, and testosterone was the prescription of choice for the condition sometimes known as andropause, or "male menopause." Some women found that Estratest, a combination of testosterone and estrogen used to relieve menopausal symptoms, had the side effect of sparking their libido. It soon became clear that estrogen-replacement therapy increased a woman's risk of breast cancer and heart disease, however, leading more doctors to prescribe simple testosterone to women to boost sexual desire.[9]

The search for an answer to women's alleged sexual problems was not over, however. In late 2004, the FDA did not approve Procter & Gamble's Intrinsa, a testosterone patch for women, due to concern about that drug's possible long-term side effects.[10] That left women with a less powerful testosterone cream, which worked best among those who experienced a decline in desire as they aged rather than those who always had a low sex drive.[11] Even if a libido drug for women did work, sexual desire was a lot different than sexual satisfaction, critics pointed out, skeptical that anything the pharmaceutical industry introduced would be successful for very long.[12]

Not everyone, however, believed that the massive effort to cure FSD was a noble or even worthwhile cause. Some argued that FSD was, like certain other medical conditions, completely fabricated by the pharmaceutical industry, which was looking for a problem it could solve in order to make money. "It's a social construction invented to benefit the drug companies," said Leonore Tiefer, a psychologist at the New York University School of Medicine who was amazed that much of the medical community had (literally) bought into the idea of FSD.[13] The way that society viewed female sexuality was the real problem, still others maintained, and the idea of "low libido" was simply not a legitimate disorder. Researcher Rosemary Basson argued that female sexual response was more circular than linear, and the male-centric model was all wrong when it came to how and why women experienced arousal and desire. Using the male model of arousal and performance as the standard for women was both bad science and a reflection of the sexism that still existed, these critics (many of them feminists) insisted; the problem was broad in scope and systematic in practice.[14]

## THE CHEMISTRY OF DESIRE

Whether real or not, sexual dysfunction among both women and men represented a main area of interest among contemporary sex researchers. Pfizer, the maker of Viagra, was funding a global survey of sex practices led by Edward Laumann, the University of Chicago sociologist who had spearheaded the 1994 *Sex in America: A Definitive Survey*. Some new research methods bypassed the problems previous students of the field had faced, notably whether participants were telling the truth. Analyzing MRI scans was one such tool, offering a peek into what was going on in men's and women's brains when exposed to sexual stimuli. Male volunteers laid in MRI machines with cuffs around their penis and watched erotic video clips while researchers measured their blood pressure, heart rate, and brain activity, a scientific if not very romantic way to study arousal. (Sonograms were thankfully replacing the cuffs.) Women's reactions to erotic stimuli were tracked via something called a photoplethysmograph, a tampon-shaped device measuring vaginal blood flow. The findings of such tests would lead to a greater understanding of mood-related sexual problems, researchers believed, something that would have made Alfred Kinsey himself proud.[15]

In trying to determine what Michael D. Lemonick of *Time* called "the chemistry of desire," sex researchers certainly had their work cut out for them. The field had obviously come a long way since the 1920s, when the scholarly study of human sexuality began in earnest. The biology of sex was as complex as any physical function, however, with hormones, neurotransmitters, and other parts of the human body working together to achieve the tri-part sequence of desire, arousal, and orgasm. (Some researchers were now discarding this linear, male-oriented progression for a more circular and flexible pattern, especially for women.) Besides a hormonal concoction of testosterone, estrogen, and oxytocin, brain chemicals like dopamine, serotonin, and norepinephrine went into the desire and arousal mix, a biological process nothing short of amazing. Further complicating research in the field was the fact that a variety of parts of the brain—the basal ganglia, anterior insula cortex, amygdala, cerebellum, and hypothalamus, to name just some—collaborated to create human sexual response. Throw in gender differences and the wild cards of setting, mood, and experience, and it became instantly clear that sex research presented challenges that even the best and brightest scientists would find daunting.[16]

Unfortunately, sex researchers often had to rely exclusively on drug companies to sponsor their work as federal funds dried up. As always, conservative politicians were uneasy about public money being used to study anything to do with sex, even if the subject was a central force in most people's lives. Budget deficits and the war on terror made sex research a particularly precarious enterprise in the mid-2000s as the National Institute of Health chose not to award grants to those working in the field. Boston University's Sexuality and Research Treatment Program, which had been studying human sexual arousal for twenty years, was one casualty, with one Republican congressman calling its work "not a wise use of taxpayer money." With Big Pharma calling the sex research shots, sexual dysfunctions were increasingly being treated with medication, with psychological aspects often left out of the process. Emotions had a strong influence on sexual feelings, obviously, but they were frequently ignored in favor of a physical condition that could be "cured" by a pill. Gaining insight into the deep psychological well of sexuality offered the possibility of improving relationships and even lowering the divorce rate, but there was much more money to be made with a pharmaceutical that promised to aid the mechanics of sex. The taboos surrounding sexuality still could be found in politicians' decisions to cut funding for sex research, and the embarrassment and shame attached to the subject resulted in a lack of answers to important questions about the mystery of sexual behavior.[17]

Still, sex research had undoubtedly revealed many important findings, many of them confirming gender stereotypes. Men had, in general, greater sexual desire in terms of both frequency and intensity than women. "Decades of data show that on average, men think more about sex, fantasize more about it, work harder to get it, place more importance on it, want to have it more, initiate it more, and masturbate more," Catherine Elton wrote in *Psychology Today* in 2010. Levels of desire varied considerably more among women than men, with both age and day of the month being important factors. Most significant, perhaps, sexual desire among women often followed arousal, something that was not true of men. Again, context was key for women, re-searchers agreed, and relationships, circumstances, emotions, and self-esteem played key roles in their relative sexual contentment. Men typically believed sex for sex's sake was entirely sufficient, in other words, while women tended to view sex within the context of a relationship. Feeling good about them-selves both emotionally and physically also was central for women's sexual desire, something that could be said to be less true for men.[18] "For men, the big sexual organ is the penis," said Leslie Schover, a psychologist and sexual-ity expert at the University of Texas in Houston, while "for women, it's the brain."[19]

But why did many happily married women, very content with the level of safety, comfort, love, and respect in their relationships, still experience a lack of desire for sex with their partners? Researchers frankly did not know, yet theories abounded. Intimacy was one thing but desire was something else, therapists proposed, and the forbidden and erotic dimensions of sex were often lost within the socially approved institution of marriage. Familiarity also diminished desire, researchers proposed, believing that innovation and "newness" were essential elements to sexual excitement. Some women found their roles as wives, mothers, and professionals to be desexualizing, making it difficult to segue from caretaker or breadwinner to sexpot. Serving mul-tiple roles could be distracting, but many experts believed there were deeper reasons for reports of widespread FSD. Some in fact suggested that the very idea of what was "normal" desire was highly subjective, and the very term was impossible to define and measure. As obsessed as we were with sex as a society, the precise workings of it remained largely a mystery, the solving of which could not be expected anytime soon.[20]

## OOPS, I DID IT AGAIN

While millions of dollars were being spent trying to figure out how to in-crease sexual desire and arousal among men and women, many Americans were equally determined to quash such feelings among teens. The sexual-abstinence movement, in which teens pledged their chastity until marriage, was still going strong in the early 2000s. Big, revival-like conferences were now being held in support of the movement, and celebrities like Enrique Iglesias and Jessica Simpson announced they adhered to the promise. And despite the suggestive title of her big hit, "Oops, I Did It Again" (and live act that rivaled Madonna's in pure, unadulterated sexuality), pop star Britney Spears maintained she too was still a virgin. (Christina Aguilera, meanwhile, made no such claim, her video "Dirrty" helping to make her the new bad girl of pop.) Abstinence was the official policy in almost a quarter of the country's school districts in 2001, with sex-ed classes focused on the merits of conjugal intercourse and high failure rate of contraceptives. There was some evidence that abstinence pledges succeeded in delaying intercourse among teenagers, although those who broke it were less likely to use birth control (and more likely to get a sexually transmitted disease [STD]). It also appeared that swearing off intercourse made one more interested in engaging in oral or anal sex, each surprisingly popular among teenagers, studies showed. In terms of maintaining one's virginity, oral sex was not much different than kissing to many teens, since each act was not seen as a violation of the commitment that "true love waits."[21]

Interestingly, as Margaret Talbot pointed out, current attitudes toward teenage sexuality seemed to be more conservative than during the so-called repressed 1950s. Talbot had recently watched the 1959 movie *A Summer Place*, starring the quintessentially wholesome Sandra Dee and Troy Donahue, and was amazed to see how sexuality was treated in the film. Although there could very well be consequences for "going all the way," the movie took it for granted that teenagers wanted to have sex. It was natural and normal for even "good girls" like Sandra Dee's seventeen-year-old character to have sexual desire and want to fulfill it, according to *A Summer Place* and similar postwar melodramas. The same idea was now more associated with "bad girls," however, a good example of the more general decline of sexuality in America over the past few decades. In her controversial *Harmful to Minors: The Perils of Protecting Children from Sex*, Judith Levine made a similar observation, that is, unlike in the not so recent past, kids today were taught that sex was dirty, dangerous, and shameful. Did the spread of STDs, as well as AIDS, cause this sea change in Americans' attitudes toward teenage sexuality? Did it stem from a need to try to shield young people from the sexual imagery and language that had proliferated in popular and consumer culture? It was not clear, but there was little doubt that Americans had become more repressed about teenage sexuality over the past half century.[22]

The passing of the Welfare Reform policy in 1996, which made public money available to schools teaching abstinence in sex-ed classes, certainly

had something to do with adults' greater fears and concerns about teenage sexuality. In just three years, one-third of all public school districts had
adopted abstinence-only curricula, propagating a decidedly sinister view of
youthful sex. In one video promoting abstinence to teens, for example, a
teenage boy asked a nurse, "What if I want to have sex before I get married?"
"Well, I guess you just have to be prepared to die," the nurse replied; the idea
of sex leading to death is extreme, to say the least. An abstinence program
called Facing Reality did not cite death as one of the possible consequences of
premarital sex but included a host of other unpleasant developments including pregnancy, fear of pregnancy, AIDS, guilt, herpes, disappointing parents,
chlamydia, inability to concentrate on school, syphilis, embarrassment, abortion, shotgun wedding, gonorrhea, selfishness, pelvic inflammatory disease,
and, last but not least, heartbreak. Although parents overwhelmingly favored
an abstinence-plus program, such an approach was viewed by conservatives
as ambiguous, capable of sending "missed messages" to teens. Ambiguity
confused young people, supporters of abstinence-only sex ed believed, although kids were facing and managing complex, multifaceted situations every
day of their lives.[23]

One of the largest abstinence-education companies in the United States
was the Dallas-based Aim for Success, which in 2001 made 2,500 presentations to middle and high school students. More than 150,000 teens heard the
Aim for Success message that year from fourteen different speakers (each
one doing a finger-puppet show involving "Ken" and "Barbie"). All kinds of
don't-do-it merchandise, including jewelry, T-shirts, and pencils, could be
purchased from the Abstinence Clearinghouse catalog, which also offered
videos, commercials, lesson plans, and advertising for forty-nine different
motivational speakers. "Virgins, Inc.," as *Rolling Stone* called it in 2002, was
big business, with quite a few abstinence entrepreneurs taking advantage of
the public money to be had. Curricula were both secular and faith based, with
humor often used to appeal to teens' tastes. As conservative as abstinence
programs were, the ultra-right believed any kind of sex education did not
belong in schools, thinking the words "condom" or "abortion" should not be
uttered. Funded programs were supposed to subscribe to the doctrine that "a
mutually faithful monogamous relationship in the context of marriage is the
expected standard of human sexual activity," but some were known to deviate
from what was called "the marriage standard." Best Friends, a program that

operated in ninety schools in fourteen states, for example, promoted abstinence until high school graduation, believing that was a much more reachable
and measurable goal than waiting until marriage.[24]

Supporters of sexual abstinence were no doubt happy to see that their programs appeared to be working. Sexual activity among teenagers had decreased
15 percent through the 1990s, according to the Centers for Disease Control
(CDC), and there had been a 20 percent decline in the teen birth rate. Still,
religious conservatives, armed with millions of dollars courtesy of Uncle Sam,
looked for new, more persuasive ways to prevent teenagers from having premarital sex. (The George W. Bush administration was even more committed
to abstinence than the Clinton administration, with sex ed as one of the key
battlegrounds in the ongoing "culture war.") One sex-ed curriculum making
the rounds was Worth the Wait, which included a graphic presentation of
STDs such as genital warts to make its point. Most doctors believed in providing students with as much information as possible and making condoms
freely available. Some physicians, however, seeing data that there had been a
rise in STDs among adolescents, were choosing to develop programs that vividly illustrated the potential consequences of casual sex. Images of lesions on
a cervix, shriveled fallopian tubes, and a distended penis covered with sores as
shown in the "Passion and Principles" workshop were not pretty sights, clearly
designed to make teens swear off sex until their wedding night.[25]

With many schools preaching abstinence, the debate over sex education
remained a contested one. Some schools had taken to passing out "ATM"
cards to students in health class, the acronym standing for "Abstinence Till
Marriage." (The cards expired when their owners got married.) Many parents and teens continued to question whether abstinence was the best (or
only) approach to take, the bigger question being if schools were teaching
kids too much about sex or not enough. Because it was grounded in what
were arguably the three most emotionally charged topics—sex, politics, and
religion—the issue would just not go away. (Only the evolution–versus–
intelligent design clash in science classes was perhaps more heated.) Sex, a
private matter, instantly became a public one when taught in schools using
government money, this only adding fuel to the fire. Three states—California,
Pennsylvania, and Maine—had turned down public funding and were taking
their own approach, recognizing that abstinence was a very narrow slice of
sex education. Although the vast majority of states accepted the government

money, curricular decisions tended to be made on a local level, with course content varying considerably from community to community. Some schools invited Planned Parenthood to make presentations, for example, while others hosted outside lecturers with a decidedly Christian point of view. The time spent on sex ed also differed greatly; some schools set aside a couple of hours for the subject while others devoted a whole semester, this alone showing how divided educators were on the topic.[26]

Although just 15 percent of parents reportedly wanted an abstinence-only curriculum taught to their kids, the dangling of federal and state funds was simply too big of a carrot for many schools to turn down when deciding about what approach to take to sex education. By 2005, 35 percent of public school districts in the United States had gone that route, with 51 percent of districts adopting an "abstinence-plus" (chastity preferred but information on birth control and preventing STDs given) approach. The remaining 14 percent used a comprehensive program covering a wide range of sex-related issues (including abortion and homosexuality), with schools neither endorsing nor discouraging premarital sex. Seventy-five percent of parents believed this approach was best, research showed, but schools, strapped for money, most often chose the abstinence course for purely economic reasons. Grassroots marketing of the abstinence message was also a powerful incentive for students to take the pledge. Teens could take a "Chastity Challenge" online, join a local "Pure Love Club," or wear "purity rings," all attempts by abstinence supporters to have more kids join the cause. There were even "WaitWear" panties for girls bearing the message "Virginity Lane. Exit when married" or "No vows. No Sex" to ward off any boy thinking he would succeed where others might have failed. Endorsements from famous women were another strategy, with Miss America 2003 declaring she was abstaining from sexual activity (as well as from drinking and drugs, quite tellingly).[27] One Virginia Beach teacher told her ninth-grade class they could be arrested for having premarital sex while teens at Bozeman High School in Montana were taught that condoms cause cancer, extreme examples of how committed some adults were to the abstinence cause.[28]

## GIRLS GONE WILD

For those who were wondering what teens were actually up to sexually, a study published in the *American Journal of Sociology* in 2004 told them everything they wanted to know (and perhaps did not want to know). Over a period of eighteen months, researchers attempted to document every romantic and sexual encounter among high school students in "Jefferson City," a midwestern town. Most of the students surveyed had at least one relationship during that time, not surprisingly, and most of these relationships involved what the authors termed an "exchange of fluids." A little more than half of the one thousand students were sexually active, with the "first time" taking place at an average age of fifteen and a half. What was most interesting about the study's findings was the network of relationships among the students; over a third of them were somehow linked together romantically in a kind of six-degrees-of-separation matrix, which posed considerable risk in terms of spreading STDs. One person abstaining from sex or using a condom would thus have a domino effect throughout the chain, in other words, something of considerable interest to the CDC's Division of STD Prevention.[29]

Because they watched a lot of it, television likely played an important role in shaping teenagers' sexual behavior. Researchers at the RAND Corporation found that a particular episode of *Friends*—the one in which Rachel became pregnant after Ross's condom broke—left a very strong imprint on teens. Rubbers were not perfect, kids recalled with vivid clarity six months after they saw the episode, a lesson whose effectiveness those teaching abstinence could only wish for.[30] Television more often served as a tutorial of the joy of sex rather than the risks involved, however. Characters on television shows popular with teens such as *7th Heaven* and *The OC* routinely lost their virginity (on what was often billed as the "very special episode"). Teens were also having sex on shows like *Desperate Housewives*, *Gilmore Girls*, and *Everwood*; all this televisual hooking up was something the more conservative were sure influenced young peoples' actual behavior.[31]

More than fictional characters, however, it was real-life young women who, for better or worse, served as role models for teen and tween girls. When it came to "bad girls" like Paris Hilton, Lindsay Lohan, and Nicole Richie, it was definitely for the worse, most agreed. Partying endlessly, regular stints in rehab, frequent brushes with the law, taping themselves having sex, and questionable decisions like appearing in public without underwear made many parents worry about their daughters' adoration for the celebrities. Miley Cyrus, fifteen years old in 2008, seemed to instantly go from good to bad with a seminaked incident, and Jamie Lynn Spears was showing all signs of following in the now naughty footsteps of her older sister by becoming pregnant at age 16. Taking their cue from these women who seemed to be having loads of fun, some girls were picking out sexy clothes, listening to music with suggestive lyrics, and flirting with boys, embracing a kind of "slut-chic" lifestyle. Was America raising a generation of "prosti-tots," some wondered, millions of "bad girls" who would grow up to be "bad women"? Fears intensified when a group of Massachusetts high schoolers reportedly agreed to all become pregnant; if true, this is certainly a real-life example of "girls gone wild." "In one generation, girls seemed to have moved from Easy-Bake to easy virtue," Belinda Luscombe quipped in *Time*; she blamed the media and celebrity culture for this scary development.[32]

The technologies that had appeared over the past generation certainly seemed to be contributing to this shift in girls' behavior. Posting revealing photos of oneself on Facebook was not unusual for teenage girls in order to get attention or become popular, nor was sending even sexier images to boys via an e-mail or text (or "sext"). Boys typically responded enthusiastically upon seeing topless or almost naked pictures of their friends from school (they had often requested them in the first place), although boyfriends were usually not as thrilled to have others share them. In one respect, it made sense that teens associated their emerging sexuality with digital technology, having grown up with it all their lives. Despite the debate over sex ed in schools, the Internet was now how most teens learned about sexuality. The tonnage of graphic information online replaced much of the need for having "the talk" with one's parents or listening to a teacher explain the mechanics of reproduction. "Inappropriate material" was hard to miss online even if one wanted to; the average age of first exposure to Internet pornography was considered to be eleven years old. Filters to block such images from computers were hardly perfect, with many a middle school student knowing how to get around censorship programs like Net Nanny. Even many teens and tweens felt online porn provided too much sexual information too soon but, since it was out there and part of life, was worth a look.[33]

If sexuality was repressed at most American high schools, it was celebrated at many colleges. Student-generated sex magazines were being published at some of America's top universities, some of them having faculty advisers, institutional funding, and corporate sponsors. Boston University had *Boink* ("user-friendly porn"), Vassar had *Squirm* (a "magazine of smut and sensibility"), Yale had *SWAY* (*Sex Week at Yale*), Harvard had *H Bomb* (a "literary arts magazine about sex and sexual issues"), the University of Chicago had *Vita Excolatur* ("Life Enriched," roughly), and Columbia had *Outlet*. Although these publications (some of them printed as hard copies and others available online) included photos, articles, and columns à la *Playboy* or *Penthouse* from the 1970s, they were a long way from your father's sex magazine. Besides their more intellectual qualities, the magazines illustrated the cultural changes that had taken place over the decades. Having grown up in an era of open sexuality and a more equal playing field in terms of gender, the "millennial generation" appeared to be perfectly comfortable with sexual content, these magazines suggested. Sex was, simply, interesting, and the rebellious aspects once associated with it were long gone.[34] As well, documenting the details of their lives through blogs and other online outlets was natural to this generation of college students. The fact that they were writing a lot about sex did not necessarily mean they were having a lot of sex, however, something that was borne out by surveys.[35]

In fact, abstinence clubs could be found at some of these same elite universities, a good example of the extreme diversity of millennials. Harvard's True Love Revolution (TLR) was founded in 2006, and its members' claim that sexual abstinence was aligned with "true feminism" was a source of considerable contention on campus. Princeton and MIT each had chapters of the Anscombe Society (named after Elizabeth Anscombe, the British philosopher and student of Ludwig Wittgenstein who argued against premarital sex), with its members also subscribing to the idea that sex should be limited to marriage between a man and woman. Although most college students did not have as many sexual partners as one might think (one study showed that nearly 80 percent reported having had one or no partner over the past year), "hookup culture" was a pervasive presence on many campuses. Abstinence groups offered an attractive alternative to students feeling pressured to be part of that culture; its countercultural message that personal fulfillment could be found outside immediate gratification was a 180-degree turn from that found on college campuses thirty or forty years earlier.[36]

Those opposed to premarital sex suffered a major blow when the Obama administration cut most federal funding of abstinence-only sex-ed programs. In her book *The Purity Myth*, however, Jessica Valenti made the case that what she called "the virginity movement" remained a powerful force.

Antifeminist groups, religious leaders, and ultraconservative politicians were using abstinence to curtail women's rights, Valenti argued, and this was the real objective of the movement. Reeling from their loss of funding and some public embarrassments (like Bristol Palin, daughter of conservative lightning rod and Tea Party member Sarah Palin, becoming pregnant), abstinence supporters were "rebranding" their cause and were not about to go away. Ironically, Bristol Palin was soon named the poster girl for the movement, promoting the message that abstinence was the best way to avoid teen pregnancy (despite her previously calling that message "unrealistic" and having a baby). "If girls realized the consequences of sex, nobody would be having sex," she said in a 2009 article in *People* magazine; the abstinence movement was proud to have a pretty and famous face attached to its cause.[37]

While the percentage of young adults reporting they were virgins increased through the 2000s, according to a National Center for Health Statistics study, the "hookup culture" was by all accounts more reflective of college students' sex lives. More students were opting for casual sex over dating or serious relationships, *USA Today* reported in 2011, with a number of reasons for the rise of "friends with benefits," as the arrangement was known. More women than men on most college campuses made the latter more in demand, for one thing, increasing the likelihood that a relationship would be brief and sexual. Many women were equally happy with such an arrangement, however, not wanting to get serious with someone so early in their lives. Serious relationships could be a real hassle, many students were deciding, especially if their plans included study abroad, graduate school, or internships. As well, juggling school and work was more difficult in a down economy, meaning there was less time to build a serious relationship. The result was that young people found themselves dating after having sex, a reversal of the traditional arc of romance and precisely the opposite of what advocates of abstinence had fought so hard for.[38]

## QUEER AS FOLK

Of course, not just teens but also all Americans were exposed to popular culture, especially television, steeped in sexuality. NBC, for example, had *Coupling*, a show about the sexual (mis)adventures of a group of thirtysomething Chicagoans (a kind of sexed-up, midwestern *Friends*). Adapted from a British cult hit, *Coupling* presented some kind of sexual fiasco in each and every episode, inspired by the apocryphal maxim that adults think about sex every six seconds.[39] Showtime had *Queer as Folk*, which, like NBC's *Will and Grace*, helped to bring gay culture further into the mainstream. "QAF opens the closet of gay TV sexuality and chucks in a neon stick of dynamite," wrote James Poniewozik of *Time* after seeing the first ten minutes of the pilot (a sex scene set in a disco).[40] The show, also adapted from a British series, tracked the lives (especially the sex lives) of five fictional gay men in Pittsburgh—that it was not set in San Francisco or New York was part of the appeal. Interestingly, half of the show's viewers were women (most of them, presumably, heterosexual), this too a sign that one did not have to be a gay man to enjoy peeking into their world. Likewise, many gay men loved *Sex and the City*, finding the lives of four straight women (again, much of the action centered around sex) to be very similar to their own. Some believed, in fact, that *Sex and the City* was really about gay men and that the straight women were simply standing in as more commercially viable surrogates. That show wound down in 2004 after a six-season run that stretched, if not completely obliterated, the boundaries of sex on television.[41]

A real-life *Sex and the City* could be found at monthly parties sponsored by CAKE, a New York based group promoting female sexual pleasure. CAKE parties were "ribald affair[s] where women rule[d] and men [were] thankful," as *Forbes* (!) described them in 2004, with hundreds of people showing up for what might be described as sexual raves themed around female fantasies. CAKE's first event in 2000 was called the "Porn Party," and its second "Striptease.a.thon," suggesting how ribald these affairs really were. The three cofounders of CAKE believed there was an opportunity to turn CAKE into an international brand centered around women's sexuality, a kind of female-centric *Playboy*. Thousands of women subscribed to the organization's online newsletter, with CAKE-branded clothing, cosmetics, and "handpicked sex accessories" available on the company's website. *A Piece of CAKE: Recipes for Female Sexual Pleasure*, a guidebook for women who wanted to explore and express their sexuality, was published in 2005, with a reality show also in the works. CAKE ran out of steam a couple of years later, however, and the financial meltdown was no doubt playing a role in crashing its men-by-invitation-only party.[42]

Alongside the ever-increasing sexualization of television and opportunity to engage in sexual "happenings," pornography had by the year 2000 become an almost inescapable presence in American culture. Its ubiquity was reflected by an episode of *Friends*, the most popular television show in the country. In the episode "The One with Free Porn," Chandler and Joey are the happy beneficiaries of a cable channel delivering continuous pornography at no cost. Worrying that their televisual windfall would suddenly stop, the two watch the channel almost twenty-four hours a day, something that shapes their general outlook on life. "I was just at the bank, and there was this really hot teller, and she didn't ask me to go do it in the vault," Chandler tells Joey, the latter equally surprised that a sexy pizza delivery woman had not tried to seduce him. "We have to turn off the porn," Chandler dryly says to his friend, advice that real-life Americans may have wanted to take. The media universe was saturated with pornography, with cable television indeed providing viewers with nonstop X-rated programming. On-demand television services such as the pay-per-view reality show *Can You be a Porn Star?* which made its debut in 2004, were another way Americans were having sexual content piped directly into their homes. HBO's 2004 six-episode documentary about the California porn industry, *Pornucopia: Going Down in the Valley*, offered a rare peek into Hollywood's multibillion-dollar business; the series was a spin-off of the channel's sexually explicit show *Real Sex*. Hollywood produced around four hundred feature films a year while the porn industry made about eleven thousand annually, a reflection of Americans' nearly insatiable demand for voyeuristic and vicarious sex.[43]

However, it was not television, videos, or DVDs but rather the Internet that was mostly responsible for the recent explosion in pornography. Affordable, easily accessed, and, most important, anonymous, online porn exponentially accelerated the consumption (and creation) of sexual content around the world. Web pages of pornography increased 1,800 percent from 1998 to 2003, with hard-core sex estimated to account for 7 percent of total Internet content. Accidentally coming across porn while surfing the Internet was not unusual, with many a teenager and even child surprised to see the kind of images that popped up on their screens. Most adult consumers of Internet porn were "recreational" users, a 2001 study showed, with most of them (overwhelmingly male) masturbating while online. Psychologists and therapists were divided on whether married men should let their wives know they enjoyed online pornography, with some wives considering the habit a kind of cheating. Many experts were concerned about how online porn affected couples' relationships, and considerable evidence showed that the activity could cause serious damage. More divorces were being blamed for a husband's excessive interest in online pornography, and many boyfriend/girlfriend relationships were suffering from the man's obsessive behavior. Some men who had once rushed home to have sex with their partner were now hurrying home with equal haste to watch porn and masturbate before their partners got home, a good example of the kind of unhealthy habits the activity could potentially cause.[44]

Given the effects it was having on people's lives, especially their relationships, it would not be an exaggeration to say that Internet pornography represented a landmark development in the history of sexuality. Never before had so much exposure to sexual imagery been available to so many. Like Chandler and Joey, heavy users developed unrealistic expectations about women's sexual behavior, with compulsiveness another serious problem. The specificity of Internet porn was where much of the appeal resided, that is, one could find the specific body, body part, act, posture, or expression by which one was most turned on. "The Internet is the crack cocaine of sexual addiction," said Jennifer Schneider, coauthor of *Cybersex Exposed: Simple Fantasy or Obsession*, making a strong case that unlimited online porn often proved damaging to one's heath, career, and relationships. "The image of a lonely, isolated man masturbating to his computer is the Willy Loman metaphor of our decade," added Mark Schwartz, director of the Masters and Johnson clinic in St. Louis. That other men ended up preferring that form of sex over that with real human beings was perhaps even more disturbing as it subverted one of the key attributes of sexuality—its unique ability to enhance intimacy between two people.[45]

For men in a committed relationship, however, was watching pornography really a form of cheating? The question was not new but, with the advent of online porn, more relevant than ever. Like the experts, ordinary Americans were divided on the subject, with men not surprisingly more likely to say "no" than women. A 2004 study found that married people who committed adultery were three times more likely to be users of Internet pornography than noncheaters, suggesting there was at least a correlation between the two activities. But lusting in thought was a lot different than lusting in action, most Americans agreed, and the betrayal that came with viewing porn on a laptop or television was a relatively minor one, if one at all. In fact, given the pervasiveness of sexual imagery in popular culture, all married people would be guilty of infidelity if a strict definition of betrayal were enforced. Fantasy was different than reality, one could fairly say, and viewing porn was not much different than consuming any other fictitious form of entertainment. "Get over it," sex columnist Dan Savage told a female reader unhappy about her boyfriend's occasional porn habit, thinking she was better off finding a woman, dog, or "blind guy" than trying to prevent the average man from looking at naked people on his computer. And despite the findings from the 2004 study, watching porn could possibly serve as a means for men to satisfy their fantasies virtually, a much lesser evil than having real-life extramarital affairs or visiting prostitutes.[46]

## THREESOMES, FOURSOMES, AND MORESOMES

Perhaps inspired by pornography, Americans were now engaging in various forms of sexuality once considered fringe. Due much in part to online social networking, interest in sadomasochistic sex was growing in the United States, both shaping and reflecting its acceptance in mainstream popular culture. Sadomasochism could be found in everything from Madonna's outfits to Anne Rice novels, *Sex and the City*, and Versace advertising, its ubiquity making once shocking Robert Mapplethorpe photographs seem not so scandalous. There were 250 SM organizations across the country in 2004, with members engaging in spanking, bondage, and a host of other activities involving domination, submission, and, frequently, a bit of pain. (Those seriously into sadomasochistic sex called it SM rather than the more popular but strictly amateur "S and M.") Restraint on bedposts, often with handcuffs, or punishment/reward fantasies (e.g., teacher/pupil, master/slave, parent/child, or owner/pet) represented the lighter end of sadomasochism, a way to add some novelty and excitement to relationships. The whip-bearing, stiletto-wearing dominatrix was the most commonly conjured image of SM, but researchers in the field found that most women taking part preferred submission over domination (and vice versa for men). Most important, it was "regular" people who enjoyed safe, consensual, sadomasochistic sex, researchers made clear, many of them attending social events, conventions, and contests dedicated to the activity, just as with any other interest or hobby.[47]

More regular folks were also now enjoying anal sex; this too was only recently considered something regular folks just did not do. Anal sex was in fact fast becoming a regular feature of heterosexual couples' bedroom activities, according to the Centers for Disease Control's National Survey of Family Growth. Thirty-eight percent of men between twenty and thirty-nine and 33 percent of women between eighteen and forty-four engaged in the practice, the survey found, substantially higher numbers than a similar study from 1992. Sex toy stores confirmed that the trend was real. One, Babeland had increased its offering of its anal-sex workshop from once to three or four times a year, the difference being that now straight women wanted to learn more about it. Couples were attracted to the practice because of its intimacy and because it remained somewhat of a taboo. More straight guys appeared to be interested in being on the receiving end of anal sex as well, with Babeland reporting higher than ever sales of "strap-ons." Another device called the Aneros was selling briskly: the doctor-created, FDA-approved prostate stimulator designed to please the male G-spot (often referred to as the P-spot or He-spot). Doctors had recently discovered that prostate stimulation could have anticancer benefits, making anal sex for men not just a kinky activity to add to one's sexual repertoire but, even better, something that was possibly good for you.[48]

Others were choosing variety over role-playing or alternative kinds of intercourse. There were probably hundreds of thousands of polyamorous Americans (some claimed they represented 2 percent of adults), all of them openly committed to loving more than one person at a time. Polyamorous people, or "polys," believed monogamy was not natural and looked to all the secretive nonmonogamous behavior going on as support for their view. (Most animal species were polyamorous, they also pointed out, even our close cousin the bonobo chimpanzee and the allegedly monogamous swan.) Importantly, most polys insisted their lifestyle choice was less about sex than love, distancing themselves from the clearly sex-based swinger culture. Rather than betray their partners or join the swinging/swapping crowd, polys accepted that they could have multiple loving relationships. More was more for the polyamorous (the term, derived from the Greek root for "many" and the Latin root for "love," was coined by one Morning Glory Zell in 1990). "Love doesn't subtract; it multiplies," wrote science fiction writer Robert Heinlein; his 1961 novel *Stranger in a Strange Land* posed the possibility of loving more than one person at a time. The book was credited with sparking the polyamorous movement, with Robert Rimmer's 1965 novel *The Harrad Experiment* also inspiring some to choose relationships not mandating sexual exclusivity. George and Nena O'Neill's 1972 self-help book *Open Marriage* accelerated the trend, as did the generally liberal climate of the counterculture. It was, again, the Internet that took the movement to a whole new level, however, as polys were now much more able to connect with each other and find multiple or "multipartner" relationships through social networks.[49]

Like sadomasochistic sex, multipartner relationships appeared to be an ascendant theme in mainstream advertising. In 2005, Chuck Klosterman observed what he called an "orgy trend" in magazine ads, the underlying message being that buying the products advertised would allow consumers to have sex with multiple partners at the same time. "To consume media these days is to be assaulted by advertising images of threesomes, foursomes, and moresomes," he wrote in *Esquire*, with group sex scenarios depicted in ads for products and services as diverse as vodka, shower gel, and a casino. Klosterman believed this was a lifestyle too unrealistic for most consumers to relate to, however; he was not sure "normal people" even wanted to have three-way sex. Even if they did, the idea that a certain brand of vodka would make it more likely to experience group sex was just too farfetched, he suggested, and ad people were clearly crossing the line with this approach.[50]

Arguably the most sexualized advertising was that being produced by the retailer American Apparel. Just as Calvin Klein had attracted attention (most of it critical) in the eighties and nineties for his highly sexual advertising, so was American Apparel getting rebuked for its racy ads in the 2000s. Unlike Abercrombie & Fitch, which was marketing its clothing to teens and young adults with an overtly sexual but still wholesome California surf aesthetic, the primary inspiration for American Apparel's advertising appeared to be retro pornography. Models in the company's T-shirt and underwear print ads were more "real" than beautiful and were often depicted in what most people would agree were sexual situations. The young men and women looked like they just had or were about to have sex or, more precisely, perform in a circa 1970s porn film or photo shoot. (Store décor featured *Penthouse* magazine covers from the 1970s and 1980s.) American Apparel's website included additional images many described as "pervy," so much so that it was considered by a trade magazine for the porn industry to be "one of the finest soft-core Web sites going these days." Dov Charney, the company's president and creator of the ads, believed its advertising aesthetic reflected the ethos and lifestyle of its target audience, a generation in tune with and eager to express their sexuality.[51]

The American retail scene was getting sexier in other ways. Shopping for erotica, an activity in which one might have (literally) bumped into sleazy men wearing little else but a London Fog, was now often a high-end retail experience. In New York's SoHo area, for example, there was Kiki de Montparnesse, the name alone suggesting this was not your don't-touch-the-magazine-unless-you're-going-to-buy-it kind of sex shop. Run by a couple of people from the fashion industry, Kiki de Montparnesse was a place to, in their words, "explore intimacy," with sex toys rebranded as "instruments of pleasure." (Dildos were referred to as "dilettos" at the store, the most expensive one being a Mi-Su titanium model going for a cool $3,750.) Original photos by Man Ray, Irving Penn, and Richard Avedon hung on the walls, with a velvet-draped dressing room in the back to try on things like a $995 cashmere robe. At Babeland's SoHo store, customers could arrange a private shopping session and have the whole place to themselves, with a sex educator included in the deal. Uptowners, meanwhile, could do their sex toy shopping at Myla, a British lingerie company on the Upper East Side. Besides the pricy bras and panties (including a bejeweled G-string), Myla sold things like the Bone, a sleek, hand-finished resin vibrator designed by Tom Dixon (and at $380, one-tenth the price of the Mi-Su).[52]

Much cheaper "dilettos" could be had at the store around the corner. Vibrators were now being advertised on MTV and sold at Duane Reade, Walgreens, and other drugstores, with condom makers targeting a mass market with very affordable models that still did the trick. Trojan's Tri-Phoria ($39.99), Lifestyle's A: Muse ($19.99), and Durex's Allure ($19.99) were all selling like hotcakes in 2011; the embarrassment that once came with purchasing the product was gone. The official outing of the vibrator was acknowledged as having taken place with the airing of a 1998 episode of *Sex and the City*, "The Turtle and the Hare" (the "hare" being the Rabbit Pearl, an actual device). Since then, vibrators have been considered rather chic, something a woman in touch with her sexuality is likely to own. Dr. Laura Berman's line of sex toys was quite popular, especially after the sex and relationship expert mentioned her company's Aphrodite model on *Oprah*. Most men were all for women owning and using a device that resembled their penis, not feeling threatened by them despite the fact they were more efficient than their phalluses (and battery powered). The iPhone even had an app for vibrators, although for the time being at least, Apple had no plans to sell the devices at their stores.[53]

## I'M NOT IN THE MOOD

While some Americans were exploring the boundaries of their sexuality to make sex exciting and perhaps daring, many others had no such interest or intent. Lots of married people in particular had not made sex a priority in their lives. "Lately, it seems, we're just not in the mood," Kathleen Deveny wrote in *Newsweek* in 2003; the sex lives of married couples with kids and busy jobs was just not what they used to be. "We're overworked, anxious about the economy—and we have to drive our kids to way too many T-ball games," she explained, and antidepressants were another possible reason for the loss of libido. Resentments toward spouses for the petty but still annoying things they did could be another factor for the lack of sparks in the bedroom, but it seemed sheer exhaustion accounted for most of it. "Sleep is the new sex," opined Margaret Carlson of *Time*, thinking overly busy American couples were finding forty winks to be more of a source of pleasure than forty minutes of intercourse.[54]

Statistics bore out the anecdotal evidence that many married Americans rarely had sex. Fifteen percent to 20 percent of couples (113 million Americans) had sex no more than ten times per year, some psychologists estimated, a frequency that qualified them for being in a "sexless marriage." A significantly larger percentage were not having sex as often as they once did, with men and women sharing equally in the lack of desire. Authors of books with titles like *The Sex-Starved Marriage*, *Rekindling Desire: A Step-by-Step Program to Help Low-Sex and No-Sex Marriages*, and *Resurrecting Sex* were making the talk show rounds, with Dr. Phil labeling the problem an "epidemic." Even former U.S. Labor secretary Robert Reich observed that something was amiss in American couples' mating habits, coining the acronym DINS (dual income, no sex) for those more interested in making money than making love.[55]

Although a standard joke in comics' routines and on sitcoms, the sexless marriage was not very funny to most people in one. Romance and passion were important elements in a marriage, elements that often disappeared when sex did. Many felt a sense of loss when sex became intermittent, something that was almost inevitable, according to the latest numbers from the General Social Survey (a research report completed every two years). Married couples under thirty years old said they had intercourse 109 times a year, while those in their sixties had it thirty-two times, the slide thus common and perhaps natural. Still, the lack of sex in a marriage was concerning for most, and the fact that we were not trained to talk about the subject in general compounded the problem. Among couples in which one partner wanted to have sex and the other did not, some were making deals to try to resolve the problem. One person could decide when to have some kind of sex while the other could choose what they would do, for example, money or gifts no doubt exchanged in other negotiating. Others were making intercourse appointments, somewhat peculiar perhaps but necessary to make sure sex would happen given how crowded most people's calendars were. Two books—*365 Nights* and *Just Do It*—documented the efforts of two couples determined to revitalize their sex lives, each "sexpedition" proving to improve their relationship and make them happier people.[56]

While most would agree that sex was one of the better things in life, was there anything wrong with being in a "sexless marriage"? Most marriage counselors believed there was, seeing sex as a significant part of a happy union. The absence of sex was usually an indicator of problems in a marriage, many felt, and a sign of a lack of intimacy in general. Still, many apparently happy couples seemed to be doing fine without sex; the activity was just not a priority in each partner's life. The norm now for married couples was 68.5 times a year (slightly more than once per week), according to a 2002 study by the National Opinion Research Center at the University of Chicago, and the frequency was about the same for working women as stay-at-home moms. Unmarried folks still had on the average slightly fewer sexual encounters, the same study found, so the notion that most single people had wild and crazy sex lives was a persistent but inaccurate belief.[57]

Interestingly, some women were choosing to be in a sexless marriage. Books with unlikely titles such as *Okay, So I Don't Have a Headache*, *I'm Not in the Mood*, and *I'd Rather Eat Chocolate* were proving quite popular, each of them making a strong case for marital celibacy. Another book, *For Women Only*, provided readers with a list of excuses to enable married women to avoid sex (ranging from embarking on nighttime household projects to the old standby, pretending one was asleep). "It has become impossible not to suspect that a large number of relatively young and otherwise healthy married people are forgoing sex for long periods of time and that many have given it up altogether," Caitlin Flanagan wrote in the *Atlantic* in 2003, with women more likely to be the primary decision maker for that state of affairs. Sex was once considered, along with cooking and cleaning, a "wifely duty" for married women, but the sexual revolution and equal rights movement had changed all that. Pleasing one's husband was no longer the principal responsibility of women, and some women were taking advantage of that gain by removing sex from their marriages when it no longer interested them.[58]

Sexless marriages were not the only example of what many experts believed was rampant dysfunction in Americans' bedrooms. The latest research showed that one-third of all adults said they had some kind of sexual problem over the past year, with no shortage of factors blamed. Women's gains in economic and social power, job stress, and simple marital monotony were behind Americans' lack of sexual desire, various critics suggested, all reasonable enough explanations. Author Elizabeth Devita-Raeburn offered a very different reason for the high incidence of sexual dysfunction, however, believing those were just symptoms of a much deeper problem. Most Americans simply did not know how to be intimate, Devita-Raeburn thought, that skill a lot more difficult than the art of romance. Intimacy required a kind of openness, honesty, and self-respect that many of us did not possess, with problems in the bedroom an almost inevitable result. "Lust for the long haul" could come only from a truly intimate connection between two people, she maintained, and all the props employed to enhance sex—different positions or settings, sexy lingerie, or even erection-inducing drugs—were helpful perhaps but generally beside the point. Sex was not "engineering" but a "language," agreed marital and sex therapist David Schnarch, and a couple's ability to speak the same language was the key to having good sex that evolved over the years. Rather than anxiety and pathology—the typical culprits in sexual dysfunction—it was personal growth and direct communication that would most likely lead to a happy sex life, Schnarch and a growing number of therapists now held.[59]

A lack of intimacy may indeed have been the root of many Americans' sexual dysfunction, but it was online pornography that was catching much of the blame. Online porn was to popular musician John Mayer "a new synaptic pathway," a heterosexual male's brain processing sexual images in a much different way than when seeing a woman's actual body. Mayer admitted he—a rock star, it need be said—partook of Internet pornography in the morning. "There have probably been days when I saw 300 vaginas before I got out of bed," he told *Playboy*; that the desirable hunk felt the urge to view naked women online illustrates how universal an experience it was to men.[60]

It was not totally clear yet how online porn was affecting men's libidos, but there was strong evidence to suggest it was making sex with a real woman less exciting. Female partners found themselves wondering why they now always had to initiate the act when in the past their mate could not wait to have sex. Delayed ejaculation also appeared to be common among heavy users of Internet pornography, and some men, unable to reach orgasm when having actual sex, were finding themselves having to fake a climax. Some men had to replay scenes of online porn in their heads in order to have an orgasm while having sex, an odd instance of life imitating art. Others were acting out scenes from porn movies, a source of puzzlement to their partners when these tableaux entered their sexual repertoire. Overmasturbating was one reason for the loss of desire for real sex, but the bigger problem was that many men simply found porn more exciting. Many men admitted to having harder erections while watching their favorite fantasies online than while having sex with their wife, girlfriend, or person they just picked up at the bar. One sex counselor had coined the term "sexual attention deficit disorder" to describe this condition, which, by all reports, appeared to be widespread and on the rise. Some therapists worried that as physical desire for one's partner faded (and as reality and fantasy further blended) so would emotional attachment, and if true, this was a much bigger concern.[61]

## WICKED VOODOO SEX

Whether due to online pornography, a lack of intimacy, or more mechanical problems, Americans were actively looking for solutions to sexual dysfunction. Sales of Viagra in the United States had reached $1.5 billion by 2008, with nineteen million prescriptions filled annually. The success of the drug had much to do with the aging of baby boomers, many of whom had no intention of giving up sex as they hit their sixties. Dropping testosterone levels among both men and women as they aged was the biggest factor in boomers' feeling less in the mood more often. Other common middle-aged medical problems further complicated things in the bedroom, making boomers try virtually anything to improve their sex lives.[62]

There was indeed quite an array of options for those interested in increasing sexual desire or arousal. Besides the various prescriptive therapies, some were opting for natural alternatives like ginkgo biloba, ginseng, L-arginine (a naturally occurring amino acid), and the aptly named horny goat weed.[63] The makers of a new herbal product for women called Avlimil sold two hundred thousand units the first month it was introduced, its alleged aphrodisiac powers difficult to resist.[64] Some products were designed to increase not one's own desire but that of others. Prominent dermatologist Nicholas Perricone, for example, was marketing a product called Synergy Anti-Aging Aromatic, a synthetic pheromone fragrance selling for $250 for less than an ounce. (Pheromones are chemicals excreted by animals to trigger a reproductive behavioral response from recipients of the same species.)[65] Others were looking to foods like watermelon, hot peppers, chocolate, and, of course, oysters to increase their sex drive and performance, although there was little scientific evidence to show that any had aphrodisiacal powers.[66]

In addition to the myriad of options available, there was no shortage of advice on how to make sex more exciting. Women's magazines routinely included articles about how to "spice up" one's sex life (the most common theme being telling your partner what you wanted). Adding zing to long-term sexual relationships was indeed a common pursuit, with all kinds of experts recommending ways to keep sex fresh and interesting. Books like *52 Invitations to Grrreat Sex* and Nancy Friday's *My Secret Garden* and *Forbidden Flowers*; movies such as *9 1/2 Weeks* and *Swept Away*; and instructional tapes with the decidedly nonsexy titles *Making Sex Fun* and *Advanced Sexual Techniques* were some of the more popular resources used for turning up the heat. Porn too was often prescribed, although it was more often men whose temperature became elevated upon seeing not very attractive people go at it like wild animals. Many sex toy boutiques held classes in sexual technique; in Babeland's "Sex Tips for Straight Men" seminar, for example, its (lesbian) instructors used vagina hand puppets as a teaching aid. Sex toy parties were also popular, with companies like Passion Parties and Temptation Parties offering guests every kind of battery-powered, penis-shaped device imaginable.[67]

If aphrodisiacs, advice, or accouterments did not resolve sexual problems, more extreme measures were sometimes felt necessary. Couples therapy remained a viable option for more serious sexual problems, especially when a specific issue (e.g., noncomplementary sex drives, an abusive past, difficulty in having an orgasm, or an addiction to Internet porn) was involved. Adjusting expectations was a big part of sex therapy, with some couples believing every occasion should conclude with the proverbial July 4 fireworks display of oohs and aahs. Even among happily married couples with normal sex lives, half of all sexual experiences were considered less than "ideal," research showed, meaning at least one partner was not completely satisfied with at least one part of the standard desire-arousal-orgasm sequence. Intercourse should take place only when each partner was at a high level of arousal, therapists advised, something that often did not take place. Homework involving erotic exercises not concluding with intercourse was frequently assigned to try to solve this particular problem.[68] If therapy was a bit too intimidating, there was of course no shortage of sex manuals to consult. Some of the newer ones included *Sex: How to Do Everything* by two women named Em and Lo, Judy Bastyra's *Best-Ever Illustrated Sex Handbook: Successful Techniques and New Ideas for Long-Term Lovers*, and Lisa Sweet's *365 Sex Positions: A New Way Every Day for a Steamy, Erotic Year*. For the less erudite, there was *The Complete Idiot's Guide to Amazing Sex* by Sari Locker and, for Wiccans, Kathleen Charlotte's *Wicked Voodoo Sex*.

Of course, the pharmaceutical industry remained keen on fixing Americans' sexual problems by offering a menu of drugs targeted to specific dysfunctions. Some companies were trying to repeat the phenomenal success of treatment for erectile dysfunction (ED) by coming up with an effective drug for premature ejaculation (PE). The FDA had in 2005 turned down a drug for PE called dapoxetine, but some doctors were prescribing the antidepressants Paxil and Prozac for the condition, which some men found to be somewhat effective (albeit with side effects). Numbing creams and gels were another option, but these were messy and made men feel like they were having sex while on Novocain. More natural solutions to the problem were the "stop and go" and "squeeze" methods, as well as therapy to resolve any psychological issues that could be at the root of it all. Again, a big part of the dissatisfaction relating to PE simply had to do with hope versus reality. Many men expected intercourse to last a half hour or more before they achieved orgasm, but the fact was that it normally lasted three to thirteen minutes; this "duration gap" was the basis for much of their unhappiness and frustration.[69]

Treating women's sexual dysfunction remained the Holy Grail for Big Pharma, however. "Forget vibrators, soft porn, and Marvin Gaye," Alexis

Jetter of *Vogue* wrote in 2010 in her report on the new wave of pills, gels, and other treatments for women's sexual problems currently in development. There were still no FDA-approved drugs to treat FSD, making pharmaceutical companies and device manufacturers all the more eager to be first in what was now estimated to be a $2 billion to $4 billion market. With shades of Woody Allen's 1973 film *Sleeper*, an orgasmatron spinal-cord stimulator was in the works, as was something called LibiGel designed to stimulate nerve centers that controlled libido in the female brain. Some continued to believe such efforts were misguided, however, and driven more out of greed than anything else. In her 2009 award-winning documentary *Orgasm Inc.*, for example, Liz Canner made a compelling case that the search to cure FSD was not just a waste of time and money but also potentially harmful to women, illustrating the medical industry at its worst.[70] By now, however, it was clear that nothing coming out of a laboratory would be, for the moment at least, strong enough to cure the nation's sexual malaise. Americans' struggle with sexuality would, for the time being, continue, our "sexidemic" an enduring feature of the nation's character.

# Conclusion

The cultural history of sex in America is not a pretty one. Americans have had a consistently contentious relationship with sexuality for decades if not centuries; the nation has struggled with it on both an individual and collective level. The United States and sex have been literally strange bedfellows, it can be said, since our public celebration of sexuality has contrasted and conflicted with its more angst-ridden role in our private lives. Too many powerful institutions have shaped the ways in which we have thought about sex and practiced it, with the government, religions, education system, and medical community all claiming a stake in what we do in our bedrooms. On a deeper level, something about the American idea and experience is at odds with sexuality, and our urge to succeed at any cost makes sex a much more complex and complicated affair than it has to be. Separately, our core consumption ethic devalued sexuality, extracting much of its extraordinariness. For as long as the country has been a country, I believe, the problems associated with sex have outweighed the pleasures it has offered in many Americans' lives and in society as a whole. Serious warning signs in American sexuality could be first detected during the Great Depression and World War II years, showing the onset of a cultural pathology that would emerge in the postwar era and mushroom over the course of the next half century. Today, our national "sexidemic" appears worse than ever, its symptoms ranging from many low- and no-sex marriages to widespread sex addiction and a rapidly growing number of individuals preferring their computer screens over their human partners as lovers.

I am hardly the only one to have observed that sexuality in this country is highly problematic for one reason or another, as recently published books and magazine articles vividly illustrate. In his *What Money Can't Buy*, for example, Michael J. Sandel convincingly argues that sexuality has been commodified, that is, sexuality is part of a market society in which every human interaction is up for sale.[1] In her *Adam and Eve after the Pill*, Mary Eberstadt looks to the paradoxes of the sexual revolution for what she sees as the "destigmatization and demystification of nonmarital sex and the reduction of sexual relations in general to a kind of hygienic reaction."[2] Marty Klein has recently updated his *America's War on Sex*, showing how sexuality in this country has become even more politicized since the first edition of the book was published in 2006.[3] As well, the medical community has not progressed much in its ignorance of sexuality. "Concerns about sexual pleasure and pain are common, but conversations about them in the exam room are not," wrote Katherine Schreiber in *Psychology Today* in the fall of 2012, citing a recent survey showing that few (14 percent) practitioners of obstetrics and gynecology discussed the topic in any detail with their patients.[4] Most concerning, perhaps, sex education in many states is still inadequate, somewhat amazing given that the subject has now been taught for about a century. In New York State, for example, a report released in September 2012 by the Civil Liberties Union revealed that only about a third of districts surveyed taught students how to use condoms in preventing pregnancy and disease. The report, "Birds, Bees and Bias," also found that more than half provided no instruction on sexual orientation, and nearly two-thirds omitted mention or depiction of female external genitalia.[5]

Is there any hope for Americans to develop healthy attitudes and behavior toward sexuality? It is easy to be as pessimistic about the country's sexual future as Albert Ellis was in 1954 when he viewed our "anti-sexual culture" as deeply engrained in the nation's firmament. A "pronounced social effort" would be required to reverse directions from the "American sexual tragedy," he felt, something that does not come around very often. One could make the case that the counterculture of the late 1960s was such a mass social movement, especially given the new ways of thinking about sexuality that were a defining part of that era. The era did not last very long, however, and the

AIDS crisis that soon followed served to make the arena of sexuality even more precarious. Patterns of the past are highly likely to continue in the future. Sexuality will undoubtedly remain central in America society—its "volume" will continue to grow and its avenues of expression will continue to proliferate. (Could anyone have anticipated "sexting," pornography on television, or dildos being sold at Walgreen's?) With sexuality in the public arena more apparent than ever, it is not surprising that many Americans are just saying no to it in private. In such a climate, it is hard to imagine sex becoming more meaningful and purposeful in the years ahead. The "age wave" certainly does not bode well for American sexuality. As the largest generation in history heads into its sixties and seventies, sex in America will become even more reliant on pharmaceuticals, not a very good scenario in which to make sexuality less stressful. Generation Y appears to be more comfortable with sexuality than overly competitive baby boomers, but the problem is too big for even them to resolve.

Just as sexuality in America entered a new paradigm every century or so, however, it is equally easy to predict that sexual attitudes and behavior will eventually change dramatically. In fact, there are clear signs we have exited the twentieth-century paradigm of sex based around individualization and commercialization and are entering something new and different. While also highly individualized and commercialized, a twenty-first-century paradigm of sexuality is destined to embrace leading-edge innovations in science and technology. (Vice industries such as sex are always at the forefront of scientific and technological advancements; erectile dysfunction drugs and online porn are just two recent examples.) Driven by information technology and biotechnology, a brave new world looms for sexuality for the remainder of the twenty-first century, prompting scenarios that George Orwell himself would have been impressed by.

What specifically might those of us who live long enough expect to encounter, sexually speaking? Today's erectile dysfunction drugs like Viagra, Levitra, and Cialis will be seen as primitive potions as a new generation of pharmaceuticals targeting human sexuality rolls out of labs over the next few decades. Getting blood to the penis is kid stuff compared to the alterations of brain chemistry that will someday be achieved. The brain, not the genitals, is where the real action is, making substances that enhance and expand desire (rather than improve performance) a much bigger opportunity.

"Neuro-aphrodisiacs" will be effective for women as well as men, as the "pink Viagra" is finally realized. More than just elevating one's libido, however, these "designer" drugs will act on the creativity and imagination sectors of the brain, making all kinds of fantasies possible (or, more accurately, "thinkable"). Brands like "Submission" and "Dominance," will be introduced, their chemical makeups acting on those parts of the gray matter that are responsible for such emotions. Out there, perhaps, but scientists are currently directing much of their energy and resources toward brain research, knowing it represents the final frontier of human understanding.

Along with advances in biotechnology, information technology will no doubt significantly reshape sexuality in the years ahead. Over the past two decades, the Internet has played an important role in doing just that, of course, and the ability to receive (and send) sexual content has altered the way we think and practice sex. Online pornography is a "game changer," I believe, a phenomenon that is already having a major impact on people's sex lives. Many men prefer the images and video they view online to sex with other people, a radical transformation in the narrative of sexuality. While people have always masturbated, often while looking at images, the volume, variety, accessibility, and immediacy of online pornography is extraordinary and unprecedented. Cindy Gallop has posed the interesting theory that online porn not only has many young men glued to their computers but also is actually changing the way they have sex with women. Through direct experience, Gallop, a middle-aged advertising executive, found that her twentysomething lovers patterned their sexual techniques after the hard-core pornography they had viewed on the Internet. Disturbed by the trend, Gallop founded MakeLoveNotPorn.tv, a website in which "amateurs" post videos of themselves having real sex. "A certain amount of re-education, rehabilitation, and reorientation has to take place," she told the *New York Times*, on a literal mission to bring authenticity back to sexuality.[6]

Again, however, as with erectile dysfunction (ED) drugs, we have just scratched the surface of "high-tech sex." The sexual entertainment industry is destined to become bigger and more legitimate as new technologies are developed that are designed, like "neuro-aphrodisiacs," to enhance and expand our sex lives. Technologies common in gaming will be applied to the arena of sexuality, allowing us to live out our wildest fantasies in make-believe worlds. Like video games, sex games ("Sex-Box"?) could be played alone or with others, allowing an infinite number and variety of sexual situations to play out. Participants will be able to choose from a menu of actors, settings, and plots or create their own custom scenarios, making possible a literally virtual universe of sexual experiences. As technology improves, it will be difficult to tell the difference between what is real and what it imaginary. After three-dimension technology will come four- and five-dimension technology, where sensory stimuli (touch, taste, and smell) are added to the experience. With new kinds of holograms, one will be able to have sex with Marilyn Monroe or Clark Gable (or both), making sex circa the early 2010s seem rather pedestrian. Combining "neuro-aphrodisiacs" with such technology will offer a one-two sexual punch that is difficult for us to even comprehend.

Is this potential paradigm of sexuality something to look forward to or something to dread? Like much about advances in science and technology, it is a little of both. Turning sex into an activity more reliant on chemicals is admittedly a scary proposition, as is the notion of turning it from an "analog" experience into a digital one. Removing any of the "naturalness" of sex seems strange and, perhaps, wrong. I believe the train has already left the station in this regard, however, with history showing that it is difficult or impossible to stop the march of scientific and technological "progress." Having sex with a device recalling the "orgasmatron" in Woody Allen's film *Sleeper* would take some getting used to, but few people imagined the prospect of millions of computer users watching people do things that satisfy their particular sexual urges (often in place of having sex with a real-life person). Regardless of one's views on the matter, rethinking the very definition of what constitutes sex is an intriguing idea, and such a radical step is perhaps the only means of curing America's nearly three-quarters-of-a-century-old "sexidemic."

# Notes

## INTRODUCTION

1. Kathy Peiss, ed., *Major Problems in the History of American Sexuality* (New York: Houghton Mifflin, 2002), xvii.

2. Julia A. Ericksen with Sally A. Steffen, *Kiss and Tell: Surveying Sex in the Twentieth Century* (Cambridge, MA: Harvard University Press, 1999), 2.

3. Laura M. Carpenter and John DeLamater, eds., *Sex for Life: From Virginity to Viagra, How Sexuality Changes throughout Our Lives* (New York: New York University Press, 2012).

4. Elizabeth Reis, *American Sexual Histories* (Malden, MA: Blackwell, 2001), 1.

5. Reis, *American Sexual Histories*, 2.

6. Reis, *American Sexual Histories*, 3.

7. John D'Emilio and Estelle B. Freedman, *Intimate Matters: A History of Sexuality in America* (New York: Harper & Row, 1988), xi–xii.

8. Gail Dines, *Pornland: How Porn Has Hijacked Our Sexuality* (Boston: Beacon, 2010); William M. Struthers, *Wired for Intimacy: How Pornography Hijacks the Male Brain* (Nottingham, UK: IVP Books, 2009); Robert Jensen's *Getting Off: Pornography and the End of Masculinity* (Cambridge, MA: South End Press, 2007); Pamela Paul, *Pornified: How Pornography Is Transforming Our Lives, Our Relationships, and Our Families* (New York: Times Books, 2005).

9. "Girl Crazy," *Women's Health*, April 2012, 38.

10. Albert Ellis, *The American Sexual Tragedy* (New York: Twayne, 1954), 264–65.

11. Maureen Dowd, "Is Pleasure a Sin?" *New York Times*, June 6, 2012, A27.

12. "'Fifty Shades of Grey' Banned from Harford Library: Five Other Controversial Erotic Books," *International Business Times* (U.S. edition), May 31, 2012.

13. Marty Klein, *America's War on Sex: The Attack on Law, Lust, and Liberty* (Westport, CT: Praeger, 2006), 1.

14. Marty Klein, *Sexual Intelligence: What We Really Want from Sex—and How to Get It* (New York: HarperOne, 2012).

15. Melissa Daly, "Most Awkward Talk Ever!" *Human Sexuality Newsletter*, April/May 2012, 1–4.

16. Roger N. Lancaster, *Sex Panic and the Punitive State* (Berkeley: University of California Press, 2011), 3.

17. Carolyn Herbst Lewis, *Prescription for Heterosexuality: Sexual Citizenship in the Cold War Era* (Chapel Hill: University of North Carolina Press, 2010), 2–4.

18. Kenneth C. W. Kammeyer, *A Hypersexual Society: Sexual Discourse, Erotica, Pornography in America Today* (New York: Palgrave MacMillan, 2008), 17–18.

19. Dagmar Herzog, *Sex in Crisis: The New Sexual Revolution and the Future of American Politics* (New York: Basic Books, 2008), xi.

20. Edwin M. Schur, *The Americanization of Sex* (Philadelphia: Temple University Press, 1988), xiii.

21. Robert T. Michael, John G. Gagnon, Edward O. Laumann, and Gina Kolata, *Sex in America: A Definitive Survey* (Boston: Little, Brown, 1994), 1.

22. Richard Godbeer, *Sexual Revolution in Early America* (Baltimore: The Johns Hopkins University Press, 2002), 2–3, 10–11.

23. D'Emilio and Freedman, *Intimate Matters*, 52. See also Merril D. Smith, ed., *Sex and Sexuality in Early America* (New York: New York University Press, 1998).

24. Faramerz Dabhoiwala, *The Origins of Sex: A History of the First Sexual Revolution* (New York: Oxford University Press, 2012). See also Lawrence Stone's *Family, Sex and Marriage in England, 1500–1800*, and Michel Foucault's epic, three-volume *History of Sexuality*.

25. D'Emilio and Freedman, *Intimate Matters*, 166–67.

26. Hanne Blank, *Straight: The Surprisingly Short History of Heterosexuality* (New York: Beacon, 2012).

27. D'Emilio and Freedman, *Intimate Matters*, 233–35.

28. Dagmar Herzog, *Sexuality in Europe: A Twentieth-Century History* (New York: Cambridge University Press, 2011).

29. Christina Simmons, *Making Marriage Modern: Women's Sexuality from the Progressive Era to World War II* (New York: Oxford University Press, 2009).

30. D'Emilio and Freedman, *Intimate Matters*, 242.

31. Marilyn E. Hegarty, *Victory Girls, Khaki-Wackies, and Patriotutes: The Regulation of Female Sexuality during World War II* (New York: New York University Press, 2007), 2.

32. Elaine Tyler May, *Homeward Bound: American Families in the Cold War Era* (New York: Basic Books, 1988).

33. Miriam G. Reumann, *American Sexual Character: Sex, Gender, and National Identity in the Kinsey Reports* (Berkeley: University of California Press, 2005), 1.

34. Beth Bailey, *Sex in the Heartland* (Cambridge, MA: Harvard University Press, 1999).

35. David Allyn, *Make Love, Not War: The Sexual Revolution; An Unfettered History* (New York: Little, Brown, 2000), 9.

36. Bailey, *Sex in the Heartland*, 1, 12.

## CHAPTER 1: PILLOW TALK

1. Robert Elliot Fitch, *The Decline and Fall of Sex: With Some Curious Digressions on the Subject of True Love* (London: Sidgwick and Jackson, 1958).

2. Dean Jennings, "Sex in the Classroom," *Reader's Digest*, February 1946, 15–17.

3. Fred Brown, "What American Men Want to Know About Sex," *Journal of Social Psychology* (February 1948): 119–25. See Marilyn E. Hegarty, *Victory Girls, Khaki-Wackies, and Patriotutes*, for a discussion of the federal government's role in what she described as "a monolithic discourse regarding both male and female sexuality" during the war.

4. "Sex and the Barn Door," *Time*, October 4, 1948, 53.

5. "Girls, Like Boys, Learn About Sex from Friends," *Science News Letter*, March 26, 1955, 200.

6. Amram Scheinfeld, "'Cold' Women—and Why," *Reader's Digest*, August 1948, 124–26. See Andrea Tone's *Devices and Desires: A History of Contraceptives in America* for a complete study of the evolution of the modern birth control industry from the 1870s to the 1970s.

7. Scheinfeld, "'Cold' Women."

8. Quoted in "Must We Change Our Sex Standards?" *Reader's Digest*, June 1948, 1–6.

9. "Sex in the Schoolroom," *Time*, March 22, 1948, 71; "Sex Education," *Life*, May 24, 1948, 55, 58, 62.

10. Catherine Mackenzie, "Simple Answers to 'Those' Questions," *New York Times Magazine*, March 27, 1949, SM38.

11. Ruth Hawthorne Fay, "Leave My Child Alone!" *Reader's Digest*, November 1950, 122–24.

12. Dorothy Barclay, "Sex Education in Home and School," *New York Times Magazine*, February 3, 1952, SM36.

13. Dorothy Barclay, "Second Thoughts on Sex Education," *New York Times Magazine*, July 5, 1953, SM25.

14. Dorothy Barclay, "When Children Ask About Sex," *New York Times Magazine*, November 15, 1953, SM47.

15. Dorothy Barclay, "When to Start Sex Education," *New York Times Magazine*, January 17, 1954, SM34.

16. "Christopher Sex Talks," *Newsweek*, July 16, 1951, 80.

17. Barclay, "Sex Education in Home and School."

18. Barclay, "Second Thoughts on Sex Education."

19. Barclay, "When Children Ask About Sex."

20. Dorothy Barclay, "Sex Education: How and How Much," *New York Times Magazine*, October 19, 1958, SM59.

21. Barclay, "Second Thoughts on Sex Education."

22. Barclay, "Sex Education: How and How Much."

23. Quoted in Dorothy Barclay, "Changing Concepts in Sex Education," *New York Times Magazine*, October 6, 1957, 70.

24. Francis Sill Wickware, "Report on Kinsey," *Life*, August 2, 1948, 87–98.

25. Ernest Havemann, "The Kinsey Report on Women," *Life*, August 24, 1953, 41–56. For much more on Kinsey and his work, see Miriam G. Reumann's *American Sexual Character: Sex, Gender, and National Identity in the Kinsey Reports* (Berkeley: University of California Press, 2005).

26. Wickware, "Report on Kinsey."

27. "How to Stop Gin Rummy," *Time*, March 1, 1948, 16.

28. Wickware, "Report on Kinsey."

29. "Behavior, after Kinsey," *Time*, April 12, 1948, 79.

30. *Time*, "How to Stop Gin Rummy."

31. Wickware, "Report on Kinsey."

32. Wickware, "Report on Kinsey."

33. Wickware, "Report on Kinsey."

34. Martin Gumpert, "The Kinsey Report," *Nation*, May 1, 1948, 471–72.

35. Gumpert, "The Kinsey Report."

36. Robert Thomas Allen, "I'm Sick of Sex," *Reader's Digest*, April 1950, 15–17.

37. "Sex and the Church," *Time*, June 7, 1948, 76.

38. "Sex before Marriage," *Time*, February 13, 1950, 57.

39. "Heroism v. Sex," *Time*, November 12, 1951, 91.

40. *Time*, "Sex before Marriage."

41. "Kinsey for Lutherans," *Time*, August 17, 1953, 54.

42. Quoted in Abraham Stone, "The Case against Marital Infidelity," *Reader's Digest*, May 1954, 11–14.

43. Paul H. Landis, "Don't Expect Too Much of Sex in Marriage," *Reader's Digest*, December 1954, 25–28.

44. Pitirim Sorokin, "The Case against Sexual Freedom: A Noted Scientist's Warning," *This Week*, March 1, 1954, 12–17. "Sex or Snake Oil," *Time*, January 11, 1954, 14.

45. David Cort, "Sex Scares the Professor," *Nation*, March 23, 1957, 255–56.

46. Goodrich C. Schauffler, "It Could Be Your Daughter," *Reader's Digest*, April 1958, 55–58.

47. "Research on Sex Aided," *Science News Letter*, August 29, 1953, 142.

48. Albert Ellis and Donald Webster Cory, "In Defense of Current Sex Studies," *Nation*, March 15, 1952, 250–52.

49. "Object Lesson," *Time*, December 25, 1950, 10.

50. "Sexual 'Pervert' Probe," *Science News Letter*, July 1, 1950, 5.

51. "Files on Parade," *Time*, February 16, 1953, 26.

52. "The Hidden Problem," *Time*, December 28, 1953, 28–29.

53. *Time*, "The Hidden Problem."

54. "A Delicate Problem," *Newsweek*, June 14, 1954, 99–102.

55. *Newsweek*, "A Delicate Problem."

56. "A Healthy Modesty," *Time*, August 12, 1957, 62.

57. "Sex Finds," *Newsweek*, July 20, 1953, 60.

58. George Milburn, "Reflections on Kinsey," *Nation*, September 19, 1953, 230–31.

59. "All About Eve: Kinsey Reports on American Women," *Newsweek*, August 24, 1953, 68–71.

60. Jane Stafford, "Kinsey's Data on Females," *Science News Letter*, August 22, 1953, 119–22.

61. Havemann, "Kinsey Report on Women."

62. Havemann, "Kinsey Report on Women."

63. Stafford, "Kinsey's Data on Females."

64. Havemann, "Kinsey Report on Women."

65. Stafford, "Kinsey's Data on Females."

66. Stafford, "Kinsey's Data on Females."

67. Stafford, "Kinsey's Data on Females."

68. "Sex vs. America," *Newsweek*, September 9, 1953, 20.

69. "Birds, Bees—and Kinsey," *Newsweek*, February 8, 1954, 55–56.

70. "Kinsey's Assembly Line," *Newsweek*, December 19, 1955, 89.

71. "More Kinsey," *Newsweek*, September 15, 1956, 77.

72. "Dr. Kinsey's Legacy," *Newsweek*, June 2, 1958, 82–83.

73. *Newsweek*, "Dr. Kinsey's Legacy."

## CHAPTER 2: EASY RIDER

1. "Trouble between the Sexes," *Time*, December 9, 1966, 68.

2. Andrew Hacker, "The Pill and Morality," *New York Times Magazine*, November 21, 1965, 138–40.

3. "Plain Talking About Sex," *Newsweek*, June 6, 1960, 108. For a full study of the American system of courtship or dating from the 1920s to the mid-1960s, see Beth Bailey's *From Front Porch to Back Seat: Courtship in Twentieth-Century America* (Baltimore: The Johns Hopkins University Press, 1988).

4. David Cort, "Sex Happiness for All," *Nation*, September 2, 1961, 118–20.

5. Albert Rosenfeld, "A Laboratory Study of Sexual Behavior," *Life*, April 22, 1966, 8–12.

6. Rosenfeld, "A Laboratory Study of Sexual Behavior."

7. "Problems of Sex," *Time*, April 29, 1966, 51.

8. "Response to 'Response,'" *Newsweek*, May 23, 1966, 94.

9. W. Bradbury, "Two Sex Researchers on the Firing Line," *Life*, June 24, 1966, 43–51.

10. "S*cr*ts of S*x," *Newsweek*, April 26, 1965, 58.

11. "Sex Under Scrutiny," *Newsweek*, April 25, 1966, 80.

12. "The $2,500 Understanding," *Newsweek*, June 10, 1968, 78.

13. "Who Are These 'Pagans,'" *Newsweek*, October 31, 1960, 58.

14. Ann Landers, "Straight Talk on Sex and Growing Up," *Life*, August 18, 1961, 74.

15. Landers, "Straight Talk on Sex."

16. "The Second Sexual Revolution," *Time*, January 24, 1964, 54–59.

17. "Sex on Campus," *Newsweek*, August 12, 1963, 75. The phrase "sexual revolution" was coined in Germany in the 1920s by Wilhelm Reich, the infamous Austrian psychoanalyst responsible for the Orgone box.

18. "The Moral Revolution on the U.S. Campus," *Newsweek*, April 6, 1964, 52–59.

19. *Newsweek*, "The Moral Revolution."

20. *Newsweek*, "The Moral Revolution."

21. *Newsweek*, "The Moral Revolution."

22. William Barry Furlong, "It's a Long Way from the Birds and Bees," *New York Times Magazine*, June 11, 1967, 24–25.

23. "The Pill and the Pupil," *Newsweek*, July 24, 1967, 72.

24. "Sex in the Classroom," *Newsweek*, July 11, 1966, 83.

25. Marybeth Weston, "Of Love and the Like, Teen-Age Division," *New York Times Magazine*, October 11, 1964, 109–10.

26. "The Fourth R," *Time*, December 31, 1965, 35.

27. Furlong, "It's a Long Way."

28. Furlong, "It's a Long Way."

29. John Kobler, "Sex Invades the Schoolhouse," *Saturday Evening Post*, June 29, 1968, 23–27, 64–66.

30. "On Teaching Children About Sex," *Time*, June 9, 1967, 36–37. Because of the sheer numbers of teenagers in the late 1960s, it is fair to say that the baby boom was mostly responsible for the dramatic rise of venereal disease, pregnancies, and abortions among teenagers.

31. Ruth and Edward Brecher, "Every Sixth Teen-Age Girl In Connecticut," *New York Times Magazine*, May 29, 1966, 6–7.

32. Katharine Davis Fishman, "Sex Becomes a Brand-New Problem," *New York Times Magazine*, Match 13, 1966, 69.

33. Kobler, "Sex Invades the Schoolhouse."

34. *Time*, "On Teaching Children About Sex."

35. Kobler, "Sex Invades the Schoolhouse."

36. "Sex and the Single Child," *Newsweek*, June 2, 1969, 102–3.

37. "Sex in the Classroom," *Time*, July 25, 1969, 50.

38. *Time*, "Sex in the Classroom."

39. *Time*, "Sex in the Classroom."

40. Lester A. Kirkendall, "Sex on the Campus," *Nation*, February 17, 1964, 165–67.

41. William A. McWhirter, "'The Arrangement' at College," *Life*, May 31, 1968, 56–62.

42. Kirkendall, "Sex on the Campus."

43. "The Free-Sex Movement," *Time*, March 11, 1966, 66.

44. Hacker, "The Pill and Morality." See Elaine Tyler May's fascinating *America and the Pill: A History of Promise, Peril, and Liberation* for everything you wanted to know about the birth control pill. The pill "was more than simply a convenient and reliable method of preventing pregnancy," May convincing argues, showing how many believed it "promised to solve the problems of the world" (2).

45. *Time*, "The Free-Sex Movement."

46. Hacker, "The Pill and Morality."

47. Hacker, "The Pill and Morality."

48. "Unstructured Relations," July 4, 1966, *Newsweek*, 78.

49. McWhirter, "'The Arrangement' at College."

50. McWhirter, "'The Arrangement' at College."

51. Albert Rosenfeld, "Student Sexuality," *Life*, May 31, 1968, 68.

52. "Ah, Wilderness," *Time*, August 16, 1968, 51–52.

53. "Close-Up," *Life*, August 23, 1968, 30.

54. J. B. Priestley, "Eroticism, Sex and Love," *Saturday Evening Post*, April 23, 1963, 10–14.

55. *Time*, "Second Sexual Revolution."

56. "Eros in Polyester," *Newsweek*, October 10, 1966, 102.

57. "Erotica on Tour," *Newsweek*, September 16, 1968, 105.

58. "Anything Goes: Taboos in Twilight," *Newsweek*, November 13, 1967, 74–78.

59. William I. Nichols, "Sex: Our Changing Times," *Vital Speeches of the Day*, May 1, 1967, 445–48.

60. Arno Karlen, "'The Sexual Revolution' Is a Myth," *Saturday Evening Post*, December 28, 1968, 10–13.

61. "Changing Standards," *Time*, May 16, 1969, 52.

62. "Sex as a Spectator Sport," *Time*, July 11, 1969, 65–66.

63. *Time*, "Sex as a Spectator Sport."

64. "Sex and the Arts: Explosive Scene," *Newsweek*, April 14, 1969, 67–70.

65. *Newsweek*, "Sex and the Arts."

66. *Time*, "Sex as a Spectator Sport."

67. *Time*, "Sex as a Spectator Sport."

68. *Newsweek*, "Sex and the Arts."

69. Robert Hatch, "Films," *Nation*, March 24, 1969, 381–82.

70. *Newsweek*, "Sex and the Arts."

71. Albert Goldman, "Wild Blue Shocker," *Life*, February 7, 1969, 58–64.

72. Desmond Smith, "Pop Sex among the Squares," *Nation*, August 25, 1969, 142–45.

73. Smith, "Pop Sex among the Squares."

74. Smith, "Pop Sex among the Squares."

## CHAPTER 3: CARNAL KNOWLEDGE

1. "Pot and Sex," *Time*, September 29, 1975, 54.

2. "Grant v. Lee," *Time*, August 31, 1970, 52–53.

3. "Sex at Sunday School," *Newsweek*, December 27, 1971, 50–51.

4. "Kids, Sex and Doctors," *Time*, November 25, 1974, 91B.

5. "The Embarrassed Virgins," *Time*, July 9, 1973, 64.

6. Joseph Lelyveld, "The New Sexual Revolution," *New York Times Magazine*, July 3, 1977, 39.

7. Albert W. Edgemon and William R. Thomas, "How We Improved Our Sex Education Program," *Educational Leadership*, December 1979, 256–58.

8. "Communist Kinseys," *Time*, June 29, 1970, 29–30.

9. Ann Landers, "Sex behind the Bamboo Curtain," *Saturday Evening Post*, September 1975, 33–36.

10. Holger Jensen and Sydney Liu, "S-e-x," *Newsweek*, January 16, 1978, 48.

11. "All About the New Sex Therapy," *Newsweek*, November 27, 1972, 65–72.

12. "Repairing the Conjugal Bed," *Time*, May 25, 1970, 49–52; Shana Alexander, "Coming Out of the Closet," *Newsweek*, February 3, 1975, 72.

13. Alexander, "Coming Out of the Closet"; Alexander believed *Human Sexual Response* and *Human Sexual Inadequacy* were "the most-bought, least-read best sellers in publishing history," which was probably true.

14. "Human Sexual Inadequacy," *Newsweek*, May 4, 1970, 90–94.

15. Mopsy Strange Kennedy, "The 'No-Nonsense' School vs. the 'Please-Give-Me-Back-My-Nonsense' School," *New York Times Magazine*, January 14, 1973, 30–35.

16. *Time*, "Repairing the Conjugal Bed."

17. "Sex before Sport?" *Time*, March 15, 1971, 54.

18. *Newsweek*, "All About the New Sex Therapy."

19. *Newsweek*, "All About the New Sex Therapy."

20. *Newsweek*, "All About the New Sex Therapy."

21. "The Sexier Sex," *Newsweek*, July 3, 1972, 71–72.

22. Kennedy, "'No-Nonsense' School."

23. Kennedy, "'No-Nonsense' School."

24. "Sex on the Phone," *Time*, July 19, 1971, 33.

25. "Re-evaluating the Pill," *Newsweek*, January 12, 1970, 66.

26. *Newsweek*, "The Sexier Sex."

27. Derek Wright, "The New Tyranny of Sexual 'Liberation,'" *Life*, November 6, 1970, 4.

28. "Group Sex Therapy," *Time*, April 1, 1974, 45A.

29. *Newsweek*, "All About the New Sex Therapy."

30. "Trick or Treatment," *Time*, June 17, 1974, 90A.

31. "Out of the Lab," *Time*, February 3, 1975, 63A.

32. JoAnn Brooks, "Transcendental Sex: A Meditative Approach to Increasing Sensual Pleasure," *Library Journal*, September 1, 1978, 1643.

33. "The Problems of 'Normal' Sex," *Science News*, July 29, 1978.

34. *Science News*, "Problems of 'Normal' Sex."

35. JoAnn Brooks, "The Hite Report: A Nationwide Study on Female Sexuality," *Library Journal*, July 1976, 1538. Radical feminist Anne Koedt first offered a clitoris-centric critique of intercourse in 1968.

36. "Hite-ing Back," *Time*, December 12, 1977, 106A.

37. "The Hite of Sexuality," *Time*, February 7, 1977, 59.

38. "True Blue," *Newsweek*, July 13, 1970, 91–92.

39. "The Rich Pornocopia," *Time*, November 16, 1970, 92.

40. *Time*, "The Rich Pornocopia."

41. "Pornography Goes Public," *Newsweek*, December 21, 1970, 26–32.

42. Jules Witcover, "Civil War Over Smut," *Nation*, May 11, 1970, 550–53.

43. John Neary, "Pornography Goes Public," *Life*, August 28, 1970, 18.

44. Neary, "Pornography Goes Public."

45. Neary, "Pornography Goes Public."

46. "How Skin Flicks Hit Bible-Belt Waterloo, Iowa," *Newsweek*, December 21, 1970, 28.

47. William Murray, "The Porn Capital of America," *New York Times Magazine*, January 3, 1971, SM8.

48. Murray, "The Porn Capital of America."

49. "The 'Throat' Case," *Newsweek*, January 15, 1973, 50; "Wonder Woman," *Time*, January 15, 1973, 46.

50. *Newsweek*, "The 'Throat' Case"; *Time*, "Wonder Woman."

51. M. J. Sobran Jr., "Playboy and Sons," *National Review*, November 26, 1976, 1294–95.

52. Sobran, "Playboy and Sons."

53. "The American Way of Swinging," *Time*, February 8, 1971, 51.

54. *Time*, "American Way of Swinging."

55. "Group Sex," *Newsweek*, June 21, 1971, 98–99.

56. *Newsweek*, "Group Sex."

57. "Swinging with the Swingers," *Newsweek*, June 21, 1971, 99.

58. "Avant-Garde Retreat?" *Time*, November 25, 1974, 100.

59. "The New Morality," *Time*, November 21, 1977, 111.

60. *Time*, "The New Morality."

61. *Time*, "Avant-Garde Retreat?"

62. "The New Bisexuals," *Time*, May 13, 1974, 79A.

63. "Bisexual Chic: Anyone Goes," *Newsweek*, May 27, 1974, 90.

64. *Time*, "The New Bisexuals."

65. "A Sex Poll (1973)," *Time*, October 1, 1973, 63B.

66. *Time*, "A Sex Poll."

67. "God Is Love," *Time*, September 1, 1975, 62B.

68. Willie Morris, "The Lending Library of Love," *Newsweek*, March 11, 1974, 12–13.

69. Bob Greene, "Beyond the Sexual Revolution," *Newsweek*, September 29, 1975, 13.

70. "Sex Rock," *Time*, December 29, 1975, 39B.

71. Jack Kroll, "Nightcrawl," *Newsweek*, October 24, 1977, 126.

72. William S. Rubens, "Sex on Television, More or Less," *Vital Speeches of the Day*, January 1, 1978, 171–74.

73. Harry F. Waters, "Sex and TV," *Newsweek*, February 20, 1978, 54.

74. Waters, "Sex and TV."

## CHAPTER 4: FATAL ATTRACTION

1. Frank Gannon, "The Spread of Sex and the Demise of Romance in the America of Our Times," *Saturday Review*, July–August 1985, 53–55.

2. Sam Keen, "A Voyeur in Plato's Cave," *Psychology Today*, 85–101.

3. Keen, "A Voyeur in Plato's Cave."

4. John M. Fuchs, "Thy Neighbor's Wife," *Library Journal*, June 15, 1980, 1403. For a contemporary survey of the borders of the nation's sexual landscape, see Suzy Spencer's *Secret Sex Lives: A Year on the Fringes of American Sexuality* (New York: Berkley, 2012).

5. Philip Nobile, "Sexual Politics: L'Affaire Talese," *New York*, April 21, 1980, 42–44.

6. Richard Corliss, "The Bodies in Question," *Time*, November 30, 1980, 100.

7. Harry F. Waters, "Jiggling into a New Season," *Newsweek*, November 10, 1980, 123.

8. "The Bum's Rush in Advertising," *Time*, December 1, 1980, 95.

9. Kim Foltz, "A Kinky New Calvinism," *Newsweek*, March 11, 1985, 65.

10. Michael Gross, "Sex Sells," *Saturday Review*, July–August 1985, 50–52.

11. Janice Castro, "Calvin Meets the Marlboro Man," *Time*, October 21, 1985, 69.

12. Jennet Conant, "Sexy Does It," *Newsweek*, September 15, 1986, 62–64.

13. Diane Weathers, "Tupperware, Step Aside," *Newsweek*, March 2, 1981, 56.

14. Bob Greene, "An Unmentionable Occasion," *Esquire*, March 1981, 15–16.

15. Pamela Abramson, "'The Erotic Is Romantic,'" *Newsweek*, January 28, 1985, 76.

16. Kenneth. L. Woodward, "The Bible in the Bedroom," *Newsweek*, February 1, 1982, 71.

17. Woodward, "Bible in the Bedroom."

18. "In Search of a Perfect G," *Time*, September 13, 1982, 102.

19. Carl Kaplan, "Filthy Rich," *Esquire*, January 1985, 41.

20. George Leonard, "The End of Sex," *Esquire*, December 1982, 70–80.

21. Leonard, "The End of Sex."

22. Leonard, "The End of Sex."

23. Peter Marin, "A Revolution's Broken Promises," *Psychology Today*, July 1983, 50–57.

24. Marin, "A Revolution's Broken Promises."

25. Lester A. Kirkendall, "The Sexual Revolution Is Here—Almost," *Humanist*, November–December 1984, 9–14.

26. Anne Hollander, "Dressed to Thrill," *New Republic*, January 28, 1985, 28–33.

27. Judith Viorst, "Rolling Back the Lust Frontier," *New York Times Book Review*, September 14, 1986.

28. Bernie Zilbergeld and Michael Evans, "The Inadequacy of Masters and Johnson," *Psychology Today*, August 1980, 29–43.

29. Matt Clark, "The Sex-Therapy Revolution," *Newsweek*, November 17, 1980, 97.

30. Clark, "The Sex-Therapy Revolution."

31. Trudy Owett, "New Sex Therapy," *Vogue*, February 1984, 270–71.

32. John Leo, "The Munchkin of the Bedroom," *Time*, July 1, 1985, 52.

33. "New Game," *New Yorker*, August 12, 1985, 22.

34. Patricia Bosworth, "Talking with Doctor Goodsex," *Ladies' Home Journal*, February 1986, 82–84.

35. Maxine Abrams, "Love, Sex and Marriage," *Ladies' Home Journal*, January 1984, 68–77.

36. Abrams, "Love, Sex and Marriage."

37. Natalie Angier, "Finding Trouble in Paradise," *Time*, January 28, 1985, 76.

38. Charles Leerhsen, "Ann Landers and 'the Act,'" *Newsweek*, January 28, 1985, 76–77.

39. Srully Blotnick, "Joggers Are Lousy Lovers," *Forbes*, June 17, 1985, 222–23.

40. Linda Wolfe, "The New Sexual Realism," *Ladies' Home Journal*, April 1987, 58.

41. Harry Stein, "How I Spent the Sexual Revolution," *Esquire*, June 1986, 147–48.

42. David Gelman, "Not Tonight, Dear," *Newsweek*, October 26, 1987, 64–66.

43. Brad Edmondson, "Selling Sex: Take Two," *American Demographics*, July 1987, 22.

44. Jill Neimark, "Beyond Promiscuity," *Mademoiselle*, March 1988, 214.

45. Neimark, "Beyond Promiscuity."

46. Constance Holden, "Doctor of Sexology," *Psychology Today*, May 1988, 45–48.

47. Kim McDonald, "Sex under Glass," *Psychology Today*, March 1988, 58–59.

48. Michael Fumento, "The AIDS Cookbook," *New Republic*, April 4, 1988, 19–21.

49. Nikki Meredith, "The Gay Dilemma," *Psychology Today*, January 1984, 56–62.

50. Donald Symons, *The Evolution of Human Sexuality* (New York: Oxford University Press, 1979).

51. Meredith, "The Gay Dilemma."

52. Nikki Meredith, "After AIDS a Walk on the Mild Side," *Psychology Today*, January 1984, 60–61.

53. Edward Cornish, "Farewell, Sexual Revolution. Hello, New Victorianism," *Futurist*, January–February 1986, 2.

54. Blayne Cutler, "Neo-Victorian," *American Demographics*, June 1988, 16.

55. Wolfe, "New Sexual Realism."

56. Wolfe, "New Sexual Realism."

57. Peter Davis, "Exploring the Kingdom of AIDS," *New York Times Magazine*, May 31, 1987, 32–36.

58. Lucy Schulte, "The New Dating Game," *New York*, March 3, 1986, 82–88.

59. Barbara Kantrowitz, "Fear of Sex," *Newsweek*, November 24, 1986, 40–42.

60. Kevin Krajick, "Private Passions and Public Health," *Psychology Today*, May 1988, 51–58.

61. Lisa Sanders, "The Worst Lie of All: What They'll Say for Sex," *Mademoiselle*, June 1989, 216.

62. Gini Sikes, "Profile of a New-Age Date," *Mademoiselle*, August 1987, 187.

63. Martha Smilgis, "The Big Chill: Fear of AIDS," *Time*, February 16, 1987, 50–53.

64. Leah Allen, "My Year of Loving Dangerously: Confessions of a Non-Condom User," *Mademoiselle*, March 1989, 221.

65. Fumento, "AIDS Cookbook."

66. David M. Alpern, "The AIDS Threat: Who's at Risk?" *Newsweek*, March 14, 1988, 42–44.

67. Fumento, "AIDS Cookbook."

68. Jean Seligmann, "The Storm Over Masters and Johnson," *Newsweek*, March 21, 1988, 78–79.

69. Christine Gorman, "An Outbreak of Sensationalism," *Time*, March 21, 1988, 58–59.

70. Steven Findlay and Joanne Silberner, "What the Press Release Left Out," *U.S. News and World Report*, March 21, 1988, 59–60.

71. Chris Norwood, "The AIDS Misinformation Explosion," *U.S. News and World Report*, May 9, 1988, 7.

72. Bernie Zilbergeld and Michael Evans, "The Inadequacy of Masters and Johnson," *Psychology Today*, August 1980, 29–43.

73. Susan Jacoby, "Hers: Risky Business," *New York Times Magazine*, April 24, 1988, 26.

74. Kenneth B. Noble, "Lansing Journal: Another Lost Species; U.S. Playboy Bunny," *New York Times*, July 29, 1988.

75. Pat Dowell, "Sex Makes a Comeback," *Psychology Today*, September 1988, 64–65.

76. Erica Abeel, "Bedroom Eyes," *Mademoiselle*, October 1987, 194–95.

77. Michael S. Kimmel, "Burning Desires: Sex in America; A Report from the Field," *Nation*, October 30, 1989, 503.

## CHAPTER 5: INDECENT PROPOSAL

1. "Heretoforeplay," *Harper's Magazine*, February 1993, 28.

2. George F. Will, "Sex amidst Semicolons," *Newsweek*, October 4, 1993, 92.

3. Jean Seligmann, "A New Survey on Sex," *Newsweek*, September 17, 1990, 58, 72.

4. Seligmann, "A New Survey on Sex."

5. Miriam Horn, "Goings-on Behind Bedroom Doors," *U.S. News and World Report*, June 10, 1991, 64; Rebecca Johnson, "Advice for the Clinton Age," *New York Times Magazine*, October 4, 1998, 59–61.

6. Philip Elmer-Dewitt, "How Safe Is Sex?" *Time*, November 25, 1991, 72–74.

7. Geoffrey Cowley, "Sleeping with the Enemy," *Newsweek*, December 9, 1991, 58–59.

8. Anastasia Toufexis, "Sex Lives and Videotape," *Time*, October 29, 1990, 104.

9. David Gelman, "Good Golly, Miss Molly," *Newsweek*, November 4, 1991, 54.

10. Michael Gross, "Sex in the '90s," *New York*, June 8, 1992, 35–42.

11. Gross, "Sex in the '90s."

12. Gross, "Sex in the '90s."

13. Gross, "Sex in the '90s."

14. Gross, "Sex in the '90s."

15. Gross, "Sex in the '90s."

16. Simon Sebag Montefiore, "Love, Lies, and Fear in the Plague Years . . . ," *Psychology Today*, September–October 1992, 30.

17. Michel Marriott, "Not Frenzied, but Fulfilled," *Newsweek*, October 17, 1994, 70–71.

18. Marriott, "Not Frenzied, but Fulfilled."

19. Philip Elmer-Dewitt, "Now for the Truth About Americans and Sex," *Time*, October 17, 1994, 62–66.

20. Jerry Adler, "Sex in the Snoring '90s," *Newsweek*, April 26, 1993, 54–57.

21. Elmer-Dewitt, "Now for the Truth About Americans and Sex."

22. Katha Pollitt, "Subject to Debate," *Nation*, October 31, 1994, 484.

23. Garrison Keillor, "It's Good Monogamy That's Really Sexy," *Time*, October 17, 1994, 62–66.

24. Elmer-Dewitt, "Now for the Truth About Americans and Sex."

25. Barbara Kantrowitz, "Sex on the Info Highway," *Newsweek*, March 14, 1994, 62–63.

26. Scott Adams, "In the '90s, Computer Skills Mean Sex Appeal," *Utne Reader*, July–August 1995, 88–89.

27. Lynn Rosellini, "Sexual Desire," *U.S. News and World Report*, July 6, 1992, 60–66.

28. Joseph P. Shapiro, "Teenage Sex: Just Say 'Wait,'" *U.S. News and World Report*, July 26, 1993, 56–59.

29. Nancy Gibbs, "How Should We Teach Our Children About Sex?" *Time*, May 24, 1993, 44–51.

30. Gibbs, "How Should We Teach Our Children About Sex?"

31. Shapiro, "Teenage Sex: Just Say 'Wait.'"

32. David Friedman, "Look Who's Teaching Sex," *Good Housekeeping*, November 1996, 74.

33. Philip Elmer-Dewitt, "Making the Case for Abstinence," *Time*, May 24, 1993, 44–51.

34. Jeff Stryker, "Abstinence or Else!" *Nation*, June 16, 1997, 19.

35. Rick Marin, "Blocking the Box," *Newsweek*, March 11, 1996, 60–62.

36. Norm Alster, "Crude Doesn't Sell," *Forbes*, January 21, 1991, 60–61.

37. Doug Marlette, "Birds, Bees, and Beavis," *Esquire*, March 1997, 112.

38. Lewis H. Lapham, "In the Garden of Tabloid Delight," *Harper's Magazine*, August 1997, 35–39.

39. David Whitman, "Was It Good for Us?" *U.S. News and World Report*, May 19, 1997, 56–60.

40. Max Frankel, "Word and Image: Steam for Sale," *New York Times Magazine*, February 7, 1999, 30.

41. Lapham, "In the Garden of Tabloid Delight."

42. Lapham, "In the Garden of Tabloid Delight."

43. Jonathan Adler, "In the Time of Tolerance," *Newsweek*, March 30, 1998, 29.

44. Johnson, "Advice for the Clinton Age."

45. Deborah Tannen, "Freedom to Talk Dirty," *Time*, February 22, 1999, 46.

46. Barbara Kantrowitz, "Mom, What's Oral Sex?" *Newsweek*, September 21, 1998, 44.

47. John Leland, "Let's Talk About Sex," *Newsweek*, December 28, 1998–January 4, 1999, 62–65. For much more on "how the little blue pill changed sex in America," as the book's subtitle reads, see Meika Loe's *The Rise of Viagra* (New York: New York University Press, 2004).

48. R. Emmett Tyrrell Jr., "No Escaping the Sexual Revolution," *American Spectator*, August 1997, 18.

49. Stanley Bing, "It's the Nineties: What's Your Sex IQ?" *Fortune*, July 21, 1997, 37–38.

50. Allan Bloom, "The Death of Eros," *New York Times Magazine*, May 23, 1993, 26–27.

51. Thomas Moore, "Sex (American Style)," *Mother Jones*, September/October 1997, 56–63.

52. Moore, "Sex (American Style)."

53. Moore, "Sex (American Style)."

54. John Tierney, "The Big City: Fab Dads and Wanton Wives," *New York Times Magazine*, February 11, 1996, 21.

55. Ron Rosenbaum, "The Coming Crisis," *Esquire*, September 1997, 48–50.

56. Rosenbaum, "Coming Crisis."

57. Brenda Maddox, "When Bad Writing Happens to Good Sex," *New York Times Book Review*, January 11, 1998, 23.

58. John Leland, "Bad News in the Bedroom," *Newsweek*, February 22, 1999, 47.

59. Wray Herbert, "Not Tonight, Dear," *U.S. News and World Report*, February 22, 1999, 57–59.

60. Miriam Karmel Feldman, "The Pharma Sutra," *Utne Reader*, July–August 1999, 16–17.

61. Dan McGraw, "A Pink Viagra?" *U.S. News and World Report*, October 5, 1998, 54.

62. Claudia Kalb, "A Little Help in the Bedroom," *Newsweek*, Spring/Summer 1999, 38–39.

63. Chris McDougall, "Joy Buzzers," *Men's Health*, June 1999, 70–71. For interesting histories of the vibrator, see Rachel P. Maines's *Technology of Orgasm: "Hysteria," the Vibrator, and Women's Sexual Satisfaction* (Baltimore: The Johns Hopkins University Press, 1998) and the 2012 movie *Hysteria*.

64. Joe Kita, "Camp Sex," *Men's Health*, January–February 1997, 50.

65. Alfred Meyer, "Patching Up Testosterone," *Psychology Today*, March–April 1997, 54.

66. Silvia Sansoni, "Battle of the Sexperts," *Forbes*, October 18, 1999, 62.

67. Johnson, "Advice for the Clinton Age."

68. Richard Turner, "Finding the Inner Swine," *Newsweek*, February 1, 1999, 52–53.

69. Richard Corliss, "In Defense of Dirty Movies," *Time*, July 5, 1999, 74.

70. James Poniewozik, "Sex on TV Is . . . Not Sexy!" *Time*, August 2, 1999, 86–87.

71. Tamala M. Edwards, "Modestly Provocative," *Time*, March 1, 1999, 59.

72. Whitman, "Was It Good for Us?"

73. John Leo, "The Joy of Sexual Values," *U.S. News and World Report*, March 1, 1999, 13.

74. George F. Will, "Modesty Is Sexy," *Newsweek*, February 1, 1999, 74.

75. Kenneth Maxwell, "Sex in the Future: Virtuous and Virtual?" *Futurist*, July–August 1997, 29–31.

76. Maxwell, "Sex in the Future."

## CHAPTER 6: ICE AGE

1. Daphne Merkin, "The Last Taboo," *New York Times Magazine*, December 3, 2000, 116.

2. Helen Gurley Brown, "Don't Give Up on Sex after 60," *Newsweek*, May 29, 2000, 55.

3. Paul Theroux, "Here's to You, Mrs. Robinson," *Harper's Bazaar*, March 2002, 228.

4. Geoffrey Cowley, "Looking Beyond Viagra," *Newsweek*, April 24, 2000, 77; Jack Hitt, "The Second Sexual Revolution," *New York Times Magazine*, February 20, 2000, 34.

5. Steve Fishman, "Sex Drugs for Women?" *Harper's Bazaar*, March 2000, 388.

6. Jan Shifren and Nancy A. Ferrari, "A Better Sex Life," *Newsweek*, May 10, 2004, 86.

7. Allisson Fass, "Quest for Desire," *Forbes*, November 29, 2004, 114–18.

8. Mary Ellen Egan, "The Love Machine," *Forbes*, July 3, 2000, 124–26.

9. David Noonan, "High on Testosterone," *Newsweek*, September 29, 2003, 50.

10. Katherine Hobson, "A Drug for Arousal," *U.S. News and World Report*, January 24, 2005, 50–51.

11. Emily Yoffe, "Passion, Interrupted," *Health*, May 2005, 66–72.

12. Fass, "Quest for Desire."

13. Hitt, "Second Sexual Revolution."

14. Catherine Elton, "Learning to Lust," *Psychology Today*, May–June 2010, 70.

15. Claudia Kalb, "Let's Talk About Sex," *Newsweek*, November 8, 2004, 48.

16. Michael D. Lemonick, "The Chemistry of Desire," *Time*, January 19, 2004, 68–72, 75.

17. Justin Clark, "The Big Turnoff," *Psychology Today*, January–February, 2005, 17–18.

18. Elton, "Learning to Lust."

19. Alexis Jetter, "Decoding Desire," *Vogue*, February 2010, 209.

20. Elton, "Learning to Lust."

21. Susan Dominus, "Abstinence Minded," *New York Times Magazine*, January 21, 2001, 9. In 2008, the Guttmacher Institute reported that the much-claimed oral sex epidemic among teens was largely a myth and that overall sexual behavior among fifteen- to nineteen-year-olds had not changed much since 1991. Jennie Yabroff, "The Myths of Teen Sex," *Newsweek*, June 9, 2008, 55.

22. Margaret Talbot, "The Young and the Restless," *New York Times Magazine*, June 30, 2002, 11.

23. Talbot, "Young and the Restless."

24. Michael Erard, "Virgins, Inc.," *Rolling Stone*, April 25, 2002, 41–51.

25. Jodie Morse, "An Rx for Teen Sex," *Time*, October 7, 2002, 64–65.

26. Katy Kelly, "Just Don't Do It!" *U.S. News and World Report*, October 17, 2005, 44–51.

27. Kelly, "Just Don't Do It!"

28. Jessica Valenti, "The Virginity Movement, Rebranded," *Nation*, July 6, 2009, 22–24.

29. Claudia Wallis, "A Snapshot of Teen Sex," *Time*, February 7, 2005, 58.

30. Walter Kirn, "Sex-Ed Night School," *New York Times Magazine*, November 16, 2003, 23.

31. Betsy Streisand, "Doing It in Prime Time," *U.S. News and World Report*, October 17, 2005, 50–51.

32. Kathleen Deveny, "Girls Gone Bad," *Newsweek*, February 12, 2007, 40; Belinda Luscombe, "The Truth About Teen Girls," *Time*, September 22, 2008, 64–69.

33. Alex Morris, "They Know What Boys Want," *New York*, February 7, 2011, 32.

34. Alexandra Jacobs, "Campus Exposure," *New York Times Magazine*, March 4, 2007, 44.

35. Jennie Yabroff, "Campus Sexperts," *Newsweek*, February 25, 2008, 46.

36. Lisa Miller, "Sexual Revolution, Part II," *Newsweek*, November 16, 2009, 26.

37. Jessica Valenti, "The Virginity Movement, Rebranded," *Nation*, July 6, 2009, 22–24.

38. Sharon Jayson, "Is Dating Dead," *USA Today*, March 31, 2011, 1A.

39. Adam Sternbergh, "Selling Your Sex Life," *New York Times Magazine*, September 7, 2003, 33.

40. James Poniewozik, "It's Here, It's Queer, Get Used to It," *Time*, November 27, 2000, 78–79.

41. Sean M. Smith, "Fan Swapping: Gay, Straight, Up Late," *Newsweek*, June 23, 2003, 65.

42. Patricia Huang, "Having Yours," *Forbes*, October 4, 2004, 68; CAKE: Entertainment for Women, home page, accessed September 19, 2012, www.cakenyc.com/.

43. Pamela Paul, "The Porn Factor," *Time*, January 19, 2004, 163.

44. Paul, "Porn Factor."

45. Paul, "Porn Factor."

46. Ross Douthat, "Is Pornography Adultery?" *Atlantic*, October 2008, 80.

47. John Cloud, "Bondage Unbound," *Time*, January 19, 2004, 104.

48. Em and Lo, "The Bottom Line," *New York*, January 8, 2007, 60.

49. Valerie White, "A Humanist Looks at Polyamory," *Humanist*, November–December 2004, 17.

50. Chuck Klosterman, "Group Sex for Sale," *Esquire*, October 2005, 112.

51. Jaime Wolf, "And You Thought Abercrombie & Fitch Was Pushing It?" *New York Times Magazine*, April 23, 2006, 58.

52. Charlotte Druckman, "Toy Time," *New York*, July 17, 2006, 56.

53. Hilary Howard, "Vibrators Carry the Conversation," *New York Times*, April 21, 2011, E1, E9.

54. Caitlin Flanagan, "Wifely Duty," *Atlantic*, January–February 2003, 171–74, 176. Kathleen Deveny, "We're Not in the Mood," *Newsweek*, June 29, 2003, 48; Margaret Carlson, "The Mummy Diaries," *Time*, October 7, 2002.

55. Deveny, "We're Not in the Mood."

56. Nicole Gregory, "From Hot . . . to Not," *Los Angeles Magazine*, October 2008, 140.

57. Deveny, "We're Not in the Mood."

58. Flanagan, "Wifely Duty."

59. Elizabeth Devita-Raeburn, "Lust for the Long Haul," *Psychology Today*, January–February 2006, 38.

60. Davy Rothbart, "He's Just Not That Into Anyone," *New York*, February 7, 2011.

61. Rothbart, "He's Just Not That Into Anyone."

62. Deborah Kotz, "Sex, Health and Happiness," *U.S. News and World Report*, September 15, 2008.

63. Sora Song, "Love Potions," *Time*, January 19, 2004.

64. Deveny, "We're Not in the Mood."

65. Caitlin Gaffey, "Can Pheromones Make You Sexier?" *Harper's Bazaar*, March 2007, 306.

66. Matthew Shulman, "A Little Aphrodisiac Science," *U.S. News and World Report*, September 15, 2008, 56.

67. Joel Stein, "Spicing It Up," *Time*, January 19, 2004.

68. Sarah Baldouf, "The Difference Sex Therapy Can Make," *U.S. News and World Report*, September 15, 2008.

69. Lindsay Lyon, Adam Volland, and Sarah Baldauf, "Coping with Sexual Woes," *U.S. News and World Report*, September 15, 2008.

70. Alexis Jetter, "Lust, Caution," *Vogue*, February 2010, 206.

## CONCLUSION

1. Michael J. Sandel, *What Money Can't Buy: The Moral Limits of Markets* (New York: Farrar, Straus and Giroux, 2012).

2. Mary Eberstadt, *Adam and Eve after the Pill: Paradoxes of the Sexual Revolution* (San Francisco: Ignatius, 2012).

3. Marty Klein, *America's War on Sex: The Continuing Attack on Law, Lust, and Liberty* (Santa Barbara, CA: Praeger, 2012).

4. Katherine Schreiber, "Don't Ask, Don't Tell," *Psychology Today*, September/ October 2012.

5. John Hildebrand, "Report: Sex Ed in NY Schools Inadequate," *Newsday*, September 13, 2012.

6. Cara Buckley, "Spreading the Word (and Pictures) on 'Real' Sex," *New York Times*, September 9, 2012, 12.

# Selected Bibliography

Allyn, David. *Make Love, Not War: The Sexual Revolution; An Unfettered History.* New York: Little, Brown, 2000.

Antonio, Gene. *The AIDS Cover-Up? The Real and Alarming Facts about AIDS.* San Francisco: Ignatius Press, 1986.

Bailey, Beth. *From Front Porch to Back Seat: Courtship in Twentieth-Century America.* Baltimore: The Johns Hopkins University Press, 1988.

———. *Sex in the Heartland.* Cambridge, MA: Harvard University Press, 1999.

Baker, Nicholson. *The Fermata.* New York: Random House, 1994.

———. *Vox.* New York: Random House, 1992.

Bartell, Gilbert D. *Group Sex: A Scientist's Eyewitness Report on the American Way of Swinging.* New York: Peter H. Wyden, 1971.

Bastyra, Judy. *The Best-Ever Illustrated Sex Handbook: Successful Techniques and New Ideas for Long-Term Lovers.* Leicester, UK: Anness, 2008.

Blank, Hanne. *Straight: The Surprisingly Short History of Heterosexuality.* New York: Beacon, 2012.

———. *Virgin: The Untouched History.* New York: Bloomsbury, 2007.

Bright, Susie. *Sexual Reality.* San Francisco: Susie/Bright, 2009.

Brown, Douglas. *Just Do It: How One Couple Turned Off the TV and Turned On Their Sex Lives for 101 Days*. New York: Crown, 2008.

Brown, Fred, and Rudolf K. Kempton. *Sex Questions and Answers*. New York: Whittlesy House, 1950.

Brown, Helen Gurley. *Sex and the Single Girl*. New York: B. Geis, 1962.

Butterfield, Oliver M. *Marriage and Sexual Harmony*. New York: Emerson Books, 1937.

Carpenter, Laura M., and John DeLamater, eds. *Sex for Life: From Virginity to Viagra, How Sexuality Changes throughout Our Lives*. New York: New York University Press, 2012.

Castallo, Mario A., and Cecilia L. Schultz Castallo. *Woman's Inside Story*. New York: Macmillan, 1948.

Chapple, Steve, and David Talbot. *Burning Desires: Sex in America*. New York: Doubleday, 1989.

Charlotte, Kathleen. *Wicked Voodoo Sex*. Woodbury, MN: Llewellyn Publications, 2008.

Chauncey, George. *Gay New York*. New York: Basic Books, 1994.

Comfort, Alex. *The Joy of Sex*. New York: Pocket Books, 1974.

———. *More Joy: A Lovemaking Companion to* The Joy of Sex. New York: Crown, 1987.

Corn, Laura. *52 Invitations to Grrreat Sex*. Oklahoma City, OK: Park Avenue, 1999.

Cory, Donald Webster. *The Homosexual in America*. New York: Greenberg, 1951.

Crenshaw, Theresa. *The Alchemy of Love and Lust*. New York: Pocket Books, 1997.

Dabhoiwala, Faramerz. *The Origins of Sex: A History of the First Sexual Revolution*. New York: Oxford University Press, 2012.

D'Emilio, John, and Estelle B. Freedman. *Intimate Matters: A History of Sexuality in America*. New York: Harper & Row, 1988.

Deutsch, Albert. *Sex Habits of American Men: A Symposium on the Kinsey Report*. New York: Prentice-Hall, 1948.

Deutsch, Helene. *The Psychology of Women: A Psychoanalytic Interpretation*. New York: Grune & Stratton, 1946.

Dickson, Ruth. *Now That You've Got Me Here, What Are We Going to Do? A Non-Marriage Manual*. New York: David McKay, 1972.

Dines, Gail. *Pornland: How Porn Has Hijacked Our Sexuality*. Boston: Beacon, 2010.

Eberstadt, Mary. *Adam and Eve after the Pill: Paradoxes of the Sexual Revolution*. San Francisco: Ignatius, 2012.

Ehrenreich, Barbara, Elizabeth Hess, and Gloria Jacobs. *Re-making Love: The Feminization of Sex*. New York: Doubleday, 1986.

Ellis, Albert. *The American Sexual Tragedy*. New York: Twayne, 1954.

———. *The Folklore of Sex*. New York: C. Boni, 1951.

Ellis, Havelock. *Studies in the Psychology of Sex*. New York: Random House, 1940.

Em and Lo. *Sex: How to Do Everything*. New York: DK Publishing, 2008.

Ericksen, Julia A., with Sally A. Steffen. *Kiss and Tell: Surveying Sex in the Twentieth Century*. Cambridge, MA: Harvard University Press, 1999.

Ernst, Morris, and David Loth. *American Sexual Behavior and the Kinsey Report*. New York: Greystone Press, 1948.

Fein, Ellen, and Sherrie Schneider. *The Rules: Time-Tested Secret for Capturing the Heart of Mr. Right*. New York: Grand Central, 1995.

Feldhahn, Shaunti. *For Women Only: What You Need to Know About the Inner Lives of Men*. Colorado Springs, CO: Multnomah Books, 2004.

Ferrare, Cristina. *Okay, So I Don't Have a Headache*. New York: St. Martin's, 1999.

Fitch, Robert Elliot. *The Decline and Fall of Sex*. New York: Harcourt Brace, 1957.

Ford, Clellan S., and Frank A. Beach. *Patterns of Sexual Behavior*. New York: Harper & Brothers, 1951.

Foucault, Michel. *The History of Sexuality*. Vol. 1, *An Introduction*. New York: Vintage, 1990.

———. *The History of Sexuality*. Vol. 2, *The Use of Pleasure*. New York: Vintage, 1990.

———. *The History of Sexuality.* Vol. 3, *The Care of the Self.* New York: Vintage, 1990.

Friday, Nancy. *Forbidden Flowers: More Women's Sexual Fantasies.* New York: Simon & Schuster, 1975.

———. *My Secret Garden: Women's Sexual Fantasies.* New York: Simon & Schuster, 1973.

———. *Women on Top: How Real Life Has Changed Women's Sexual Fantasies.* New York: Simon & Schuster, 1991.

Fromm, Erich. *The Art of Loving.* New York: HarperTrade, 1974.

Fromme, Allan. *The Psychologist Looks at Sex and Marriage.* New York: Prentice-Hall, 1950.

Gaddam, Sai, and Ogi Ogas. *A Billion Wicked Thoughts: What the World's Largest Experiment Reveals about Human Desire.* New York: Dutton Adult, 2011.

Gallagher, Melinda, and Emily Kramer. *A Piece of Cake: Recipes for Female Sexual Pleasure.* New York: Atria, 2005.

Garrity, Joan. *The Sensuous Woman: The First How-To Book for the Female Who Yearns to Be All Woman.* New York: Dell, 1971.

Gebhard, Paul H., Wardell B. Pomery, Clyde E. Martin, and Cornelia V. Christenson. *Pregnancy, Birth, and Abortion.* London: Heinemann Medical Books, 1959.

Gillies, Jerry. *Transcendental Sex: A Meditative Approach to Increasing Sensual Pleasure.* New York: Holt, Rinehart and Winston, 1978.

Gittelson, Natalie. *The Erotic Life of the American Wife.* New York: Delacorte Press, 1972.

Godbeer, Richard. *Sexual Revolution in Early America.* Baltimore: The Johns Hopkins University Press, 2002.

Greene, Gael. *Sex and the College Girl.* New York: Delacorte, 1964.

Hegarty, Marilyn E. *Victory Girls, Khaki-Wackies, and Patriotutes: The Regulation of Female Sexuality during World War II.* New York: New York University Press, 2007.

Heinlein, Robert. *Stranger in a Strange Land.* New York: Putnam, 1961.

Herzog, Dagmar. *Sex in Crisis: The New Sexual Revolution and the Future of American Politics*. New York: Basic Books, 2008.

——. *Sexuality in Europe: A Twentieth-Century History*. New York: Cambridge University Press, 2011.

Hite, Shere. *The Hite Report: A Nationwide Study on Female Sexuality*. New York: Macmillan, 1976.

Hollander, Xavier. *The Happy Hooker: My Own Story*. New York: Dell, 1973.

Hunt, Morton. *Sexual Behavior in the 1970s*. Chicago: Playboy Press, 1974.

James, E. L. *Fifty Shades of Grey*. London: Arrow Books, 2012.

Jensen, Robert. *Getting Off: Pornography and the End of Masculinity*. Cambridge, MA: South End Press, 2007.

Kammeyer, Kenneth C. W. *A Hypersexual Society: Sexual Discourse, Erotica, Pornography in America Today*. New York: Palgrave MacMillan, 2008.

Kaplan, Helen Singer. *Disorders of Sexual Desire and Other Concepts and Techniques in Sex Therapy*. New York: Simon & Schuster, 1979.

——. *The Evaluation of Sexual Disorders: Psychological and Medical Aspects*. New York: Brunner/Mazel, 1983.

——. *The New Sex Therapy: Active Treatment of Sexual Dysfunctions*. London: Routledge, 1974.

Kensington Ladies Erotica Society. *Ladies' Home Erotica*. Berkeley, CA: Ten Speed Press, 1984.

Kinsey, Alfred C., Wardell B. Pomeroy, and Clyde E. Martin. *Sexual Behavior in the Human Male*. Philadelphia: Saunders, 1948.

Kinsey, Alfred C., Wardell B. Pomeroy, Clyde E. Martin, and Paul H. Gebhard. *Sexual Behavior in the Human Female*. Philadelphia: Saunders, 1953.

Kirkendall, Lester. *Premarital Intercourse and Interpersonal Relations*. Westport, CT: Praeger, 1984.

Klein, Marty. *America's War on Sex: The Attack on Law, Lust, and Liberty*. Westport, CT: Praeger, 2006.

——. *America's War on Sex: The Continuing Attack on Law, Lust, and Liberty*. 2nd ed. Santa Barbara, CA: Praeger, 2012.

——. *Sexual Intelligence: What We Really Want from Sex—and How to Get It*. New York: HarperOne, 2012.

Ladas, Alice Kahn, Beverly Whipple, and John D. Perry. *The G Spot and Other Recent Discoveries About Human Sexuality*. New York: Holt, Rinehart and Winston, 1982.

LaHaye, Tim, and Beverly LaHaye. *The Act of Marriage: The Beauty of Sexual Love*. Grand Rapids, MI: Zondervan, 1976.

Lancaster, Roger N. *Sex Panic and the Punitive State*. Berkeley: University of California Press, 2011.

Landers, Ann. *Since You Ask Me*. New York: Prentice-Hall, 1961.

Levine, Judith. *Harmful to Minors: The Perils of Protecting Children from Sex*. Minneapolis: University of Minnesota Press, 2002.

Lewis, Carolyn Herbst. *Prescription for Heterosexuality: Sexual Citizenship in the Cold War Era*. Chapel Hill: University of North Carolina Press, 2010.

Locker, Sari. *The Complete Idiot's Guide to Amazing Sex*. New York: Alpha, 1999.

Loe, Meika. *The Rise of Viagra: How the Little Blue Pill Changed Sex in America*. New York: New York University Press, 2004.

Lorand, Rhoda L. *Love, Sex and the Teenager*. New York: Macmillan, 1966.

Maines, Rachel P. *The Technology of Orgasm: "Hysteria," the Vibrator, and Women's Sexual Satisfaction*. Baltimore: The Johns Hopkins University Press, 1998.

Masters, William H., and Virginia E. Johnson. *Human Sexual Response*. Boston: Little, Brown, 1966.

——. *Human Sexual Inadequacy*. Boston: Little, Brown, 1970.

Masters, William H., Virginia E. Johnson, and Robert Kolodny. *Crisis: Heterosexual Behavior in the Age of AIDS*. New York: Grove Press, 1988.

Masters, William, Virginia Johnson, and Robert J. Levin. *The Pleasure Bond*. Boston: Little, Brown, 1974.

Maxwell, Kenneth. *A Sexual Odyssey: From Forbidden Fruit to Cybersex*. New York: Plenum, 1996.

May, Elaine Tyler. *America and the Pill: A History of Promise, Peril, and Liberation*. New York: Basic Books, 2010.

———. *Homeward Bound: American Families in the Cold War Era*. New York: Basic Books, 1988.

McCarthy, Barry W., and Emily J. McCarthy. *Rekindling Desire: A Step-by-Step Program to Help Low-Sex and No-Sex Marriages*. London: Routledge, 2003.

McCarthy, Tara. *Been There, Haven't Done That: A Virgin's Memoir*. New York: Warner Books, 1997.

Michael, Robert T., John G. Gagnon, Edward O. Laumann, and Gina Kolata. *Sex in America: A Definitive Survey*. Boston: Little, Brown, 1994.

Moody, Rick. *Purple America*. Boston: Little, Brown, 1997.

Moore, Thomas. *The Soul of Sex*. New York: HarperCollins, 1998.

Muller, Charla, and Betsy Thorpe. *365 Nights: A Memoir of Intimacy*. New York: Berkley Trade, 2008.

O'Neill, Nena, and George O'Neill. *Open Marriage: A New Life Style for Couples*. New York: M. Evans, 1972.

———. *Shifting Gears: Finding Security in a Changing World*. New York: Avon, 1975.

Packard, Vance. *The Sexual Wilderness: The Contemporary Upheaval in Male-Female Relationships*. New York: David McKay, 1968.

Patterson, James, and Peter Kim. *The Day America Told the Truth: What People Really Believe About Everything That Really Matters*. New York: Prentice-Hall, 1991.

Paul, Pamela. *Pornified: How Pornography Is Transforming Our Lives, Our Relationships, and Our Families*. New York: Times Books, 2005.

Peiss, Kathy, ed. *Major Problems in the History of American Sexuality*. New York: Houghton Mifflin, 2002.

Reichman, Judith. *I'm Not in the Mood: What Every Woman Should Know About Improving Her Libido*. New York: William Morrow, 1998.

Reinisch, June Machover, with Ruth Beasley. *The Kinsey Institute New Report on Sex: What You Must Know to Be Sexually Literate*. New York: Pharos Books, 1990.

Reis, Elizabeth. *American Sexual Histories*. Malden, MA: Blackwell, 2001.

Reiss, Ira. *Premarital Sexual Standards in America*. Glencoe, IL: Free Press, 1960.

Reuben, David. *Everything You Always Wanted to Know About Sex—But Were Afraid to Ask*. New York: David McKay, 1969.

Reumann, Miriam G. *American Sexual Character: Sex, Gender, and National Identity in the Kinsey Reports*. Berkeley: University of California Press, 2005.

Rimmer, Robert. *The Harrad Experiment*. Dover, MA: Sherborn Press, 1966.

Rossner, Judith. *Looking for Mr. Goodbar*. New York: Simon & Schuster, 1975.

Roth, Philip. *Portnoy's Complaint*. New York: Random House, 1969.

Sandel, Michael J. *What Money Can't Buy: The Moral Limits of Markets*. New York: Farrar, Straus and Giroux, 2012.

Schnarch, David, and James Maddock. *Resurrecting Sex: Solving Sexual Problems and Revolutionizing Your Relationship*. New York: Harper, 2003.

Schneider, Jennifer, and Robert Weiss. *Cybersex Exposed: Simple Fantasy or Obsession*. Center City, MN: Hazelden, 2001.

Schur, Edwin M. *The Americanization of Sex*. Philadelphia: Temple University Press, 1988.

Seaman, Barbara. *Free and Female: The Sex Life of the Contemporary Woman; Sex Respect*. Greenwich, CT: Fawcett, 1973.

Sewell, Joan. *I'd Rather Eat Chocolate: Learning to Love My Low Libido*. New York: Broadway, 2007.

Shalit, Wendy. *A Return to Modesty: Discovering the Lost Virtue*. New York: Free Press, 1999.

Shedd, Charlie, and Martha Shedd. *Celebration in the Bedroom*. Waco, TX: World Books, 1979.

Sherfey, Mary Jane. *The Nature and Evolution of Female Sexuality*. New York: Random House, 1972.

Simmons, Christina. *Making Marriage Modern: Women's Sexuality from the Progressive Era to World War II*. New York: Oxford University Press, 2009.

Slung, Michele, ed. *Slow Hand: Women Writing Erotica*. New York: HarperCollins, 1992.

Smith, Merril D., ed. *Sex and Sexuality in Early America*. New York: New York University Press, 1998.

Sohn, Amy. *Run Catch Kiss: A Gratifying Novel*. New York: Simon & Schuster, 1999.

Sorokin, Pitirim. *The American Sex Revolution*. Boston: Porter Sargent, 1956.

Spencer, Suzy. *Secret Sex Lives: A Year on the Fringes of American Sexuality*. New York: Berkley, 2012.

Stone, Abraham, and Hannah Stone. *A Marriage Manual: A Practical Guide-Book to Sex and Marriage*. New York: Simon & Schuster, 1935.

Stone, Lawrence. *The Family, Sex and Marriage in England, 1500–1800*. New York: Harper & Row, 1977.

Struthers, William M. *Wired for Intimacy: How Pornography Hijacks the Male Brain*. Nottingham, UK: IVP Books, 2009.

Susann, Jacqueline. *The Love Machine*. New York: Simon & Schuster, 1969.

———. *Valley of the Dolls*. New York: B. Geis, 1966.

Sweet, Lisa. *365 Sex Positions: A New Way Every Day for a Steamy, Erotic Year*. Berkeley, CA: Amorata Press, 2009.

Symons, Donald. *The Evolution of Human Sexuality*. New York: Oxford University Press, 1979.

Talese, Gay. *Thy Neighbor's Wife*. Garden City, NY: Doubleday, 1980.

Tone, Andrea. *Devices and Desires: A History of Contraceptives in America*. New York: Hill and Wang, 2001.

Turner, Christopher. *Adventures in the Orgasmatron: How the Sexual Revolution Came to America*. New York: Farrar, Straus and Giroux, 2011.

Valenti, Jessica. *The Purity Myth: How America's Obsession with Virginity Is Hurting Young Women*. Berkeley, CA: Seal Press, 2009.

von Krafft-Ebing, Richard. *Psychopathia Sexualis*. New York: Stein & Day, 1965.

Weiner-Davis, Michele. *The Sex-Starved Marriage: A Couple's Guide to Boosting Their Marriage Libido*. New York: Simon & Schuster, 2003.

Wheat, Ed, and Gaye Wheat. *Intended for Pleasure: Sex Technique and Sexual Fulfillment in Christian Marriage*. Grand Rapids, MI: Fleming H. Revell, 1977.

Wright, Derek. *The Psychology of Moral Behavior*. New York: Penguin, 1971.

# Index

# About the Author

Lawrence R. Samuel is the founder of Culture Planning LLC, a Miami- and New York–based resource offering cultural insight to Fortune 500 organizations. He is the author of *Freud on Madison Avenue: Motivation Research and Subliminal Advertising in America*, *Supernatural America: A Cultural History*, *The American Dream: A Cultural History*, and a number of other books.